ON FREUD'S
"FEMININITY"

CONTEMPORARY FREUD
Turning Points and Critical Issues

Series Editor: Leticia Glocer Fiorini

IPA Publications Committee
Leticia Glocer Fiorini (Buenos Aires), Chair; Samuel Arbiser (Buenos Aires); Mary Kay O'Neil (Montreal); Gail S. Reed (New York); Paulo Cesar Sandler (São Paulo); Gennaro Saragnano (Rome); Christian Seulin (Lyon); David Coe (London), Ex-officio as Director General

On Freud's "Analysis Terminable and Interminable"
edited by Joseph Sandler

Freud's "On Narcissism: An Introduction"
edited by Joseph Sandler, Ethel Spector Person, Peter Fonagy

On Freud's "Observations on Transference-Love"
edited by Ethel Spector Person, Aiban Hagelin, Peter Fonagy

On Freud's "Creative Writers and Day-Dreaming"
edited by Ethel Spector Person, Peter Fonagy, Sérvulo Augusto Figueira

On Freud's "A Child Is Being Beaten"
edited by Ethel Spector Person

On Freud's "Group Psychology and the Analysis of the Ego"
edited by Ethel Spector Person

On Freud's "Mourning and Melancholia"
edited by Leticia Glocer Fiorini, Thierry Bokanowski, Sergio Lewkowicz

On Freud's "The Future of an Illusion"
edited by Mary Kay O'Neil & Salman Akhtar

On Freud's "Splitting of the Ego in the Process of Defence"
edited by Thierry Bokanowski and Sergio Lewkowicz

ON FREUD'S
"FEMININITY"

Edited by

Leticia Glocer Fiorini & Graciela Abelin-Sas Rose

CONTEMPORARY FREUD
Turning Points and Critical Issues

KARNAC

First published in 2010 by
Karnac Books
118 Finchley Road
London NW3 5HT

British Library Cataloguing in Publication Data

A C.I.P. for this book is available from the British Library

ISBN: 978–1–85575–701–1

Edited, designed, and produced by Communication Crafts

Printed in Great Britain

www.karnacbooks.com

CONTENTS

CONTEMPORARY FREUD

IPA Publications Committee

This significant series was founded by Robert Wallerstein and was first edited by Joseph Sandler, Ethel Spector Person, and Peter Fonagy, and its important contributions have greatly interested psychoanalysts of different latitudes.

The objective of this series is to approach Freud's work from a present and contemporary point of view. On the one hand, this means highlighting the fundamental contributions of his work that constitute the axes of psychoanalytic theory and practice. On the other, it implies the possibility of getting to know and spreading the ideas of present psychoanalysts about Freud's *oeuvre*, both where they coincide and where they differ.

This series considers at least two lines of development: a contemporary reading of Freud that reclaims his contributions, and a clarification of the logical and epistemic perspectives from which he is read today.

Freud's theory has branched out, and this has led to a theoretical, technical, and clinical pluralism that has to be worked through. It has therefore become necessary to avoid a snug and uncritical coexistence of concepts in order to consider systems of increasing complexities that take into account both the convergences and the divergences of the categories at play.

Consequently, this project has involved an additional task—that is, gathering psychoanalysts from different geographical regions representing, in addition, different theoretical stances, in order to be able to show their polyphony. This also means an extra effort for the reader that has to do with distinguishing and discriminating, establishing relations or contradictions, which each reader will eventually have to work through.

Being able to listen to other theoretical viewpoints is also a way of exercising our listening capacities in the clinical field. This means that the listening should support a space of freedom that would allow us to hear what is new and original.

In this spirit we have brought together authors deeply rooted in the Freudian tradition and others who have developed theories that had not been explicitly taken into account in Freud's work.

Freud's "Femininity" shows his final thoughts concerning femininity, feminine sexuality, and motherhood; his ideas have been thoroughly discussed by post-Freudian and contemporary psychoanalysts. This volume encompasses different viewpoints on femininity and enlightens the debatable aspects as well as the contributions of Freudian proposals. In this way, our purpose has been to go beyond a single, uniform line of thought in order to sustain differences, which each reader might also process and expand.

The authors of the chapters accepted the challenge to reconsider Freudian proposals and their expansions, implications, and contradictions in the light of contemporary psychoanalysis.

Special thanks are due to the contributors to this volume, which enriches the Contemporary Freud series.

Leticia Glocer Fiorini
Series Editor
Chair of the Publications Committee

EDITORS AND CONTRIBUTORS

Graciela Abelin-Sas Rose is a member of the New York Psychoanalytic Institute and of the Association for Psychoanalytic Medicine. She is a member of CAPS (Center for the Advancement of Psychoanalysis). She is the founder and former Chairperson of the New York Psychoanalytic Institute's Colloquium with Visiting Authors, where psychoanalysts from all over the world, with different perspectives in psychoanalysis, presented their points of view. She served for several years as the Foreign Editor of the *Journal of Clinical Psychoanalysis* and is at present a member of the Committee for Foreign Book Reviews for the *Journal of the American Psychoanalytic Association*. She is in private practice and conducts private seminars and supervisions. Her published works include: "To Mother or Not to Mother: Abortion and its Challenges" (1992); "Discovering One's Own Responsibility in a Judgmental System" (1996); "The Headless Woman: Scheherazade's Syndrome" (1994). "The First Interview: From Psychopathology to Psychoexistential Diagnosis" (1997); "The Internal Interlocutor" (2002); "Malignant Passionate Attachments" (2004); and "Implicit Theories of the Psychoanalyst about Femininity" (2009). She has been the guest lecturer at many national and international institutions, presenting on topics including: "Expanding Worlds: Women's

Development after Forty-Five" (1995); "Working Through" (2007); "Coupledom", "A Case of Inhibition of Creativity", and "Winnicott's 1968 Visit to the New York Psychoanalytic Institute" (2008); "The Synergizing Effect of Individual and Couple Therapy" (2009); "The Perilous Road to Hope" (2010).

Mariam Alizade is a psychiatrist and training analyst of the Argentine Psychoanalytic Association. She is also scientific consultant at the Argentine Psychoanalytical Association; COWAP Latin American co-chair of the IPA Committee on Women and Psychoanalysis (COWAP 1998–2001); co-chair for Latin America of the programme committee of the International Psychoanalytical Association for the Nice Congress held in July 2001; overall chair of COWAP (2001–05); and scientific Secretary of FEPAL (Latin American Psychoanalytical Federation, 2006–2008). She is the author of *Feminine Sensuality* (1992); *Near Death: Clinical Psychoanalytical Studies* (1995); *Time for Women* (1996); *The Lone Woman* (1999); *Psychoanalysis and Positivity* (2002; 2010). *Farewell to Blood: Psychoanalytic Essay on Menopause* (2005) *The Broken Couple: Essay on Divorce* (2008). She has been Editor of the IPA–COWAP–Karnac Series (*The Embodied Female; Studies on Femininity; Masculine Scenarios; Motherhood in the XXIst century*) and of the collected papers of the *COWAP Latin-American Intergenerational Dialogues*.

Thierry Bokanowski, a member of the International Psychoanalytical Association, is a training and supervising analyst of the Paris Psychoanalytical Society (*Société Psychanalytique de Paris*: SPP); he is a former secretary of the Paris Psychoanalytical Institute, a former Editor of the *Revue Française de Psychanalyse*, and a former member of the IPA Publications Committee. He has published several papers in various psychoanalytic reviews and several books, including *Sándor Ferenczi*, and *De la pratique analytique*, translated under the title *The Practice of Psychoanalysis*.

Emilce Dio Bleichmar (Universidad Buenos Aires), is a PhD in the programme "Principles and Developments in Psychoanalysis" (Universidad Autónoma Madrid); a full member of the Argentine Psychoanalytic Association and the International Psychoanalytical Association; Director of and Professor in the postgraduate course: "Clinic and Psychoanalytic Psychotherapy of the Child and His/Her Family", ELIP-

SIS, teaching institution of Universidad Pontificia Comillas, Madrid; Vice-President of the Forum Psychoanalytic Psychotherapy Society in Madrid, founded by her together with Hugo Bleichmar in 1995; editorial reader of the journal *International Forum of Psychoanalysis* (Sweden); and Member of the International Attachment Network (IAN). She is the author of the following books: *Fears and Phobias: Genesis Conditions on Infancy* (1982); *The Spontaneous Feminism of the Hysteria* (1985) [Clara Campoamor Award Essay, Women Institute, Madrid]; *Depression in Women* (1991); *Feminine Sexuality: From Child to Woman* (1998); *Gender, Psychoanalysis, Subjectivity* (1996) (edited with Mabel Burin); *Manual of Psychotherapy of the Relation between Parent and Children* (2005). She is also the author of a number of articles in edited books and specialized journals in Argentina, Brazil, the United States, and Spain.

Leticia Glocer Fiorini is a training and supervising psychoanalyst of the Argentine Psychoanalytic Association. She is also current chair (since 2005) of the Publications Committee of the International Psychoanalytical Association; former chair of the Publications Committee of the Argentine Psychoanalytic Association and former member of the Editorial Board of the *Revista de Psicoanálisis*, Buenos Aires. She is General Editor of the IPA Publications Committee's Series. She has been awarded the Celes Cárcamo Prize for her paper: "The feminine position: A heterogeneous construction" (APA, 1994). She is also the author of *Lo femenino y el pensamiento complejo* (2001), published in English as *Deconstructing the Feminine: Psychoanalysis, Gender and Theories of complexity* (2007); co-editor of *On Freud's Mourning and Melancholia* (2007) and of *The Experience of Time* (2009). She is also Editor, in Spanish, of: *The Other in the Intersubjective Field* (2004); *Time, History and Structure* (2006); *Labyrinths of Violence* (2008); and *The Body: Languages and Silences* (2008). She has also published numerous papers about femininity in books and in psychoanalytic journals in Spanish, English, Portuguese, and Italian.

Deanna Holtzman is a training and supervising analyst and past president of the Michigan Psychoanalytic Institute. She is an associate professor in the Department of Psychiatry, School of Medicine at Wayne State University and an adjunct professor of psychology at the University of Detroit. She is well known for her work on female psychology and sexuality and has many publications, including

Nevermore: The Hymen and the Loss of Virginity (1996), and *A Story of Her Own: The Female Oedipus Complex Reexamined and Renamed* (2008), of which she is co-author, with Nancy Kulish. She has published articles in the *Journal of the American Psychoanalytic Association*, the *International Journal of Psychoanalysis*, and the Film Forum's "Projections", and she was a contributor to *Female Psychology: An Annotated Psychoanalytic Bibliography* as well as *The Freud Encyclopedia*. The current president of the Sigmund Freud Archives, she is in private practice in Bloomfield Hills, Michigan.

Mikyum Kim is in private practice in psychiatry and psychoanalysis in New York City. She is a member of the William Alanson White Psychoanalytic Society and a supervisor of psychotherapy at the William Alanson White Psychoanalytic Institute. She was born in Seoul, Korea, and graduated from Ewha Womans University Medical School. She had her psychiatric residency at the New Jersey College of Medicine, Newark, New Jersey, and at the Albert Einstein Medical School, Bronx, New York.

Nancy Kulish is an Adjunct Professor of Psychology, University of Detroit/Mercy and Professor, Department of Psychiatry, Wayne State Medical School, and Training and Supervising Analyst at the Michigan Psychoanalytic Institute. Currently she is on the Editorial Boards of the *Psychoanalytic Quarterly* and the *International Journal of Psychoanalysis*. She has published and presented on topics ranging from female sexuality, gender, transference/countertransference, adolescence to termination. With Deanna Holtzman, she is the co-author of *Nevermore: The Hymen and the Loss of Virginity* (1996), about the loss of virginity, and *A Story of Her Own: The Female Oedipus Complex Reexamined and Renamed* (2008). She is in private practice in Birmingham, Michigan. She was chosen as the National Woman Psychoanalytic Scholar, for 2005, of the American Psychoanalytic Association.

Mary Kay O'Neil, a Supervising and Training Analyst of the Canadian Institute of Psychoanalysis (CIP), is in private practice as a psychoanalyst and psychologist in Montreal, Quebec. Currently, she is Director of the Canadian Institute of Psychoanalysis (Quebec English) and secretary/treasurer of the CIP. She completed her PhD at the University of Toronto, where she was on the staff at the University of Toronto Psychiatric Service and Assistant Professor in the Department of Psychiatry. Her psychoanalytic training was completed at the Toronto Institute of Psychoanalysis. She is author of *The Unsung Psychoanalyst: The Quiet Influence of Ruth Easser* and co-editor of *Confidentiality: Ethical Perspectives and Clinical Dilemmas; On Freud's "The Future of an Illusion"*; and *On Freud's "Beyond the Pleasure Principle"*. Her research and publications include articles on depression and young adult development, emotional needs of sole-support mothers, post-analytic contacts, and psychoanalytic ethics. She has served on psychoanalytic ethics committees at local, national, and international levels, on the IPA finance committee, and as a reviewer for the *Journal of the American Psychoanalytic Association* and the *Canadian Journal of Psychoanalysis*, and is on the North American Editorial Board of the *International Journal of Psychoanalysis*.

Joan Raphael-Leff is a Fellow of the British Society. For 35 years she has specialized in clinical practice and academic work on reproductive issues, with over 100 single-author publications and 9 books, including *Psychological Processes of Childbearing; Pregnancy: The Inside Story; Parent–Infant Psychodynamics: Wild Things, Mirrors and Ghosts; Between Sessions and Beyond the Couch; Spilt Milk: Perinatal Loss and Breakdown; Ethics of Psychoanalysis*; and *Female Experience: Four Generations of British Women Psychoanalysts on Work with Women* (co-edited with R. Jozef Perelberg). Previously Professor of Psychoanalysis in the Centre for Psychoanalytic Studies, University of Essex, and head of the MSc in Psychoanalytic Developmental Psychology at University College London, she now leads the Academic Faculty for Psychoanalytic Research at the Anna Freud Centre, where she also heads a training programme for practitioners working with teenage parents. She was Founding Chair of COWAP (IPA's Committee on Women & Psychoanalysis) in 1998; she lectures and teaches worldwide and acts as consultant to perinatal and women's projects in many high- and low-income countries, including South Africa where she is Visiting Professor, Stellenbosch University.

Barbara S. Rocah, MD, is a Training and Supervising Analyst and Faculty at the Chicago Institute for Psychoanalysis, Geographic Rule Supervising Analyst at the Wisconsin Psychoanalytic Institute, and Past President of the Chicago Psychoanalytic Society. She is a member of the Center for Advanced Psychoanalytic Studies. She

has taught many courses and workshops, including Freud's Clinical
Theory, Advanced Freud Studies, and The Psychology of Women:
Current and Historical Views. Her publications and presentations
include "The Impact of the Analyst's Pregnancy on a Vulnerable
Child: A Case Presentation with Discussion by Miss Anna Freud"
(2009); *Links Between the Personal and the Theoretical: Some Insights
from Freud's Self-analysis That Influenced Later Conceptualizations* (presentation, Prague, Czech Republic, May 2006); "The Language of
Flowers: Freud's Adolescent Language of Love, Lust, and Longing"
(2002); *Personal Reflections on the Continuing Significance of Infantile Sexuality to Pathogenesis* (presentation to the American Psychoanalytic Association, 1987); *A Pluralistic Conception of Gender Identity*
(presentation to the American Psychoanalytic Association, 1986);
"Fixation in Late Adolescent Women: Negative Oedipus Complex,
Fear of Being Influenced, and Resistance to Change" (1984).

Jacqueline Schaeffer as a full member of and training analyst with
the Paris Psychoanalytical Society (*Société Psychanalytique de Paris:*
SPP); a training analyst in adult psychoanalysis and psychodrama
with the Paris Institute of Psychoanalysis; former training analyst
(1994–2006) in child and adolescent psychoanalysis at the Ste Anne
psychiatric hospital, Paris; Editor (1988–1997) of the *Revue Française
de Psychanalyse,* published by the Presses Universitaires de France;
Series co-editor (1995—2000) of the *Débats de psychanalyse* [Psycho-
analytic debates] collection, published by Presses Universitaires de
France. She was awarded the Maurice Bouvet Prize in 1987.

Introduction

Leticia Glocer Fiorini & Graciela Abelin-Sas Rose

We have assembled in this book a group of contemporary psycho-analytic authors dedicated to studies on women and the feminine, with the objective of displaying points of concordance and discord-ance in relation to Freudian proposals.

Discourse on women has changed greatly since Freud's time. It coincides with deep changes experienced by women and the feminine position, at least in most of the Western world. It is common knowledge that contraceptives, assisted fertilization, advances in women's rights, growingly evident sublimational capacities, and demonstrations of professional success have definitely changed ideas regarding an eternal and immutable feminine nature. We are interested in illuminating ways in which these changes have or have not influenced psychoanalytic debate in relation to the feminine. This implies renewing the question of what "feminine" means and whether there is any essential truth concerning the feminine.

We selected as a starting point "Femininity" (1933), Lecture XXXIII in *New Introductory Lectures on Psycho-Analysis* (1933a), a paper in which Freud reflects, and at the same time expands, ideas developed in previous texts that state his concepts on femininity.

1

Although he leaves some questions open, he also establishes some conclusions that we need to revisit with fresh questions.

Much has been discussed about Freudian proposals concerning the psychosexual development of girls, and the feminine in general. Although this is perhaps one of the most controversial subjects in Freud's works, debates and polemics are always lateralized rather than being integrated into fundamental theoretical lines. Consequently, these contributions are generally relegated to addenda to the main theory without actually interacting with theoretical nuclei to which they refer.

No single text could include the enormous quantity of post-Freudian and contemporary psychoanalytic contributions on this subject as well as contributions by gender theory and different types of feminisms (this comprehensive bibliography is amply reflected in different contributions to this book). To these we may add texts produced by social studies, which require multidisciplinary work.

Notwithstanding, this volume aims to manifest the most significant debates provoked by readings of Freudian texts.

First: major controversy centres on Freud's postulation of primary masculinity in girls, because of which girls are able to access femininity only through a complex itinerary guided by penis envy. This issue generated intense debate over primary versus secondary femininity and consequently over whether penis envy is primary or secondary. At this time there is no unanimity on these points in the psychoanalytic field. Besides, other questions are implied: Is penis envy a concept that may be applied universally to the psychosexual development of women? How does this concept relate to narratives and myths about masculine/feminine relations? Also, how could this concept be made compatible with the notion of bisexuality, considering that other theoretical lines provide yet another alternative to phallic-monism-versus-primary-femininity option: the concept of primary psychic bisexuality?

Second: how do we interpret the famous dictum that "anatomy is destiny"? How might we categorize the larger presence of the biological and the body in women (e.g., in menarche, pregnancy, and menopause)? What is our thinking on the role of genetic, hormonal, and morphological determinations in the constitution of femininity? Also, how could we include a fact thoroughly discussed by diverse authors—namely, that anatomy is also interpreted and that, in this sense, cultural discourses and norms do inevitably exert influence? Although Freud referred to social restrictions that weigh on the psychosexual development of women, he never concluded his development of these ideas. This, in turn, leads us to another series of debates on the nature–culture relation. We consider that we need to include the concept of complementary series in this debate if we are to avoid bias towards one of the terms of this polarity, favouring neither pure biologism nor extreme culturalism. It is only at the meeting point of these two variables that we may work on intersections between social discourse and norms and the drive field.

Third, and a subject of utmost importance: Is maternity the *princeps* aim of femininity, as Freud defined it? In this sense, what place do we assign to feminine sexuality independent of maternity? This subject also brings up the issue of the extent to which maternity corresponds to instinctive life.

Finally, why would access to femininity be so difficult, according to Freud? Do girls have options other than the Oedipus and castration complexes?

Also, a large number of psychoanalysts have countered Freud's ideas that the feminine superego is weaker than the masculine, that women's capacities of sublimation are poorer, and that their autonomy and capacity for planning are minimal.

In this Introduction we have undoubtedly omitted a great many polemical issues that will be discussed in different chapters of this book. However, we do wish to add another point in reference to relations between gender theories and psychoanalysis, both articulations and oppositions. These relations have already been discussed by various authors, who contributed to our understanding of the complex determinations of sexuated identity. The issue is whether gender theories are part of the psychoanalytic field and whether gender is a priority in relation to sexuality, topics also discussed in this book.

To these we may add other questions that invite us to reflect on the concept of femininity, such as the desire for children in lesbian women or the status of the feminine in single women with children who have no wish for a partner, as well as the desire for children and parentality in men who form homosexual couples. New forms of family organization are observed in the frame of

multiculturalism and globalization. In some sectors, the downfall of
the *pater familiae* generates fears of "feminization" in culture. New
forms of subjectivity have been identified. All these developments
question the traditional place of women. In other words, we should
ask ourselves how these experiences may be included in theory.
Does theory encompass enough? In this line, it is important to examine complex relations between theory and experience.

Yet another point that attracts heated polemics is feminine
masochism. Although Freud described it predominantly in men,
the term itself points to something seemingly inherent in women.
For some authors it is an essential part of access to femininity.
Others consider it a cultural construction.

To these questions we may even add others: What happens to
the concept of femininity in the course of a woman's life? Is it the
same when maternity has been realized in its most demanding facets and when, for various reasons, it has not been? What happens
in relation to physical decline in mid-life, considering that physical
beauty is a cultural value for women? These questions imply unavoidable relations between temporality and femininity.

All these questions present complex problems that attempt to
illuminate and delimit the questions being debated. They pinpoint
weak points of Freudian theory. When we examine the latter, we are
induced to reflect on subjacent logics and epistemological foundations of Freudian concepts on women and the feminine.

With respect to some debates presented, we think that there are
aspects of psychosexual and sublimational development of women
that find no satisfactory explanation in Freudian theory. However,
we also need to recall that, although Freud considers anatomy to
be destiny, his conception of the Oedipus complex—in the sense
of the process the girl needs to follow in order to access femininity—contributes elements in favour of the opinion that girls'
psychosexual development is quite far from any naturalistic determination. Hence, on the one hand, Freud creates an explanatory
path for access to the feminine position beyond anatomy, whereas
on the other hand, the feminine Oedipus leads into problems
without solution within this frame. In this sense, the proposal of
primary femininity and gender theories both contribute different
viewpoints on these issues.

We also point out that Freud lends a previously unknown ear

to the problems of women through his relation with his hysteric patients. His discovery of the [pre]oedipal phase also introduces interesting ideas on primary mother–daughter relations at the root of many problems in a woman's life, as long as this is not interpreted as an attempt to infantilize women.

Freud was repeatedly accused of phallocentrism, and it is true that his theories on girls' psychosexual development hinge on penis envy and its symbolic substitutions, which, at best, lead into maternity, ultimately a substitute for constitutional lack. Phallic/castrated polarity, as an infantile sexual theory on sexual difference, is implicitly extended to the whole theory and made equivalent to a masculine/feminine polarity, the feminine interpreted in terms of castration. In this sense, Freud maintains a gender theory based on a phallic/castrated dichotomy.

Freud's immense contributions to theories on psychosexuality, the drives, and the unconscious certainly revolutionized previously accepted conceptions of the subject. However, his works, which we consider multicentred and complex, also contain contradictions and blind spots, mainly in the field of the feminine and sexual difference; Freud examined them only partially, and they continue to be debated.

A review of the chapters included in this volume reveals many of these debates. Nancy Kulish and Deanna Holtzman question the Oedipus myth and propose that the myth of Persephone best explains the girl's psychosexual dynamic. Joan Raphael-Leff's concept of generative identity presents an explanatory model based on post-oedipal psychic construction of oneself as a *potential (pro)creator*. Leticia Glocer Fiorini studies epistemological bases subjacent to Freudian discourse on femininity and analysts' meta-theories on sexual difference and the feminine. Thierry Bokanowski reiterates the need to work on the feminine dimension and bisexuality in men and to listen in the transference to the bisexuality of both *partenaires* as a way to avoid bedrock. The role of bisexuality in connection with creativity in women is explored by Barbara Rocah. Jacqueline Schaeffer proposes the existence of a feminine erotic dimension beyond infantile sexual theories and beyond the phallic dimension. She postulates feminine erotogenic masochism as essential for access to "ecstatic pleasure" through sexual interchange. Graciela Abelin-Sas Rose, instead, states that feminine masochism is neither innate nor an instinctual vicissitude inherent in women but is, rather, a solution to complex infantile object relations reproduced in adulthood. Mary Kay O'Neil considers feminine autonomy in terms of an autonomous self, as either desires or projects, independent of sexuality. Emilce Dio Bleichmar discusses implicit gender theories in psychoanalysis and proposes the incorporation of the concept of gender in psychoanalysis in order to listen to legitimate desires for expansion of the feminine self. Mariam Alizade postulates a human dimension based on pre-sexual and non-sexual aspects previous to assignment of the newborn as a boy or a girl. In her view, gender and psychoanalysis have some points in common as well as other aspects that diverge. Finally, characteristics of the feminine position in three generations of Korean women in different historical circumstances and contexts are analysed by Mikyum Kim, who emphasizes that drastic changes in these women's lives coexist with the survival of cultural ideals in spite of these changes.

This itinerary evidences an enormous variety of problems and the inconceivability of universalizing conclusions on the feminine and on women. To this we may add complex interactions—both hetero- and homosexual—between men and women, which determine weighty and significant variants in terms of distributions of functions and roles. Ultimately, each woman—like each man—is a singularity "in process", and clinical work needs to consider her as such. Although she may share characteristics with other women, the way determining variants intersect is always totally singular and unique.

PART I

Lecture XXXIII: "Femininity" (1933)

Sigmund Freud

LECTURE XXXIII

FEMININITY[1]

LADIES AND GENTLEMEN,—All the while I am preparing to talk to you I am struggling with an internal difficulty. I feel uncertain, so to speak, of the extent of my licence. It is true that in the course of fifteen years of work psycho-analysis has changed and grown richer; but, in spite of that, an introduction to psycho-analysis might have been left without alteration or supplement. It is constantly in my mind that these lectures are without a *raison d'être*. For analysts I am saying too little and nothing at all that is new; but for you I am saying too much and saying things which you are not equipped to understand and which are not in your province. I have looked around for excuses and I have tried to justify each separate lecture on different grounds. The first one, on the theory of dreams, was supposed to put you back again at one blow into the analytic atmosphere and to show you how durable our views have turned out to be. I was led on to the second one, which followed the paths from dreams to what is called occultism, by the opportunity of speaking my mind without constraint on a department of work in which prejudiced expectations are fighting to-day against passionate resistances, and I could hope that your judgement, educated to tolerance on the example of psycho-analysis, would not refuse to accompany me on the excursion. The third lecture, on the dissection of the personality, certainly made the hardest demands upon you with its unfamiliar subject-matter; but it was impossible for me to keep this first beginning of an ego-psychology back from you, and if we had possessed it fifteen years ago I should have had to mention it to you then. My last lecture, finally, which you were probably

[1] [This lecture is mainly based on two earlier papers: 'Some Psychical Consequences of the Anatomical Distinction between the Sexes' (1925*j*) and 'Female Sexuality' (1931*b*). The last section, however, dealing with women in adult life, contains new material. Freud returned to the subject once again in Chapter VII of the posthumous *Outline of Psycho-Analysis* (1940*a* [1938]).]

112

8

able to follow only by great exertions, brought forward necessary corrections—fresh attempts at solving the most important
conundrums; and my introduction would have been leading
you astray if I had been silent about them. As you see, when one
starts making excuses it turns out in the end that it was all inevitable, all the work of destiny. I submit to it, and I beg you to
do the same.

To-day's lecture, too, should have no place in an introduction; but it may serve to give you an example of a detailed piece
of analytic work, and I can say two things to recommend it. It
brings forward nothing but observed facts, almost without any
speculative additions, and it deals with a subject which has
a claim on your interest second almost to no other. Throughout
history people have knocked their heads against the riddle of
the nature of femininity—

> Häupter in Hieroglyphenmützen,
> Häupter in Turban und schwarzem Barett,
> Perückenhäupter und tausend andre
> Arme, schwitzende Menschenhäupter. . . .[1]

Nor will *you* have escaped worrying over this problem—
those of you who are men; to those of you who are women this
will not apply—you are yourselves the problem. When you
meet a human being, the first distinction you make is 'male or
female?' and you are accustomed to make the distinction with
unhesitating certainty. Anatomical science shares your certainty at one point and not much further. The male sexual product, the spermatozoon, and its vehicle are male; the ovum and
the organism that harbours it are female. In both sexes organs
have been formed which serve exclusively for the sexual functions; they were probably developed from the same [innate]
disposition into two different forms. Besides this, in both sexes
the other organs, the bodily shapes and tissues, show the influence of the individual's sex, but this is inconstant and its
amount variable; these are what are known as the secondary

[1] Heads in hieroglyphic bonnets,
  Heads in turbans and black birettas,
  Heads in wigs and thousand other
  Wretched, sweating heads of humans. . . .
       (Heine, *Nordsee* [Second Cycle, VII, 'Fragen'].)

sexual characters. Science next tells you something that runs
counter to your expectations and is probably calculated to con-
fuse your feelings. It draws your attention to the fact that por-
tions of the male sexual apparatus also appear in women's
bodies, though in an atrophied state, and vice versa in the
alternative case. It regards their occurrence as indications of
bisexuality,[1] as though an individual is not a man or a woman
but always both—merely a certain amount more the one than
the other. You will then be asked to make yourselves familiar
with the idea that the proportion in which masculine and feminine are mixed in an individual is subject to quite considerable fluctuations. Since, however, apart from the very rarest
cases, only one kind of sexual product—ova or semen—is nevertheless present in one person, you are bound to have doubts
as to the decisive significance of those elements and must conclude that what constitutes masculinity or femininity is an unknown characteristic which anatomy cannot lay hold of.

Can psychology do so perhaps? We are accustomed to em-
ploy 'masculine' and 'feminine' as mental qualities as well, and
have in the same way transferred the notion of bisexuality to
mental life. Thus we speak of a person, whether male or female,
as behaving in a masculine way in one connection and in a
feminine way in another. But you will soon perceive that this
is only giving way to anatomy or to convention. You cannot
give the concepts of 'masculine' and 'feminine' *any* new connotation. The distinction is not a psychological one; when you
say 'masculine', you usually mean 'active', and when you say
'feminine', you usually mean 'passive'. Now it is true that a relation of the kind exists. The male sex-cell is actively mobile and
searches out the female one, and the latter, the ovum, is im-
mobile and waits passively. This behaviour of the elementary
sexual organisms is indeed a model for the conduct of sexual
individuals during intercourse. The male pursues the female for
the purpose of sexual union, seizes hold of her and penetrates
into her. But by this you have precisely reduced the character-

[1] [Bisexuality was discussed by Freud in the first edition of his *Three
Essays on the Theory of Sexuality* (1905d), *Standard Ed.*, 7, 141–4. The
passage includes a long footnote to which he made additions in later
issues of the work.]

istic of masculinity to the factor of aggressiveness so far as psychology is concerned. You may well doubt whether you have gained any real advantage from this when you reflect that in some classes of animals the females are the stronger and more aggressive and the male is active only in the single act of sexual union. This is so, for instance, with the spiders. Even the functions of rearing and caring for the young, which strike us as feminine *par excellence*, are not invariably attached to the female sex in animals. In quite high species we find that the sexes share the task of caring for the young between them or even that the male alone devotes himself to it. Even in the sphere of human sexual life you soon see how inadequate it is to make masculine behaviour coincide with activity and feminine with passivity. A mother is active in every sense towards her child; the act of lactation itself may equally be described as the mother suckling the baby or as her being sucked by it. The further you go from the narrow sexual sphere the more obvious will the 'error of superimposition'[1] become. Women can display great activity in various directions, men are not able to live in company with their own kind unless they develop a large amount of passive adaptability. If you now tell me that these facts go to prove precisely that both men and women are bisexual in the psychological sense, I shall conclude that you have decided in your own minds to make 'active' coincide with 'masculine' and 'passive' with 'feminine'. But I advise you against it. It seems to me to serve no useful purpose and adds nothing to our knowledge.[2]

One might consider characterizing femininity psychologically as giving preference to passive aims. This is not, of course, the same thing as passivity; to achieve a passive aim may call for a large amount of activity. It is perhaps the case that in a woman, on the basis of her share in the sexual function, a preference for passive behaviour and passive aims is carried over into her life to a greater or lesser extent, in proportion to the

[1] [I.e. mistaking two different things for a single one. The term was explained in *Introductory Lectures*, XX, *Standard Ed.*, **16**, 304.]

[2] [The difficulty of finding a psychological meaning for 'masculine' and 'feminine' was discussed in a long footnote added in 1915 to the *Three Essays* (1905*d*), *Standard Ed.*, **7**, 219–20 and again at the beginning of a still longer footnote at the end of Chapter IV of *Civilization and its Discontents* (1930*a*), ibid., **21**, 105–6.]

limits, restricted or far-reaching, within which her sexual life thus serves as a model. But we must beware in this of under-estimating the influence of social customs, which similarly force women into passive situations. All this is still far from being cleared up. There is one particularly constant relation between femininity and instinctual life which we do not want to over-look. The suppression of women's aggressiveness which is pre-scribed for them constitutionally and imposed on them socially favours the development of powerful masochistic impulses, which succeed, as we know, in binding erotically the destruc-tive trends which have been diverted inwards. Thus masochism, as people say, is truly feminine. But if, as happens so often, you meet with masochism in men, what is left to you but to say that these men exhibit very plain feminine traits?

And now you are already prepared to hear that psychology too is unable to solve the riddle of femininity. The explanation must no doubt come from elsewhere, and cannot come till we have learnt how in general the differentiation of living organ-isms into two sexes came about. We know nothing about it, yet the existence of two sexes is a most striking characteristic of organic life which distinguishes it sharply from inanimate nature. However, we find enough to study in those human in-dividuals who, through the possession of female genitals, are characterized as manifestly or predominantly feminine. In con-formity with its peculiar nature, psycho-analysis does not try to describe what a woman is—that would be a task it could scarcely perform—but sets about enquiring how she comes into being, how a woman develops out of a child with a bisexual dis-position. In recent times we have begun to learn a little about this, thanks to the circumstance that several of our excellent women colleagues in analysis have begun to work at the ques-tion. The discussion of this has gained special attractiveness from the distinction between the sexes. For the ladies, whenever some comparison seemed to turn out unfavourable to their sex, were able to utter a suspicion that we, the male analysts, had been unable to overcome certain deeply-rooted prejudices against what was feminine, and that this was being paid for in the partiality of our researches. We, on the other hand, standing on the ground of bisexuality, had no difficulty in avoiding impoliteness. We had only to say: 'This doesn't apply to *you*.

You're the exception; on this point you're more masculine than feminine.'

We approach the investigation of the sexual development of women with two expectations. The first is that here once more the constitution will not adapt itself to its function without a struggle. The second is that the decisive turning-points will already have been prepared for or completed before puberty. Both expectations are promptly confirmed. Furthermore, a comparison with what happens with boys tells us that the development of a little girl into a normal woman is more difficult and more complicated, since it includes two extra tasks, to which there is nothing corresponding in the development of a man. Let us follow the parallel lines from their beginning. Undoubtedly the material is different to start with in boys and girls: it did not need psycho-analysis to establish that. The difference in the structure of the genitals is accompanied by other bodily differences which are too well known to call for mention. Differences emerge too in the instinctual disposition which give a glimpse of the later nature of women. A little girl is as a rule less aggressive, defiant and self-sufficient; she seems to have a greater need for being shown affection and on that account to be more dependent and pliant. It is probably only as a result of this pliancy that she can be taught more easily and quicker to control her excretions: urine and faeces are the first gifts that children make to those who look after them [see p. 100 above], and controlling them is the first concession to which the instinctual life of children can be induced. One gets an impression, too, that little girls are more intelligent and livelier than boys of the same age; they go out more to meet the external world and at the same time form stronger object-cathexes. I cannot say whether this lead in development has been confirmed by exact observations, but in any case there is no question that girls cannot be described as intellectually backward. These sexual differences are not, however, of great consequence: they can be outweighed by individual variations. For our immediate purposes they can be disregarded.

Both sexes seem to pass through the early phases of libidinal development in the same manner. It might have been expected that in girls there would already have been some lag in aggres-

13

siveness in the sadistic-anal phase, but such is not the case. Analysis of children's play has shown our women analysts that the aggressive impulses of little girls leave nothing to be desired in the way of abundance and violence. With their entry into the phallic phase the differences between the sexes are completely eclipsed by their agreements. We are now obliged to recognize that the little girl is a little man. In boys, as we know, this phase is marked by the fact that they have learnt how to derive pleasurable sensations from their small penis and connect its excited state with their ideas of sexual intercourse. Little girls do the same thing with their still smaller clitoris. It seems that with them all their masturbatory acts are carried out on this penis-equivalent, and that the truly feminine vagina is still undiscovered by both sexes. It is true that there are a few isolated reports of early vaginal sensations as well, but it could not be easy to distinguish these from sensations in the anus or vestibulum; in any case they cannot play a great part. We are entitled to keep to our view that in the phallic phase of girls the clitoris is the leading erotogenic zone. But it is not, of course, going to remain so. With the change to femininity the clitoris should wholly or in part hand over its sensitivity, and at the same time its importance, to the vagina. This would be one of the two tasks which a woman has to perform in the course of her development, whereas the more fortunate man has only to continue at the time of his sexual maturity the activity that he has previously carried out at the period of the early efflorescence of his sexuality.

We shall return to the part played by the clitoris; let us now turn to the second task with which a girl's development is burdened. A boy's mother is the first object of his love, and she remains so too during the formation of his Oedipus complex and, in essence, all through his life. For a girl too her first object must be her mother (and the figures of wet-nurses and foster-mothers that merge into her). The first object-cathexes occur in attachment to the satisfaction of the major and simple vital needs,[1] and the circumstances of the care of children are the same for both sexes. But in the Oedipus situation the girl's father has become her love-object, and we expect that in the normal course of development she will find her way from

[1] [Cf. *Introductory Lectures*, XXI, *Standard Ed.*, 16, 328–9.]

this paternal object to her final choice of an object. In the course of time, therefore, a girl has to change her erotogenic zone and her object—both of which a boy retains. The question then arises of how this happens: in particular, how does a girl pass from her mother to an attachment to her father? or, in other words, how does she pass from her masculine phase to the feminine one to which she is biologically destined?

It would be a solution of ideal simplicity if we could suppose that from a particular age onwards the elementary influence of the mutual attraction between the sexes makes itself felt and impels the small woman towards men, while the same law allows the boy to continue with his mother. We might suppose in addition that in this the children are following the pointer given them by the sexual preference of their parents. But we are not going to find things so easy; we scarcely know whether we are to believe seriously in the power of which poets talk so much and with such enthusiasm but which cannot be further dissected analytically. We have found an answer of quite another sort by means of laborious investigations, the material for which at least was easy to arrive at. For you must know that the number of women who remain till a late age tenderly dependent on a paternal object, or indeed on their real father, is very great. We have established some surprising facts about these women with an intense attachment of long duration to their father. We knew, of course, that there had been a preliminary stage of attachment to the mother, but we did not know that it could be so rich in content and so long-lasting, and could leave behind so many opportunities for fixations and dispositions. During this time the girl's father is only a troublesome rival; in some cases the attachment to her mother lasts beyond the fourth year of life. Almost everything that we find later in her relation to her father was already present in this earlier attachment and has been transferred subsequently on to her father. In short, we get an impression that we cannot understand women unless we appreciate this phase of their pre-Oedipus attachment to their mother.

We shall be glad, then, to know the nature of the girl's libidinal relations to her mother. The answer is that they are of very many different kinds. Since they persist through all three phases of infantile sexuality, they also take on the characteristics of the different phases and express themselves by oral, sadistic-anal and phallic wishes. These wishes represent active as well as passive impulses; if we relate them to the differentiation of the sexes which is to appear later—though we should avoid doing so as far as possible—we may call them masculine and feminine. Besides this, they are completely ambivalent, both affectionate and of a hostile and aggressive nature. The latter often only come to light after being changed into anxiety ideas. It is not always easy to point to a formulation of these early sexual wishes; what is most clearly expressed is a wish to get the mother with child and the corresponding wish to bear her a child—both belonging to the phallic period and sufficiently surprising, but established beyond doubt by analytic observation. The attractiveness of these investigations lies in the surprising detailed findings which they bring us. Thus, for instance, we discover the fear of being murdered or poisoned, which may later form the core of a paranoic illness, already present in this pre-Oedipus period, in relation to the mother. Or another case: you will recall an interesting episode in the history of analytic research which caused me many distressing hours. In the period in which the main interest was directed to discovering infantile sexual traumas, almost all my women patients told me that they had been seduced by their father. I was driven to recognize in the end that these reports were untrue and so came to understand that hysterical symptoms are derived from phantasies and not from real occurrences. It was only later that I was able to recognize in this phantasy of being seduced by the father the expression of the typical Oedipus complex in women. And now we find the phantasy of seduction once more in the pre-Oedipus prehistory of girls; but the seducer is regularly the mother. Here, however, the phantasy touches the ground of reality, for it was really the mother who by her activities over the child's bodily hygiene inevitably stimulated, and perhaps even roused for the first time, pleasurable sensations in her genitals.[1]

[1] [In his early discussions of the aetiology of hysteria Freud often mentioned seduction by adults as among its commonest causes (see, for instance, the second paper on the neuro-psychoses of defence (1896b), Standard Ed., 3, 164 and 'The Aetiology of Hysteria' (1896c), ibid., 208). But nowhere in these early publications did he specifically inculpate the girl's father. Indeed, in some additional footnotes written in 1924 for the

I have no doubt you are ready to suspect that this portrayal of the abundance and strength of a little girl's sexual relations with her mother is very much overdrawn. After all, one has opportunities of seeing little girls and notices nothing of the sort. But the objection is not to the point. Enough can be seen in the children if one knows how to look. And besides, you should consider how little of its sexual wishes a child can bring to pre-conscious expression or communicate at all. Accordingly we are only within our rights if we study the residues and consequences of this emotional world in retrospect, in people in whom these processes of development had attained a specially clear and even excessive degree of expansion. Pathology has always done us the service of making discernible by isolation and exaggeration conditions which would remain concealed in a normal state. And since our investigations have been carried out on people who were by no means seriously abnormal, I think we should regard their outcome as deserving belief.

We will now turn our interest on to the single question of what it is that brings this powerful attachment of the girl to her mother to an end. This, as we know, is its usual fate: it is destined to make room for an attachment to her father. Here we come upon a fact which is a pointer to our further advance. This step in development does not involve only a simple change of object. The turning away from the mother is accompanied by hostility; the attachment to the mother ends in hate. A hate of that kind may become very striking and last all through life; it may be carefully overcompensated later on; as a rule one part

Gesammelte Schriften reprint of *Studies on Hysteria*, he admitted to having on two occasions suppressed the fact of the father's responsibility (see *Standard Ed.*, **2**, 134 n., and 170 n.). He made this quite clear, however, in the letter to Fliess of September 21, 1897 (Freud, 1950a, Letter 69), in which he first expressed his scepticism about these stories told by his patients. His first published admission of his mistake was given several years later in a hint in the second of the *Three Essays* (1905d), *Standard Ed.*, **7**, 190, but a much fuller account of the position followed in his contribution on the aetiology of the neuroses to a volume by Löwenfeld (1906a), ibid., **7**, 274–5. Later on he gave two accounts of the effects that this discovery of his mistake had on his own mind—in his 'History of the Psycho-Analytic Movement' (1914d), ibid., **14**, 17–18 and in his *Autobiographical Study* (1925d), ibid., **20**, 33–5. The further discovery which is described in the present paragraph of the text had already been indicated in the paper on 'Female Sexuality' (1931b), ibid., **21**, 238.]

of it is overcome while another part persists. Events of later years naturally influence this greatly. We will restrict ourselves, however, to studying it at the time at which the girl turns to her father and to enquiring into the motives for it. We are then given a long list of accusations and grievances against the mother which are supposed to justify the child's hostile feelings; they are of varying validity which we shall not fail to examine. A number of them are obvious rationalizations and the true sources of enmity remain to be found. I hope you will be interested if on this occasion I take you through all the details of a psycho-analytic investigation.

The reproach against the mother which goes back furthest is that she gave the child too little milk—which is construed against her as lack of love. Now there is some justification for this reproach in our families. Mothers often have insufficient nourishment to give their children and are content to suckle them for a few months, for half or three-quarters of a year. Among primitive peoples children are fed at their mother's breast for two or three years. The figure of the wet-nurse who suckles the child is as a rule merged into the mother; when this has not happened, the reproach is turned into another one—that the nurse, who fed the child so willingly, was sent away by the mother too early. But whatever the true state of affairs may have been, it is impossible that the child's reproach can be justified as often as it is met with. It seems, rather, that the child's avidity for its earliest nourishment is altogether insatiable, that it never gets over the pain of losing its mother's breast. I should not be surprised if the analysis of a primitive child, who could still suck at its mother's breast when it was already able to run about and talk, were to bring the same reproach to light. The fear of being poisoned is also probably connected with the withdrawal of the breast. Poison is nourishment that makes one ill. Perhaps children trace back their early illnesses too to this frustration. A fair amount of intellectual education is a prerequisite for believing in chance; primitive people and uneducated ones, and no doubt children as well, are able to assign a ground for everything that happens. Perhaps originally it was a reason on animistic lines. Even to-day in some strata of our population no one can die without having been killed by someone else—preferably by the doctor.

And the regular reaction of a neurotic to the death of someone closely connected with him is to put the blame on himself for having caused the death.

The next accusation against the child's mother flares up when the next baby appears in the nursery. If possible the connection with oral frustration is preserved: the mother could not or would not give the child any more milk because she needed the nourishment for the new arrival. In cases in which the two children are so close in age that lactation is prejudiced by the second pregnancy, this reproach acquires a real basis, and it is a remarkable fact that a child, even with an age difference of only 11 months, is not too young to take notice of what is happening. But what the child grudges the unwanted intruder and rival is not only the suckling but all the other signs of maternal care. It feels that it has been dethroned, despoiled, prejudiced in its rights; it casts a jealous hatred upon the new baby and develops a grievance against the faithless mother which often finds expression in a disagreeable change in its behaviour. It becomes 'naughty', perhaps, irritable and disobedient and goes back on the advances it has made towards controlling its excretions. All of this has been very long familiar and is accepted as self-evident; but we rarely form a correct idea of the strength of these jealous impulses, of the tenacity with which they persist and of the magnitude of their influence on later development. Especially as this jealousy is constantly receiving fresh nourishment in the later years of childhood and the whole shock is repeated with the birth of each new brother or sister. Nor does it make much difference if the child happens to remain the mother's preferred favourite. A child's demands for love are immoderate, they make exclusive claims and tolerate no sharing.

An abundant source of a child's hostility to its mother is provided by its multifarious sexual wishes, which alter according to the phase of the libido and which cannot for the most part be satisfied. The strongest of these frustrations occur at the phallic period, if the mother forbids pleasurable activity with the genitals—often with severe threats and every sign of displeasure—activity to which, after all, she herself had introduced the child. One would think these were reasons enough to account for a girl's turning away from her mother. One would judge, if so, that the estrangement follows inevitably from the nature of children's sexuality, from the immoderate character of their demand for love and the impossibility of fulfilling their sexual wishes. It might be thought indeed that this first love-relation of the child's is doomed to dissolution for the very reason that it is the first, for these early object-cathexes are regularly ambivalent to a high degree. A powerful tendency to aggressiveness is always present beside a powerful love, and the more passionately a child loves its object the more sensitive does it become to disappointments and frustrations from that object; and in the end the love must succumb to the accumulated hostility. Or the idea that there is an original ambivalence such as this in erotic cathexes may be rejected, and it may be pointed out that it is the special nature of the mother-child relation that leads, with equal inevitability, to the destruction of the child's love; for even the mildest upbringing cannot avoid using compulsion and introducing restrictions, and any such intervention in the child's liberty must provoke as a reaction an inclination to rebelliousness and aggressiveness. A discussion of these possibilities might, I think, be most interesting; but an objection suddenly emerges which forces our interest in another direction. All these factors—the slights, the disappointments in love, the jealousy, the seduction followed by prohibition—are, after all, also in operation in the relation of a *boy* to his mother and are yet unable to alienate him from the maternal object. Unless we can find something that is specific for girls and is not present or not in the same way present in boys, we shall not have explained the termination of the attachment of girls to their mother.

I believe we have found this specific factor, and indeed where we expected to find it, even though in a surprising form. Where we expected to find it, I say, for it lies in the castration complex. After all, the anatomical distinction [between the sexes] must express itself in psychical consequences. It was, however, a surprise to learn from analyses that girls hold their mother responsible for their lack of a penis and do not forgive her for their being thus put at a disadvantage.

As you hear, then, we ascribe a castration complex to women as well. And for good reasons, though its content cannot be the same as with boys. In the latter the castration complex arises after they have learnt from the sight of the female genitals that the organ which they value so highly need not necessarily accompany the body. At this the boy recalls to mind the threats he brought on himself by his doings with that organ, he begins to give credence to them and falls under the influence of fear of castration, which will be the most powerful motive force in his subsequent development. The castration complex of girls is also started by the sight of the genitals of the other sex. They at once notice the difference and, it must be admitted, its significance too. They feel seriously wronged, often declare that they want to 'have something like it too', and fall a victim to 'envy for the penis', which will leave ineradicable traces on their development and the formation of their character and which will not be surmounted in even the most favourable cases without a severe expenditure of psychical energy. The girl's recognition of the fact of her being without a penis does not by any means imply that she submits to the fact easily. On the contrary, she continues to hold on for a long time to the wish to get something like it herself and she believes in that possibility for improbably long years; and analysis can show that, at a period when knowledge of reality has long since rejected the fulfilment of the wish as unattainable, it persists in the unconscious and retains a considerable cathexis of energy. The wish to get the longed-for penis eventually in spite of everything may contribute to the motives that drive a mature woman to analysis, and what she may reasonably expect from analysis—a capacity, for instance, to carry on an intellectual profession—may often be recognized as a sublimated modification of this repressed wish.

One cannot very well doubt the importance of envy for the penis. You may take it as an instance of male injustice if I assert that envy and jealousy play an even greater part in the mental life of women than of men. It is not that I think these characteristics are absent in men or that I think they have no other roots in women than envy for the penis; but I am inclined to attribute their greater amount in women to this latter influence. Some analysts, however, have shown an inclination to depreciate the importance of this first instalment of penis-envy in the phallic phase. They are of opinion that what we find of this attitude in women is in the main a secondary structure which has come about on the occasion of later conflicts by regression to this early infantile impulse. This, however, is a general problem of depth psychology. In many pathological—or even unusual—instinctual attitudes (for instance, in all sexual perversions) the question arises of how much of their strength is to be attributed to early infantile fixations and how much to the influence of later experiences and developments. In such cases it is almost always a matter of complemental series such as we put forward in our discussion of the aetiology of the neuroses.[1] Both factors play a part in varying amounts in the causation; a less on the one side is balanced by a more on the other. The infantile factor sets the pattern in all cases but does not always determine the issue, though it often does. Precisely in the case of penis-envy I should argue decidedly in favour of the preponderance of the infantile factor.

The discovery that she is castrated is a turning-point in a girl's growth. Three possible lines of development start from it: one leads to sexual inhibition or to neurosis, the second to change of character in the sense of a masculinity complex, the third, finally, to normal femininity. We have learnt a fair amount, though not everything, about all three.

The essential content of the first is as follows: the little girl has hitherto lived in a masculine way, has been able to get pleasure by the excitation of her clitoris and has brought this activity into relation with her sexual wishes directed towards her mother, which are often active ones; now, owing to the influence of her penis-envy, she loses her enjoyment in her phallic sexuality. Her self-love is mortified by the comparison with the boy's far superior equipment and in consequence she renounces her masturbatory satisfaction from her clitoris, repudiates her love for her mother and at the same time not infrequently represses a good part of her sexual trends in general. No doubt her turning away from her mother does not occur all at once, for to begin with the girl regards her castration as an individual misfortune, and only gradually extends it to other females and finally to her mother as well. Her love was directed to her *phallic* mother; with the discovery that her mother is castrated it becomes possible to drop her as an object, so that

[1] [See *Introductory Lectures*, XXII and XXIII, *Standard Ed.*, 16, 347, 362 and 364.]

the motives for hostility, which have long been accumulating, gain the upper hand. This means, therefore, that as a result of the discovery of women's lack of a penis they are debased in value for girls just as they are for boys and later perhaps for men.

You all know the immense aetiological importance attributed by our neurotic patients to their masturbation. They make it responsible for all their troubles and we have the greatest difficulty in persuading them that they are mistaken. In fact, however, we ought to admit to them that they are right, for masturbation is the executive agent of infantile sexuality, from the faulty development of which they are indeed suffering. But what neurotics mostly blame is the masturbation of the period of puberty; they have mostly forgotten that of early infancy, which is what is really in question. I wish I might have an opportunity some time of explaining to you at length how important all the factual details of early masturbation become for the individual's subsequent neurosis or character: whether or not it was discovered, how the parents struggled against it or permitted it, or whether he succeeded in suppressing it himself. All of this leaves permanent traces on his development. But I am on the whole glad that I need not do this. It would be a hard and tedious task and at the end of it you would put me in an embarrassing situation by quite certainly asking me to give you some practical advice as to how a parent or educator should deal with the masturbation of small children.[1] From the development of girls, which is what my present lecture is concerned with, I can give you the example of a child herself trying to get free from masturbating. She does not always succeed in this. If envy for the penis has provoked a powerful impulse against clitoridal masturbation but this nevertheless refuses to give way, a violent struggle for liberation ensues in which the girl, as it were, herself takes over the role of her deposed mother and gives expression to her entire dissatisfaction with her inferior clitoris in her efforts against obtaining satisfaction from it. Many years later, when her

---

[1] [Freud's fullest discussion of masturbation was in his contributions to a symposium on the subject in the Vienna Psycho-Analytical Society (1912*f*), *Standard Ed.*, **12**, 241 ff., where a number of other references are given.]

masturbatory activity has long since been suppressed, an interest still persists which we must interpret as a defence against a temptation that is still dreaded. It manifests inself in the emergence of sympathy for those to whom similar difficulties are attributed, it plays a part as a motive in contracting a marriage and, indeed, it may determine the choice of a husband or lover. Disposing of early infantile masturbation is truly no easy or indifferent business.

Along with the abandonment of clitoridal masturbation a certain amount of activity is renounced. Passivity now has the upper hand, and the girl's turning to her father is accomplished principally with the help of passive instinctual impulses. You can see that a wave of development like this, which clears the phallic activity out of the way, smooths the ground for femininity. If too much is not lost in the course of it through repression, this femininity may turn out to be normal. The wish with which the girl turns to her father is no doubt originally the wish for the penis which her mother has refused her and which she now expects from her father. The feminine situation is only established, however, if the wish for a penis is replaced by one for a baby, if, that is, a baby takes the place of a penis in accordance with an ancient symbolic equivalence [p. 100 f.]. It has not escaped us that the girl has wished for a baby earlier, in the undisturbed phallic phase: that, of course, was the meaning of her playing with dolls. But that play was not in fact an expression of her femininity; it served as an identification with her mother with the intention of substituting activity for passivity. *She* was playing the part of her mother and the doll was herself: now she could do with the baby everything that her mother used to do with her. Not until the emergence of the wish for a penis does the doll-baby become a baby from the girl's father, and thereafter the aim of the most powerful feminine wish. Her happiness is great if later on this wish for a baby finds fulfilment in reality, and quite especially so if the baby is a little boy who brings the longed-for penis with him.[1] Often enough in her combined picture of 'a baby from her father' the emphasis is laid on the baby and her father left unstressed. In this way the uncient masculine wish for the possession of a penis is still faintly visible through the femininity now achieved. But per-

[1] [See p. 133 below.]

haps we ought rather to recognize this wish for a penis as being *par excellence* a feminine one.

With the transference of the wish for a penis-baby on to her father, the girl has entered the situation of the Oedipus complex. Her hostility to her mother, which did not need to be freshly created, is now greatly intensified, for she becomes the girl's rival, who receives from her father everything that she desires from him. For a long time the girl's Oedipus complex concealed her pre-Oedipus attachment to her mother from our view, though it is nevertheless so important and leaves such lasting fixations behind it. For girls the Oedipus situation is the outcome of a long and difficult development; it is a kind of preliminary solution, a position of rest which is not soon abandoned, especially as the beginning of the latency period is not far distant. And we are now struck by a difference between the two sexes, which is probably momentous, in regard to the relation of the Oedipus complex to the castration complex. In a boy the Oedipus complex, in which he desires his mother and would like to get rid of his father as being a rival, develops naturally from the phase of his phallic sexuality. The threat of castration compels him, however, to give up that attitude. Under the impression of the danger of losing his penis, the Oedipus complex is abandoned, repressed and, in the most normal cases, entirely destroyed [see p. 92], and a severe super-ego is set up as its heir. What happens with a girl is almost the opposite. The castration complex prepares for the Oedipus complex instead of destroying it; the girl is driven out of her attachment to her mother through the influence of her envy for the penis and she enters the Oedipus situation as though into a haven of refuge. In the absence of fear of castration the chief motive is lacking which leads boys to surmount the Oedipus complex. Girls remain in it for an indeterminate length of time; they demolish it late and, even so, incompletely. In these circumstances the formation of the super-ego must suffer; it cannot attain the strength and independence which give it its cultural significance, and feminists are not pleased when we point out to them the effects of this factor upon the average feminine character.

To go back a little. We mentioned [p. 126] as the second possible reaction to the discovery of female castration the development of a powerful masculinity complex. By this we mean that the girl refuses, as it were, to recognize the unwelcome fact and, defiantly rebellious, even exaggerates her previous masculinity, clings to her clitoridal activity and takes refuge in an identification with her phallic mother or her father. What can it be that decides in favour of this outcome? We can only suppose that it is a constitutional factor, a greater amount of activity, such as is ordinarily characteristic of a male. However that may be, the essence of this process is that at this point in development the wave of passivity is avoided which opens the way to the turn towards femininity. The extreme achievement of such a masculinity complex would appear to be the influencing of the choice of an object in the sense of manifest homosexuality. Analytic experience teaches us, to be sure, that female homosexuality is seldom or never a direct continuation of infantile masculinity. Even for a girl of this kind it seems necessary that she should take her father as an object for some time and enter the Oedipus situation. But afterwards, as a result of her inevitable disappointments from her father, she is driven to regress into her early masculinity complex. The significance of these disappointments must not be exaggerated; a girl who is destined to become feminine is not spared them, though they do not have the same effect. The predominance of the constitutional factor seems indisputable; but the two phases in the development of female homosexuality are well mirrored in the practices of homosexuals, who play the parts of mother and baby with each other as often and as clearly as those of husband and wife.

What I have been telling you here may be described as the prehistory of women. It is a product of the very last few years and may have been of interest to you as an example of detailed analytic work. Since its subject is woman, I will venture on this occasion to mention by name a few of the women who have made valuable contributions to this investigation. Dr. Ruth Mack Brunswick [1928] was the first to describe a case of neurosis which went back to a fixation in the pre-Oedipus stage and had never reached the Oedipus situation at all. The case took the form of jealous paranoia and proved accessible to therapy. Dr. Jeanne Lampl-de Groot [1927] has established the incredible phallic activity of girls towards their mother by some assured observations, and Dr. Helene Deutsch [1932] has shown that the erotic actions of homosexual women reproduce the relations between mother and baby.

It is not my intention to pursue the further behaviour of femininity through puberty to the period of maturity. Our knowledge, moreover, would be insufficient for the purpose. But I will bring a few features together in what follows. Taking its prehistory as a starting-point, I will only emphasize here that the development of femininity remains exposed to disturbance by the residual phenomena of the early masculine period. Regressions to the fixations of the pre-Oedipus phases very frequently occur; in the course of some women's lives there is a repeated alternation between periods in which masculinity or femininity gains the upper hand. Some portion of what we men call 'the enigma of women' may perhaps be derived from this expression of bisexuality in women's lives. But another question seems to have become ripe for judgement in the course of these researches. We have called the motive force of sexual life 'the libido'. Sexual life is dominated by the polarity of masculine-feminine; thus the notion suggests itself of considering the relation of the libido to this antithesis. It would not be surprising if it were to turn out that each sexuality had its own special libido appropriated to it, so that one sort of libido would pursue the aims of a masculine sexual life and another sort those of a feminine one. But nothing of the kind is true. There is only one libido, which serves both the masculine and the feminine sexual functions. To it itself we cannot assign any sex; if, following the conventional equation of activity and masculinity, we are inclined to describe it as masculine, we must not forget that it also covers trends with a passive aim. Nevertheless the juxtaposition 'feminine libido' is without any justification. Furthermore, it is our impression that more constraint has been applied to the libido when it is pressed into the service of the feminine function, and that—to speak teleologically—Nature takes less careful account of its [that function's] demands than in the case of masculinity. And the reason for this may lie—thinking once again teleologically—in the fact that the accomplishment of the aim of biology has been entrusted to the aggressiveness of men and has been made to some extent independent of women's consent.

The sexual frigidity of women, the frequency of which appears to confirm this disregard, is a phenomenon that is still insufficiently understood. Sometimes it is psychogenic and in that case accessible to influence; but in other cases it suggests the hypothesis of its being constitutionally determined and even of there being a contributory anatomical factor.

I have promised to tell you of a few more psychical peculiarities of mature femininity, as we come across them in analytic observation. We do not lay claim to more than an average validity for these assertions; nor is it always easy to distinguish what should be ascribed to the influence of the sexual function and what to social breeding. Thus, we attribute a larger amount of narcissism to femininity, which also affects women's choice of object, so that to be loved is a stronger need for them than to love. The effect of penis-envy has a share, further, in the physical vanity of women, since they are bound to value their charms more highly as a late compensation for their original sexual inferiority.[1] Shame, which is considered to be a feminine characteristic *par excellence* but is far more a matter of convention than might be supposed, has as its purpose, we believe, concealment of genital deficiency. We are not forgetting that at a later time shame takes on other functions. It seems that women have made few contributions to the discoveries and inventions in the history of civilization; there is, however, one technique which they may have invented—that of plaiting and weaving. If that is so, we should be tempted to guess the unconscious motive for the achievement. Nature herself would seem to have given the model which this achievement imitates by causing the growth at maturity of the pubic hair that conceals the genitals. The step that remained to be taken lay in making the threads adhere to one another, while on the body they stick into the skin and are only matted together. If you reject this idea as fantastic and regard my belief in the influence of lack of a penis on the configuration of femininity as an *idée fixe*, I am of course defenceless.

The determinants of women's choice of an object are often made unrecognizable by social conditions. Where the choice is able to show itself freely, it is often made in accordance with the narcissistic ideal of the man whom the girl had wished to

[1] [Cf. 'On Narcissism' (1914c), *Standard Ed.*, **14**, 88-9.]

become. If the girl has remained in her attachment to her father
—that is, in the Oedipus complex—her choice is made according to the paternal type. Since, when she turned from her
mother to her father, the hostility of her ambivalent relation
remained with her mother, a choice of this kind should guarantee a happy marriage. But very often the outcome is of a kind
that presents a general threat to such a settlement of the
conflict due to ambivalence. The hostility that has been left
behind follows in the train of the positive attachment and
spreads over on to the new object. The woman's husband, who
to begin with inherited from her father, becomes after a time
her mother's heir as well. So it may easily happen that the
second half of a woman's life may be filled by the struggle
against her husband, just as the shorter first half was filled by
her rebellion against her mother. When this reaction has been
lived through, a second marriage may easily turn out very
much more satisfying.[1] Another alteration in a woman's
nature, for which lovers are unprepared, may occur in a
marriage after the first child is born. Under the influence of a
woman's becoming a mother herself, an identification with her
own mother may be revived, against which she had striven up
till the time of her marriage, and this may attract all the available libido to itself, so that the compulsion to repeat reproduces
an unhappy marriage between her parents. The difference in
a mother's reaction to the birth of a son or a daughter shows
that the old factor of lack of a penis has even now not lost its
strength. A mother is only brought unlimited satisfaction by her
relation to a son; this is altogether the most perfect, the most
free from ambivalence of all human relationships.[2] A mother
can transfer to her son the ambition which she has been obliged
to suppress in herself, and she can expect from him the satisfaction of all that has been left over in her of her masculinity
complex. Even a marriage is not made secure until the wife

---

[1] [This had already been remarked upon earlier, in 'The Taboo of
Virginity' (1918a), *Standard Ed.*, **11**, 206.]
[2] [This point seems to have been made by Freud first in a footnote to
Chapter VI of *Group Psychology* (1921c), *Standard Ed.*, **18**, 101 *n*. He
repeated it in the *Introductory Lectures*, XIII, ibid., **15**, 206 and in *Civilization and its Discontents* (1930a), ibid., **21**, 113. That exceptions may occur
is shown by the example above, p. 66.]

has succeeded in making her husband her child as well and in acting as a mother to him.

A woman's identification with her mother allows us to distinguish two strata: the pre-Oedipus one which rests on her affectionate attachment to her mother and takes her as a model, and the later one from the Oedipus complex which seeks to get rid of her mother and take her place with her father. We are no doubt justified in saying that much of both of them is left over for the future and that neither of them is adequately surmounted in the course of development. But the phase of the affectionate pre-Oedipus attachment is the decisive one for a woman's future: during it preparations are made for the acquisition of the characteristics with which she will later fulfil her role in the sexual function and perform her invaluable social tasks. It is in this identification too that she acquires her attractiveness to a man, whose Oedipus attachment to his mother it kindles into passion. How often it happens, however, that it is only his son who obtains what he himself aspired to! One gets an impression that a man's love and a woman's are a phase apart psychologically.

The fact that women must be regarded as having little sense of justice is no doubt related to the predominance of envy in their mental life; for the demand for justice is a modification of envy and lays down the condition subject to which one can put envy aside. We also regard women as weaker in their social interests and as having less capacity for sublimating their instincts than men. The former is no doubt derived from the dissocial quality which unquestionably characterizes all sexual relations. Lovers find sufficiency in each other, and families too resist inclusion in more comprehensive associations.[1] The aptitude for sublimation is subject to the greatest individual variations. On the other hand I cannot help mentioning an impression that we are constantly receiving during analytic practice. A man of about thirty strikes us as a youthful, somewhat unformed individual, whom we expect to make powerful use of the possibilities for development opened up to him by analysis. A woman of the same age, however, oftens frightens us by her psychical rigidity and unchange-

[1] [Cf. some remarks on this in Chapter XII (D) of *Group Psychology* (1921c), *Standard Ed.*, **18**, 140.]

ability. Her libido has taken up final positions and seems incapable of exchanging them for others. There are no paths open to further development; it is as though the whole process had already run its course and remains thenceforward insusceptible to influence—as though, indeed, the difficult development to femininity had exhausted the possibilities of the person concerned. As therapists we lament this state of things, even if we succeed in putting an end to our patient's ailment by doing away with her neurotic conflict.

That is all I had to say to you about femininity. It is certainly incomplete and fragmentary and does not always sound friendly. But do not forget that I have only been describing women in so far as their nature is determined by their sexual function. It is true that that influence extends very far; but we do not overlook the fact that an individual woman may be a human being in other respects as well. If you want to know more about femininity, enquire from your own experiences of life, or turn to the poets, or wait until science can give you deeper and more coherent information.

PART II

Discussion of "Femininity"

1

Femininity and the Oedipus complex

Nancy Kulish & Deanna Holtzman

The question before us is, "Is a woman's sexual life based on the Oedipus complex?" Our answer is both "Yes and No". Yes, we believe that conflicts and issues from the triangular phase or "Oedipus stage", which spans the ages of around 3–6 years, are central to a little girl's future development. These conflicts and issues are important organizing influences on female development in general and on sexual development specifically. And No, while providing powerful explanations of human experience in general, the dynamics of the Oedipus complex, as laid down originally by Freud, are not, in our opinion, strictly accurate or appropriate when applied to females. In his essay on "Femininity" (1933), Freud set forth his "last word" on female development, including the "female Oedipus complex". In the years that followed, these propositions have been revised, reformulated and rejected. We will focus only on the conceptualizations pertaining more narrowly to the "Oedipus" or triangular period. Among the ideas found in this paper that are problematic are:

1. The girl must change her original libidinal object (from the mother to the father) in order to achieve a feminine position.

2. The girl's preoedipal attachment to the mother is inordinately strong and long.

3. The girl's castration complex and penis envy bring the end of the attachment to the mother and entry into the oedipal phase.

4. Penis envy is a lifelong feminine characteristic originating in the lack of a penis.

5. The wish for a baby cannot be considered a feminine wish; rather, it is an unconsciously displaced wish for a penis.

6. Girls remain in the oedipal complex for an indeterminate length of time, in comparison to boys, because they lack the motivation of castration anxiety needed for its resolution.

We will argue that what has been called "the female Oedipus complex" is based on a male model, and we will offer an alternative viewpoint for female development, based on another ancient Greek myth—the myth of Persephone and Demeter. We have come to name this triadic phase the Persephonal phase, and the conflicts associated with it *the Persephone complex*. We have argued that the concept of a "female Oedipus complex" is an oxymoron.

Changing concepts often requires changing language. The words we use for our concepts, and the names we chose to describe them, establish the context in which we understand them. Language shapes perception and expectation: it organizes our thinking. When thinking about "Oedipus", we think about "castration" and "penis envy", not about "pregnancy" or "vagina"; when we talk about the "phallic–oedipal" phase in little girls, we distract ourselves from—and thereby foreclose on—the girl's crucial developmental needs to identify with her mother and her discovery of the pleasures and intricacies of her own female body. We have proposed, therefore, that the myth of Persephone and Demeter is a better fit for the female triangular situation, and better suited to name it (Kulish & Holtzman, 1998, 2008). We assert that this name change is not superficial but substantial: as the story itself shows, a change of name is a vital act of re-identification. It allows us to shed old and erroneous ways of thinking about girls and women and take on a new capacity to think about their development and lives in terms truer to their experience.

What, then, are the areas of the girl's triangular or "oedipal" complex that we think necessitate a re-examination in the light of contemporary psychoanalytic thinking? The first is the *entry into the triangular situation*. A second area needing re-examination is *the role of identification with the mother*. The central importance of the girl's identification with the mother was not appreciated by Freud, in its important influences on the girl's desire for a baby, to take the mother's role, and to fashion herself like her in a myriad of ways. A third important consideration concerns the *dynamics of the triangular situation itself*. The shape of triangular object relations is different for boys and girls, and aggression and competitive strivings are expressed differently as a function of these differing dynamics. A fourth area calling for reformulation involves the *female body*. In his formulations of the female triangular phase, Freud emphasized what the female lacks. Nowhere were there ideas—now falling under the umbrella of "primary femininity"—about the *role played by the female body in the triadic phase in terms of what the girl has,* and not what she lacks. Fifth is the *important issue of the resolution of the triangular situation and the formation of the superego*. Freud's assertion that girls, lacking the motivation of castration anxiety that boys have, can never resolve the triangular situation and that their superego development is therefore compromised is untenable. We disagree with the notion that castration anxiety is necessary for the resolution of the Oedipus conflict and for the development of a "mature" superego.

The myth of Persephone and Demeter

As we stated above, we think that triangular conflicts and issues in females are better captured by the Persephone myth than the Oedipus myth. Both myths delineate the dilemmas that we must all navigate—the "oedipal" conflicts that enmesh men, the "persephonal" ones that entrap women. The myth of Persephone and Demeter captivated the ancient world and has over the centuries inspired widespread religious beliefs and rites in the general populace, as well as a myriad poets, philosophers, and artists across many cultures.

There are many versions of this myth. The oldest and most complete is *The Homeric Hymn to Demeter* (Foley, 1994); we will refer to Foley's 1994 translation. The story is as follows: Kore is the lovely young daughter of Demeter, Goddess of Grain, and Zeus, King of the Gods, who are sister and brother. Kore is gathering flowers in a meadow with other young girls. Attracted by a particularly beautiful narcissus, she wanders from her mother's side and plucks it,[1] whereupon the earth suddenly opens and Hades, God of the Underworld and Death, abducts her into his dominion. (Hades is Zeus's brother and therefore Persephone's uncle.) No one hears her cries. When Kore next appears in the Homeric Hymn, she is with Hades in the underworld: he is "reclining on a bed with his shy spouse, strongly reluctant" (p. 20). Some versions of the story make a rape more explicit. It is important to note that prior to her abduction and the loss of her virginity, the girl is known only as "Kore", which in Greek literally means "maiden" or virgin. *Afterwards, she takes on a new name—Persephone, Queen of the Underworld.*

Demeter is bereft. She descends from Olympus to search the earth frantically for her daughter. In grief and anger she causes droughts and famines that will plague the earth until Persephone is found. Disguised as an old woman, the goddess offers herself as a servant to a mortal family to care for their infant boy, Demophoon. "Voiceless with grief" (Foley, 1994, p. 12), Demeter refuses to take food and drink. An older servant woman, Baubo (sometimes known as Iambe), jokes with the despondent visitor by lifting up her skirt and displaying her genitals. Demeter laughs at this raucous jest, and comes out of her depression enough to eat and drink.

Zeus, moved by the catastrophe engulfing the earth, intervenes. He persuades Hades to release Persephone. In the bargain struck between the two gods, Persephone is to be released only if she does not eat in the underworld. Hades "stealthily passing it around her" enjoins Persephone to eat a pomegranate seed (in some versions seven or several seeds), an action that undermines the bargain. When questioned later by her mother, Persephone says that Hades "compelled me against my will and by force to taste it" (Foley, p. 22, line 413). In other versions of the story the act of eating the pomegranate is variously and ambiguously interpreted as voluntary or involuntary, with or without the girl's awareness.[2] In any case, having broken the injunction against eating in the underworld, Persephone is now bound to Hades for some part of the year. In classical mythology, as in psychoanalytic theory, "eating the seed" symbolically implies sexual union, binding her to Hades (Foley, pp. 56–57).[3] Thus, a compromise is worked out between the gods, by which Persephone spends two-thirds of the year with her mother and one third of the year as queen of the underworld with Hades. This compromise serves as an ancient explanation of the origin of the seasons. Winter rules while Persephone is with her husband in the underworld of the dead, and the earth flowers in spring and summer when she returns to her mother above. The poem ends with Demeter's founding of the popular Eleusinian rites.

We argue that the Persephone myth captures the female "oedipal" conflict and its typical resolution better than the male-modelled Oedipus story does.[4] Several psychoanalytic writers read the Persephone myth, as we do, as an evocation of important female dynamics (Burch, 1997; Chodorow, 1994a; Tyson, 1996). We emphasize in our argument four aspects of the story: (1) its representation of the girl's loss of virginity and entry into adult heterosexuality: the girl's step into the world of adult sexuality and inevitably away from her mother revives earlier conflicts of loyalty and separation from the triadic period; (2) its dramatization of the themes of separation and rapprochement between mother and daughter, which we feel are central to the female triangular situation; (3) its depiction of a compromise formation, however flawed, designed to resolve conflicts over love, desire, and loyalty towards mother and father; and (4) its depiction of the clearly female themes of cyclicality, fertility, and pregnancy.

The tale of Persephone and Demeter is an incestuously erotic story, as is the Oedipus story. It begins with abduction and a seduction, or possibly a rape. Some see Persephone straying from her mother willingly, attracted by the sensual unknown, the beautiful flower she longs to pluck. She may go unwillingly into the arms of Hades at first—as we have said—but she is not so single-minded about leaving him. Her ambivalence is manifest in the seeds that she eats, a symbolically sexual act in which she participates perhaps by trickery, but perhaps with intent.

Demeter, too, is a figure attracted by the erotic. She is brought out
of her catastrophic depression by Baubo's display of the female
genitals.

This tale may also be seen as depicting homoerotic love. Demeter's love for Persephone is passionate and intense. Foley (1994)
tells us that the Greek language of Demeter's lament for her lost
daughter is that of an erotic love poem. She notes a passage that
seems to emphasize eye contact between mother and daughter,
which implies sexual desire. "Normally in Greek poetry, such language is suggestive of erotic motifs: for the Greeks, love begins with
the eyes" (p. 58). And when separated, Persephone and Demeter
pine for each other with desire—with *pothos*—a word in Greek having sexual overtones (p. 131).

As in many stories about young girls, including fairy tales and
myths, Persephone is presented as a passive object to whom things
happen, not as the initiator of the narrative. This stance is in sharp
contrast to the adventurous and aggressive hero Oedipus and other
male protagonists in fairy tales and myths. Bad things—dangerous,
sexual things—happen to Persephone, as to other female heroines,
when she leaves her mother's protection. This is one moral of
the tale of Persephone: it warns that leaving mother's protection
exposes the daughter to the dangers of sexuality. Yet to become an
adult and sexual woman, a girl must leave her mother's domain and
enter her own. Persephone becomes Queen of the Underworld.
Note that the change of name—from Kore, virgin, to Persephone,
married woman—clearly represents sexual initiation, just as it does
in our society.

We think that the myth demonstrates several important psychic realities: the first is that a psychic separation is necessary for
achieving the female adult role. A second psychic reality depicted
in this myth is the characteristic defensive way in which females
deal with sexuality and aggression. It is difficult for girls to deal
directly and openly with their sexual feelings and actions, sexual and aggressive. Psychoanalysts and psychotherapists are aware
of the guilt and anxieties that many women experience about
sex—which they perceive as owned by the mother, and thus of
their common defensive tactic of unconsciously abdicating agency
and responsibility for their own actions. Like Persephone, many

women disavow their own desires, convincing themselves and others that they have been forced or tricked into sexuality.[5] The triangular situation raises the dangers of direct competition with mother. In the myth, the competition between females is hidden, but it is discernable in both in Persephone's disobedience and in Demeter's rage. Persephone comes into her own, seemingly without such overt competition; again she is "forced" into becoming a powerful queen of her own world. Even as she has competitive wishes to take mother's place with father, a little girl certainly does not want to lose her mother. The Persephone tale finds a solution to such a dilemma: it allows her to keep her mother and have her father (uncle) too—to be taken as a *metaphoric* but not an ideal *unconscious* resolution of such conflicts. The third psychic reality that this story elucidates is the girl's anxiety about the catastrophic consequences of severing the bonds between mother and daughter.

In summary, we see the triangular situation for the girl—the ultimate psychological reality depicted in this tale—as a balancing of loyalties and relationships (Kulish & Holtzman, 1998, 2008). The myth of Persephone and her mother Demeter, the goddess of grain and fertility, is above all a female's story. Life, death, and rebirth are in the power of the female, and these are themes throughout the narrative, which dramatizes the cyclical nature of the female experience.

The female triangular situation

Despite much critical re-evaluation of Freud's theories about female development, the female triadic phase—referred to as the "female oedipal" phase—has not received much attention. We have attempted to integrate contemporary psychoanalytic thinking about female development and its attendant structures and conflicts into a cohesive picture of this important period. We will describe some of these theoretical implications for girls and women in terms of *separation issues and entry into the triadic stage, aggression and competition, superego and triadic guilt, the female body, and adolescence.*

Separation issues and entry into the triadic stage

What do these new perspectives tell us about the female triangular situation?

First, that a girls' entry into the persephonal/triadic stage is not motivated by penis envy and accompanying disappointment and hostility towards her mother. Penis envy and hostility exist as important aspects of female development, of course, but they do not serve as the central stimuli for progression into the triangular phase. The following is a brief summary of the arguments brought forth by many psychoanalytic thinkers that refute the idea that castration anxiety and angry renunciation are the central forces for female development into the triadic phase. Both Horney and Jones mounted early and serious—and, to our minds, compelling—challenges to Freud's ideas about the centrality of castration. Horney (1924) asserted that the girl's inferiority complex and penis envy were secondary and culturally based. Jones (1933), too, argued that the girl's "phallic phase" was essentially defensive.

Challenges have also come from a series of studies stemming from infant and child observation. Kleeman (1976), for example, confirmed the importance of learning, cognitive functions, and language, compared to penis envy in the emergence of femininity. He stated that toddlers' discovery of sexual differences came much earlier than Freud had thought and hence logically could not serve as the initiator of the much later oedipal phase. Parens (1990; Parens, Pollock, Stern, & Kramer, 1976) found that it is not castration anxiety but, rather, the emergence of genitality—that is, a biologically programmed differentiation of the sexual drive—that motivates or drives the toddler into the oedipal phase.

Many others through the years have offered rich clinical understandings of the role of penis envy in female development, but from perspectives very different from Freud's (Lerner, 1976). Most clinicians (Moulton, 1970) have linked penis envy to problems between the girl and her mother and conceptualize it not as an inevitable or necessary cog in a stepwise schema, but as a passing experience of childhood (Chasseguet-Smirgel, 1970; Frenkel, 1996). In an influential paper, Grossman and Stewart (1976) examine the concept of penis envy, emphasizing the need to analyse its meanings and functions when it appears, rather than reflexively taking it as "bedrock".

We characterize the entry into the triadic phase as multi-faceted—biological, psychological, familial, and social. We have listed six possible influences on the entry into the triangular phase for both girls and boys: the compelling fantasies of the primal scene, innate biological pressures, bisexuality, cognitive factors, the role of the father, and the role of the mother. No one component in and of itself provides a unitary and satisfactory explanation for the developmental shift.

1. The Kleinians view primitive unconscious knowledge of the primal scene known to the child as a given (Britton, 1989). In other psychoanalytic views, such awareness of the primal scene comes to the fore between the ages of 3 and 6, as the child can more fully appreciate the difference between genders and generations. The primal scene is seen as the prototypical recognition and experience of triangularity for both genders, with the concomitant feelings of desire, exclusion, and humiliation.

2. Many analysts, such as Parens (Parens et al., 1976, Parens, 1990), whom we mentioned above, argue that a biologically programmed differentiation of the sexual drive moves the toddler into the oedipal or triangular phase. In terms of other biological pressures towards triangularity, we suggest the girl's body disposes her to fantasies of being pregnant and, often, being penetrated by her father. But what determines future object-choice—that is, heterosexual or homosexual—at this stage? After reviewing research on the biological domain and sexual preference, Young-Bruehl (2003) concluded that no causal biological explanation for object choice has yet been found, but that biological factors seem to have some unspecified but as yet unknown influence. She emphasized other factors, particularly how internal objects are layered or blended from disparate identifications with individuals of either sex.

3. A related and longstanding notion of psychoanalysis, which has never been refuted, is bisexuality—both psychic and physical (Elise, 1998b; Freud, 1937c). Given an inborn bisexuality, we argue that everyone has sexual feelings towards both the same

and the opposite sex. Strong societal forces, however, reinforce heterosexuality and thus entry into the "positive" oedipal situation. Homoerotic interests are, typically, discouraged, negatively reinforced, and repressed (Butler, 1995). Chodorow (1994b) argued that both heterosexuality and homosexuality result from compromise formations that include bisexual feelings.

4. Cognitive development allows for the capacity to understand relationships in more complexity and in three dimensions (Mahon, 1991). For example, the perception of the reality of the primal scene seems connected to the child's cognitive development—the ability to notice that an intimate sexual relationship, however conceptualized, exists between the parents.

5. Triangulation is said to be promoted by the role of the father who breaks into or interrupts the early maternal dyad and becomes a "third" object for the infant of either gender (Abelin, 1971). Brown (2002) delineated an early "preoedipal" stage of triangularity and corresponding conflicted relationships.

6. Many contemporary authors other than ourselves elucidate the importance of the role of the mother in the girl's entry into the triangular stage. The mother serves as an object of identification and communicates her conscious and unconscious sexual attitudes to her daughter. Benjamin (1988), for example, has described the complicated acquisition of feminine desire for the girl as she identifies with her mother and her mother's attitudes towards sex. Elise (2007) cites the importance of the mother in offering her daughter an image of maternal sexuality for identification.

Second, separation from the mother is a crucial issue for girls at this stage and an inescapable aspect of their triangular conflicts (Holtzman & Kulish, 2000). One reason for this is the pattern of object relationships at the time the girl approaches the "oedipal" stage of development (Chodorow, 1978). At this time, the typical family pattern, in which the mother is the primary caregiver, poses a major dilemma for girls, compared to boys. With the onset of the triangular stage, children usually become more competitive with the parent of the same sex. (This is the heterosexual or so-called "positive oedipal" scenario.) A dangerous conflict is created as the mother, the parent on whom the girl usually depends for her day-to-day well-being—such as being fed or nurtured—now becomes the girl's rival. In contrast, a boy's feelings of murderous rivalry are not usually directed at his caregiver, his mother.

Thus, fears of the loss of mother and her love come to the fore for girls in the context of triangular erotic conflicts and emanate from the triadic conflict itself. Therefore the conflicts around separation that are regularly seen in women and girls are not necessarily a representation of unresolved fixations at the preoedipal levels: they arise because the girl has to separate from, and later comes to compete with, the same-sexed caregiver. We argue that this picture emerges not because the little girl has yet to resolve "preoedipal" conflicts, nor, as Freud and psychoanalytic theory would have had it, because she has no penis and is therefore not motivated by castration anxiety. It is separation from the mother and the threat of abandonment by her that is central in the girl's triangular situation. The fear of the loss of mother or her love represents a major "triadic" or persephonal punishment for the little girl. Her solutions for this dilemma are intended to avoid this potential life-threatening catastrophe. We maintain that these dynamics are an important part of the period of triangulation; they are inherent in it and not simply a carry-over from earlier developmental phases.

Because genital activity for girls, in general, is met with by disapproval, erotic impulses towards *either* father or mother lead to fears of loss of the mother or her love and approval, fears that may become very frightening. (Feelings towards mother—homoerotic feelings—have been labelled the "negative oedipal" scenario.) In contrast, genital activity is typically more acceptable for males, although it may be accompanied by fears of a castration by the father if incestuous impulses are directed towards the mother. The loss of the mother and her caretaking, however, are not inherently at stake.

Third, girls do not change love objects, shifting their attention from mother to father, as psychoanalytic thinking assumed for many years; rather, they add another erotic object, the father, to create a triangular relationship. Much contemporary writing argues against the view that women undergo a simple change of object in their entry into the triangular phase (Fischer, 2002; Kulish, 2006; Ritvo, 1989). A girl's attention and her sexual interest oscillate between both parents, forming patterns that may be repeated throughout development. Characteristic of this phase are issues of balancing loyalty: girls can feel caught by their urges towards mother and father. We do not concur with the idea of a normative sequence of the so-called "negative oedipal phase", a period of homosexual object choice that precedes the normative heterosexual phase for girls. Others (Edgecumbe, Lunberg, Markowitz, & Salo, 1976) have reiterated that there is no evidence of this separate phase and its proposed timing.

Aggression and competition

Aggression, like sexuality, is an integral part of the triangular period. But the expression of aggression differs for girls and boys, just as it does in the myths of Oedipus and Persephone (Holtzman & Kulish, 2003). In the Oedipus story, the aggression of the protagonist, Oedipus, is overt and deadly: he kills his father and eventually blinds himself in a self-punitive, symbolic castration. In the Persephone myth, the heroine is passive; the aggression lies in the hands of Demeter, displaced, as in most fairy tales and myths, onto the mother.

Many authors have written about the general cultural prohibitions against the expression of anger by girls and women (Bernardez-Bonesatti, 1978; Lerner, 1980; Person, 2000). We acknowledge these powerful influences but focus on the psychological forces stemming from the triadic period. As we described above, it is highly dangerous for a little girl to acknowledge and express her sexual wishes towards her father. She wants to be her father's chosen love and to outdo and replace her mother. Yet she needs to remain bonded to and taken care of—nurtured and nourished—by her mother/caretaker. Thus, she must hide her aggressive and rivalrous fantasies towards her mother from herself and from others. Homoerotic impulses, which also become highly charged in this phase, also bring with them conflicted aggression: anger at the mother for preferring the father or brothers, angry jealousy towards rivals for mother's favours. These sources of anger towards the male rivals also call for defensive measures.

The more tenuous the mother–daughter relationship, the more

difficult and frightening it may be for a girl to tolerate her own aggressiveness (Reenkola, 2002). We do not see disappointment and anger at the mother as the main motivating factors for developmental progression either into or out of the triangular situation, as Freud postulated.

For a little boy, the destruction and reanimation of his oedipal rival is repeatedly expressed in active aggressive play. For a little girl, a more careful route must be traversed, in order to preserve the relationship with her mother. Murderous and passionate aggression and rivalry must be denied or repressed. Thus, inhibition of a subjective sense of themselves as aggressive agents becomes a pervasive defence for women and girls (Hoffman, 1999). Girls' aggression will typically take indirect channels. Because of their inhibitions, girls typically express their aggression differently from boys, in what has been called "relational aggression". While bullying, punching, and other forms of overt aggression are the preferred outlets for boys in the schoolyard, girls resort to cattiness, backbiting, secretiveness, and social exclusion to express their aggression and competitiveness (Talbot, 2002).

Superego and triadic guilt

In our work with women we have seen no gendered differences in structure, strength, and functioning of the superego, as Freud suggested. Nor do we believe that castration anxiety is the necessary motivator for superego development for females. (We are not certain that castration anxiety is the central motivator for boys, either.) Rather, we find in women the central motivator for the continued development of superego is fear of loss of love and/or fear of loss of the object. It is important to note that these fears of loss are not necessarily primitive or "preoedipal". These fears of loss are consonant with the specific triadic task of separation with the same sex caregiver. We agree with those who describe superego development for girls and boys as a gradual accretion of functions, acquired step by step through identifications and learning (Lichtenberg, 2004) and not a sudden transformation brought on by fear of castration. Furthermore, we have found no differences in the process or function of identification for males and females.

On the other hand, we do find that there are gendered differences in *contents* of the superego—a conclusion made by Bernstein (1993) in her study of the female superego. The content of girls' superego fears often relates to the mother. For example, we have seen that whenever the girl contemplates taking the step of assuming active, competitive sexual activity, from age 3 in fantasy or in young adulthood in reality, the mother is—consciously or unconsciously—psychically present, and the daughter begins to worry about her disapproval or even her loss. For example, a young woman, in treatment said, "When I was little and wanted my Daddy's attention, I wanted my mother out of the picture. But then I remember feeling guilty and scared, thinking, who would take care of us?"

We do think that there are major gendered differences in the ways guilt is defended against and handled, just as defences against aggression differ. Oedipus tolerates his guilt by maintaining, "I didn't know I did it." Persephone tolerates hers by insisting, "Hades made me do it." For males the defences are disavowal, negation, and denial; for females, repression and, once again, abdication of a sense of agency.

We argue that the superego is not the heir to the Oedipus complex, which rests on resolution of triangular conflicts. Nevertheless, the triadic phase stands as an important point in the timeline of superego development. It is then that the child must grapple with intense conflicts of—and consequent guilt about—sexual desire, death wishes towards rivals, and competition. In terms of object relations, it is a time for dealing with three objects instead of two, which requires a balancing act that must in some way engender guilt and anxiety. This is so for boys as well as girls.

The female body

In 1933 Freud pictured the development of femininity in terms of a sense of lack and shame, an absence of desired masculinity. But long before a little girl reaches the triadic phase, she has become aware of her body and has developed an early and positive sense of femaleness (Elise, 1997). By the age of 2, her core gender identity is solid: she knows she is a girl and is beginning to experience what her gender means for her—its limits and possibilities. By the time she is 3, she has a solid body map, which includes a sense of her genitals and the pleasure they might bring. Contrary to what Freud thought, it has been documented that girls experience intense erotic—vaginal—sensations from early infancy (Greenacre, 1952; Plaut & Hutchinson, 1986); genital self stimulation has been observed in little girls before the age of 2, somewhat later, and less focused, than in boys (Kleeman, 1976). With the entry into the triangular persephonal phase, the girl's sexuality becomes more genitally focused and intense. With her blossoming sexual feelings and her new capacities to appreciate the complexities of the inter-personal sphere around her, her fantasy life becomes richer and more complex. Already identified with her mother and mothering functions, her earlier interest in babies takes a new turn: now she wishes to have a baby *with* someone.

Girls can have babies, and boys cannot; what does this fact mean in the development of the triangular situations in boys and girls? By the time a little girl is 4 or so, she usually knows that her body will someday be able to accommodate a baby. This formidable idea, however rudimentary, colours her experience of the trian-gular situation as she fantasizes, from her little-girl's point of view, what it might mean. She thinks that she might be a Mummy, with her Daddy as partner (or with her mother as her partner). Our colleagues who work with children tell us how often these fantasies occur in their little girl patients. The desire to get big with child and give birth is part of the triadic family dynamic and reflects the little girl's identification with her mother and her competition with her as well. Fears about penetration and one's body being able to accommodate a baby or a penis occur in addition. Of course, little boys fantasize that they can make babies, too, but it is only little girls who will be able to actualize these wishes when they grow up and who see that they have bodies that will be like their mothers' bodies someday.

Freud reduced the girl's maternal instincts to penis envy, with the baby a displacement for the envied penis, but contemporary psychoanalysts (Balsam, 1996; Benjamin, 1988; Chodorow, 1978; Parens, et al., 1976; Tyson & Tyson, 1990) have abandoned that one-sided conceptualization in favour of the complex process of identification. They see the girl's wish to have babies as coming from positive sources—recognition of the potentials of her own body and identification with her mother and her mothering functions. For example, in their observations, Parens and colleagues identify as early as 12 to 14 months the appearance of an interest in babies in girls, associated with identification with the mother. Balsam argues that the image of the pregnant mother's body to the little girl is "the most important icon of grown-up physical femaleness" (Balsam, 2001, p. 1341).

For little girls and boys, as genital erotic desires emerge more fully in the triadic phase, the comparison of their bodies and their genitals with the bodies and genitals of the adults around them leads to feelings of inadequacy and other narcissistic concerns. As Fast (1979) and Kubie (1974) have suggested, young children's sense of their gender possibilities is limitless: they want it all. In this context penis envy may certainly arise, but so can breast and womb envy. The response from the immediate environment to these narcissistic wounds will determine their intensity and whether or not they become symptomatic.

The girl's body also becomes a vehicle of competition with her mother, as the boy's does with his father. She compares her body with her mother's. Balsam (1996) presents clinical material that demonstrates the importance of the mother's body on a girl's perception of her shape, size, abdomen, breasts, buttocks, genitals, skin, and hair. The effects of these female-to-female comparisons and perceptions are apparent in the analyses of adult women and help to explain both the particulars of women's body images and also the pleasures and anxieties about them that we see so often in our clinical practices.

Alice, a patient in analysis, is worried to find that her new lover, a recently divorced man, had to meet with his ex-wife, whom she sees as a potential threat. Her worries and competition are fanned by his report that in a moment of passionate anguish, the ex-wife ripped her blouse open and cried, "Aren't my breasts better than Alice's?" This behaviour is a bodily, female-to-female competition in the triadic mode.

The father's response to the girl's sexuality and body can also have consequences, negative or positive, that reverberate throughout her life. Another patient recalled that as a very little girl of 4 years, she had dressed up in her mother's high heels and put lipstick on. Her father's angry response was traumatizing. A strict and overly religious man, he yelled, "No daughter of mine will be a slut!" This central memory became the core of this patient's long-standing sexual inhibitions and bad feelings about herself and her body.

Adolescence

The specifically female concerns of the triangular phase intensify as girls grow into the sexual maturity and psychological separateness of adolescence. The added stress of societal pressures against women's ownership of their own sexuality makes the challenges of adolescence more rigorous than they might otherwise be. Competition, envy, and incestuous longings reclaim the psychological foreground in adolescence, and the issues of maturity and autonomy that appear first in the triangular period come to a far more definitive blossoming in adolescence. We emphasize *not* a recrudescence of the original triangular phase at adolescence, but a new chapter in life, with its own powerful triadic dynamics and issues.

The onset of puberty delivers immense bodily changes for the girl. It arouses feelings, fantasies, and conflicts about her body with a new intensity. Insistent sexual urges are more and more pressing. Now the girl can actually have babies and can compete with the mother on a grown-up level for male attention. She compares her sexually mature body with her mother's. While these rivalries with mother and other females intensify, girls are frequently devastated when their girlfriends begin to date, and they lose the attention and intimacy that they had enjoyed before this. One adolescent patient complained: "Rita doesn't call me any more. All she is interested in is her boyfriend." Sexual and affectionate interests in adolescence oscillate, as they did in the earlier triangular period, between homoerotic and heterosexual objects.

These triadic issues that come up in adolescence are easily discernable, and they appear in the analyses of women of every age, both in memories of adolescence and at later turning points of sexuality and maturation. In our clinical experience with adult females who describe their first experiences of intercourse and the loss of virginity, we have found in *every* case that thoughts of their mothers occur in some form or another (Holtzman & Kulish, 1996, 1997). These thoughts reflect what we feel are the main dynamics and issues of the triadic phase: anxiety about loss of the mother and her love for having crossed the threshold and entered into her realm of sexuality, or rivalrous feelings and thoughts of victory over her.

We feel that these dynamics are clearly and beautifully portrayed by the tale of Persephone, who encounters danger as she leaves her mother and crosses the threshold into the underworld of sexuality.

Clinical vignette: "Ann"

Ann reported a memory that she was fascinated by the story of Persephone when she was a child. In her mid-thirties, Ann had been in analysis for several years. Her father had met her mother, who was a nurse, when he was in the army as a medic and stationed in France. The family's visits to France over the years to see relatives were special occasions for Ann. These visits, and the parents' chronic arguments and differences, had induced in Ann a conflict of loyalty between the father and mother, and between France and the United States. The patient's symptoms were chronic depression, a lack of assertiveness and being able to stick up for herself, and an inability to enjoy sex with her husband.

Her mother's funeral was the occasion of her going through family belongings. She came upon her mother's letters, which were to and from the maternal grandmother whom the mother missed and longed to join.

In one session shortly after the funeral, Ann remembered the story of Persephone. What stood out vividly for her about this story was that Persephone picked a flower, and the earth opened up beneath her. The patient talked about Persephone's separation from Demeter and feeling so sad. And then she said, "I can identify with Persephone because I love flowers and have talked about finding happier times with her mother within myself." At this point the analyst noted that she had left out the entire part of the story about Persephone being snatched away/abducted and raped by Hades. (In telling the narrative in this way, the patient made the story dyadic.) The patient responded to the analyst's intervention by reporting her obsessive fears, which had followed her into adult life. She had the fantasy that she would be "sold into white slavery". She said she feared that she would be drugged when she went into a doctor's office and had to have some kind of procedure. (This is also a transference anxiety that the analyst/doctor will lure and entrap her.) This patient then talked in further sessions about how she had lost her virginity in her late adolescence. She could only engage in sex by getting herself so drunk that she was "unconscious" and then couldn't remember that she had had sex, or with whom. (Thus she avoided responsibility for her sexuality and any aware-ness of her unconsciously incestuous object choices.) In this material, there is a clear connection to triadic dynamics: mother and father and daughter are the principal players in the mate-rial; the patient's fear of rape is a projected incestuous wish, especially apparently in the fact that the it would occur in a doc-tor's office (her father was a medic); the persephonal theme of oscillating between different worlds—France/United States or consciousness/unconsciousness—is present; she clearly articu-lates her issues around separation in her yearnings for earlier, happier times with her mother; the whole train of thought is stimulated by the loss of the mother.

Discussion and conclusions

If we do not have in mind that the girl's Persephone phase is differ-ent from the boy's oedipal phase, then we run the risk of misper-ceiving and misinterpreting women patients. Thinking "oedipal" may tunnel the therapist's vision, blocking out important aspects of a female patient's experience. Allegiance to older, erroneous theories about female development perpetuates individual blind spots and encourages the infantilization, preoedipalization, and cultural stereotyping of females. This limits the effectiveness of their analyses.

Current theories and training often contribute to these ellipses. For many reasons, the Oedipus complex is going out of style, and unfortunately the current emphasis in psychoanalysis has abandoned the unconscious and sexuality for the study of attachment, interaction, and enactment. This turn has recently been articulated by one of the predominant researchers in the area of attachment, Fonagy (2008). Our hope is that practitioners and students in the mental health fields might become more responsive and attentive to triadic and persephonal incestuous unconscious dynamics and the sometimes difficult countertransferences and transferences that accompany them. A heightened sensitivity to persephonal triangular conflicts in our patients requires self-vigilance on the part of the analyst, male or female.

In summary, the triadic phase is fundamentally as important for females as it is for males, but not in the ways that Freud presented his ideas. His theory about women, as exemplified in the essay "Femininity", was phallocentric and misleading. We are, however, in accord with his notions that for both boys and girls a crucial period between the ages of 3 and 6 becomes the hierarchical organizer of fantasy life, with its major determinants of sex and aggression.

The triadic or persephonal period is indeed a crucible out of which core psychic structures emerge. The Persephone myth—not the Oedipus story—is, we feel, the best fit for explaining these dynamics from the vantage point of the little girl. Many myths have something to tell us about the psychology of women, yet none capture the female *triangular* situation as elegantly, as comprehensively, and as compellingly as the Persephone/Demeter story. It is the story about a young woman's separation from and eventual reunion with her mother; about her first negotiations of adult sexuality with a father figure; and about how loving and close relationships with *both* mother and father might be balanced. It is a triangular tale of incest and intense emotions. In addition, it captures the cyclical nature of woman's experience: the ebbing and flowing of fertility and childbearing. These uniquely feminine and triadic experiences are central in defining femininity.

Notes

1. The narcissus that proliferates so easily is a symbol of fertility. Foley suggest that Persephone's attraction to the seductive flower demonstrates

her readiness for a new phase of life. Girls in myth are traditionally carried off while gathering flowers in a meadow. (Foley, p. 127).

2. The ambiguity and variability in the telling and retelling the story of the seeds in the different versions of the myth first suggested to us the idea of conflict and defensiveness around the question of the volition of woman's sexual impulses. Freud (1900a) wrote that modifications, repetition, vagaries and circumlocutions in dreams are evidence of censorship and conflict. Acknowledging the cultural, historical, and other reasons in variability in myth, however, we know that there is a danger in leaping to interpretations of myth as dream.

3. In psychoanalytic practice, the idea of eating seeds is a common children's fantasy of oral impregnation.

4. Like the Oedipus myth, the tale of Persephone and Demeter has a central theme of incest. Demeter and Zeus are brother and sister, who have a child, Persephone; Hades is the brother of Zeus and Demeter and hence is Persephone's uncle.

5. We have observed another common defensive tactic in contemporary young women, who deny their sexual anxiety with a counterphobic promiscuity.

2

Contemporary views on femininity, gender, and generative identity

Joan Raphael-Leff

> When you meet a human being, the first distinction you make
> is "male or female?"
>
> Freud, "Femininity" (1933, p. 113)

Much has changed since Freud's day. Although our primary curiosity still prevails, in the West today this male/female distinction is no longer made with the "unhesitating certainty" Freud ascribed to it (1933, p. 113). Physical distinctions between the sexes are blurred by unisex clothes, hairstyles, and mannerisms. Difference may be deliberately annulled by self-ascriptive intersexuality, presentations of transvestism, or gender-queer "*poser* or *passer*" performance. Female/male identity may be physiologically reversed by sex-change surgery, sometimes with unforeseen consequences, such as the Canadian case of a bearded transsexual man who recently gave birth.

This chapter addresses some dramatic modifications in the seemingly eternal and universal facts of life, dwelling on how our relation to "femininity"—including body schemata and identificatory introjects—has altered since Freud's time, partly through his own influence. A fundamental shift has occurred in the psychoso-cial order, not least due to efficient female-based contraception and safe legalized abortions. Consciously assumed awareness of rights to body ownership, reproductive control, and sexual self-determina-tion, coupled with educational parity and greater access to public power and economic resources, has altered the close connection between "femininity" and motherhood, with almost a fifth of Eu-ropean women of childbearing age now choosing to remain child-less. Conversely, men have gained admission to the birth-chamber, nursery, and kitchen.

Thus present-day psychoanalytic work is embedded in a new context: one of cultural plurality significant for both psychic in-teriority and theorizing of gender. Due to feminist subversion of power-relations, revised conceptualizations of "femininity" are now located within expanded and much liberated normative boundaries, offering many choices for expression of generative agency. These have invalidated some of the "social customs" and repressive constraints that Freud noted "force women into passive situations" (1933, p. 116). Indeed, looking back to women's lack of economic or political rights in nineteenth-century Europe, prescribed "femi-ninity" may be seen as a kind of "prolonged infancy" that not only defined women as "other", set aside from the "ideal of the race", but "enfeebled her mind" (Beauvoir, 1949).

Aware of the phallocentric constraints of his time, Freud said: "If you want to know more about femininity, enquire from your own experiences of life, or turn to the poets, or wait until science can give you deeper and more coherent information" (1933, p. 135). In this chapter I draw on all three—poetry, self-analysis, and scien-tific inquiry—believing that interdisciplinary research enriches our understanding. Nonetheless, despite Bob Dylan's claim that "the poet is a naked person", I am aware that even poetry, like scientific methodology and interpretation of research findings, is subject to unconscious influences and prejudices of contemporary ideology. Epistemology and knowledge themselves are profoundly affected by gender considerations.

With the aid of an explanatory concept—*generative identity*—I attempt here to undertake the astonishing task advanced by Freud: to "set about" enquiring how today's "woman develops out of a child with a bisexual disposition" (1933, p. 135).[1]

Gender and gender identity today

> I worked with Freud in Vienna. We broke over the concept of
> penis envy. He thought it should be limited to women.
>
> Woody Allen, *Zelig*

Freud understood that far from being innate, gender categories are
psychosexually determined and socioculturally defined. This set the
scene for empirical distinction between *"sex"* (chromosomal status
at birth) and *"gender"* as a self-categorizing construct. Biological sex,
studied through embryo, genetic, and endocrinal manipulation, is
seen to consist of diverse interactive components, including genes,
anatomy, hormonal determination of prenatal internal/external
genitalia, and post-pubertal secondary sex characteristics. I argue
here that gender, too, is multivariate, based on intersubjective
meanings of changing bodily experience. Its broad scope becomes
evident, through cross-cultural and cross-species studies, as an inter-
penetration of historical, psychosocial, and cultural forces along a
continuum, rather than discretely dichotomized male/female traits
and identifying features.

Increasingly, the dualistic nature/nurture debate has had to
encompass complex multi-factorial interweaving of *both* innate and
environmental processes, affecting anatomical sex, gender differentiation, and sex differences in behaviour (even between identical
twins).[2] *Gender binaries (whether essentialist or constructivist) are no longer tenable.* Furthermore, medical technology now enables gender
fantasy to be actualized in reality, demonstrating Freud's revelation
that gender is not predetermined by biology but constituted within
the context of insatiable desire.

Such interdisciplinary research has allowed us to tease out conflated constituents of *"gender identity"*. The basic concept has undergone commensurate changes since early psychoanalytic debates on
"the riddle of femininity" and "female sexuality" were subsumed
under headings of *core gender, gender role,* and *sexual orientation* (see
Tyson, 1994). Today, far from a fixed entity, *gender formation is seen as
a lifelong process emerging dialectically through primary relationships and
intra-psychic, bodily, and sociocultural experience.* In Western societies
gender itself is now regarded as just one fluid aspect of intricate
self–other representations, freeing "gender identity" to manifest

differently according to age, context, and company and to undergo revisions at life's nodal points.

To accommodate present-day thinking, I recategorize the three headings of *gender identity* as: sexual "*embodiment*" [femaleness], gender "*representation*" [femininity], and erotic "*desire*" [sexuality], adding a fourth, "*generative identity*", with inevitable overlappings. These categories are addressed here from the perspective of intersubjective structuring of the psyche–soma, interdisciplinary contributions to understanding, and the effect of technological advances on lived psychosocial experience of gender and generativity.

Embodiment

Sexed subjectivity is dependent on psychic meanings rather than anatomy. Far from innate, these are interactively constituted from the moment of birth, and even before.[3] Whatever the biochemical mechanisms of transmission, "raw" foetal material is moulded within the maternal uterine milieu. Hormonal influences are psychically primed by the expectant mother's personal experience of pregnancy—her expectations (including the desired sex of her baby), anxieties, unconscious wishes and projections. During gestation her feelings operate on the foetus, directly through fluctuating cortisol levels and indirectly through her lifestyle, her intake of nutritious and toxic substances, her ambulatory activities, and attitude to antenatal care.

Psychoanalytic perinatal psychotherapy and qualitative and quantitative research[4] confirm that maternal orientations to pregnancy and mothering reflect each woman's own subjective representations of connectedness with her baby, including fantasies of her own baby-self with carer, laden with residual sex/gender configurations from her own archaic primary caregivers. Permutations may be charted as an idealized, depressive, persecutory, anxiety-ridden, obsessional, or detached *"placental paradigm"*, predictive of postnatal interchange (Raphael-Leff, 1986, 1993, 2010b).

Today this complex trans-generational interplay of psychosocial–biochemical forces has further social and ethical implications, as parents can actively *choose the preferred sex of offspring.* Assisted conception allows for the possibility of sexing an embryo before implantation, and knowledge of foetal sex through ultrasound imaging and amniocentesis has led to sex-selective antenatal terminations.[5]

Bodily schemata

Once the baby comes into the world, s/he is inserted into the dynamic intricacies of a boy- or girl-gendered space, primed for him or her in the parent's mind. Parental unconscious assignment is not always commensurate with the baby's sex ["I know perfectly well that you are a man but I am listening to a girl, and I am talking to a girl" says Winnicott to the middle-aged man on his couch, as together they uncover his mother's covert desire for a girl baby (1966, p. 73)]. Parental emotions are conveyed in a myriad direct and subliminal ways. Sex attributions manifest in subtleties of adaptation, caressing, holding, roughhousing, rhythmic responsivity, pitch, tone and tempo of vocalization—all of which influence the pre-verbal infant's developing body image, colouring even auto-erotic cathexes. Many of these "primeval" subsymbolic introjects will remain forever inaccessible to consciousness, saturated with unconscious meanings ascribed by the caregiver to his/her own male or female body and to that of the baby.

Pre-discursive subjectivity is limited and initially *ungendered* from the baby's but not from the parents' point of view. However, I stress that there can be no time before culture. As I find in my cross-cultural work, already *in utero* babies are exposed to societal variation—mediated influences such as environmental sounds, music and language-specific phonemes, maternal dietary prescriptions, sanctioned ambulatory and work habits, tactile pressures, recommended maternity care, and childbirth procedures and ritual practices to contain and counter maternal anxieties about gestational formation, transformation, and sustenance. Similarly, puerperal practices like discarding colostrum as "dirty" or feeding the newborn sugared water, or the circumcised male alcohol, signify insertion into culture before mother's milk ever whets the palette (cf. Raphael-Leff, 1991).

Neonatal research has established that pre-symbolic procedural representations are *co-created* interactively within the early dyadic dialogue (Beebe, Lachman, & Jaffe, 1997; Lyons-Ruth, 1999; Stern, 1985; Trevarthen & Aitken, 2001; Tronick, 1989). As Freud noted in "Femininity" (1933, p. 129) somato-sensory experience is initially stimulated within physical baby care. Representations of both proprioceptive and extroceptive aspects of sensuality are aroused, heightened, and acquire their meanings through intimate interaction with significant others. Self–other bodily interchanges are impregnated with the carer's attitudes to sexuality and narcissistic investment, with their unconscious prohibitions and intimate expression of incestuous desires and taboos, transgressions of which constitute seductions. Hence, *body schemata, too, are interpersonally co-constructed.* Empirical studies corroborate that core gender as a *self-evaluation of maleness or femaleness* is a complex mix of gene regulation, parental attributions, and subjectivity.[6]

In today's climate of "hands-on" fathers, caregiving is no longer a maternal or even a female prerogative. Yet many psychoanalysts continue to demarcate a sexed dichotomy of "expressive" functions (nurture/possession/merger) as maternal and "instrumental" functions (goal directed/limit-setting) as paternal. Psychoanalytic studies of fathers who do the bulk of baby care demonstrate that they can be as sensitive and responsive to cues as mothers, since attunement depends not on gender but on the degree of intimacy and amount of time carer and infant spend together (Pruett, 1998).

Breastfeeding is the only aspect of parenting that is sex-specific. Ultimate awareness of having grown within, emerged from, and been fed by juices of a female body engenders fantasies of intra- and extra-uterine existence and has as profound an influence on the sexed embodiment of both boys and girls as does symbolic phallic dominance. Elsewhere Freud made little distinction between mothers, wet-nurses, and nannies in arousing rage by primary seduction followed by prohibition. However, in "Femininity" he noted a preoedipal litany of accusations and grievances explicitly against the biological mother, ranging from too little milk and, hence, lack of love to the child's fierce jealousy and cruel disappointment at her "faithlessness" in producing a new baby leading to "dethronement" of the current one. These, like his sex-specific

notion that "girls hold their mother responsible for their lack of a
penis" may be directed at the mother of pregnancy. With shared
care and greater awareness of paternal input to baby-making, boys
may equally berate the archaic father for withholding a larger penis,
or the capacity to be pregnant.

Failure to distinguish theoretically between the gestatory mother's "placental"/lactatory function and caregiving designates *the
archaic as female,* a conflation due to the historical fact that Western primary carers were invariably women.[7] These days, with each
subsequent generation of shared care, mothers are less affected by
ramifications of an inferior social position and their sole account-
ability for the child's well-being, although unconscious guilt about
incubatory formation and malformation may be as great.

Similarly, while Freud ascribed nineteenth-century repudiation
of femininity by both sexes to disillusionment in discovering the
preoedipal mother's non-phallic nature, twentieth-century feminists emphasized the continued omnipotence of the female primary carer—who lacked other outlets. The girl and boy child's
previous frustrated dependency on the desired, feared, and hated
all-powerful mother as source of derision towards all things female (Dinnerstein, 1976), counterbalanced by defensive inflation
of paternal powers (Chasseguet-Smirgel, 1970) may change in the
twenty-first century to encompass the baby-care couple.

In sum, a male or female child's interactively constituted embodiment in a mixed-sex family of shared care encompasses a variety of inputs, with multiple conscious and unconscious cross-sex
identifications adhering to his/her basic sense of gendered self,
to be articulated or inhibited as the specific psychosocial milieu
allows.

Awareness of sex

I have proposed here that each infant's lived biological body is *a
dual conduit* for "mapping" a sense of femaleness/maleness that
is both internally and externally primed. But at first there is no
conscious schismatic division of sex. Although the baby's male or
female body is salient for the parents from the start, for the toddler

his/her sex becomes significant only retrospectively—*après coup*—and is revised time and again, especially with bodily changes in adolescence.

Thus, although urethral, anal, and genital sensations contribute to the growing body image, for the infant these implicit experiences are not specifically linked to a sexed self-representation.[8] This interpersonal dimension of embodiment indicates that, like all other experience, *bodily sensations are filtered through implicit mental constructs before becoming subjectively "incorporated".* It is only in the second year that the sexed meaning of genitalia is retroactively interpreted in relation to sexual differentiation, to be reworked again at later stages.

Throughout life, our body representations and gender identity continue to be revised and mediated by the responses and ideas of others. Needless to say, male and female body image is also heavily influenced by public opinion and manipulated by the media. Over the last few decades, hitherto unrealizable aspects of the desired body have been able to materialize. While swoon-inducing whalebone corseting transfigured some nineteenth-century women's physiques, today's transformations are less reversible. *Medical biotechnology can now be utilized to realize ideal embodiment,* blurring the dividing line between the imaginary and the real by permitting actualization of impossible desires, no longer confined to fantasy. Compulsive exercising, appetite suppressants, Botox treatments, skin lightening, hormone-replacement therapy, breast implants, face lifts, liposuction, and other forms of cosmetic surgery are commonplace; men indulge in hair implants, anabolic steroids, and penile enhancements to incorporate an optimal Western embodiment for their sex. This may hook into concrete disavowal of limitations set by our sexed bodies. Lacking boundaries, enactments prevail, with confabulatory externalized displacements of poorly internalized prohibitions, of oedipal parents and their ancestral superegos.

In sum, "core gender", no longer synonymous with a solipsistic "body ego", must be recognized as an intersubjectively co-constructed body configuration that continues to influence—and is influenced by—life's experiences, anxieties, conflicts, unconscious fantasies, and desires. Hence my preference here for a category of "embodiment" signifying that corporeality is an *ongoing process,* undermined by fluctuations and discontinuities in different contexts and at different stages of the life-course.

Gender representations

> Woman is not born: she is made. In the making, her humanity
> is destroyed. She becomes symbol of this, symbol of that:
> mother of the earth, slut of the universe; but she never
> becomes herself because it is forbidden for her to do so.
>
> Andrea Dworkin [radical feminist writer and activist
concerned with sexual violence and antipornography laws]

In patriarchal societies, envisaged as alterity, woman reflects the dominant projections and counter-fantasies of the era, a mythology that serves to repress female sexuality to further men's control over her reproductive capacities. Treating gender definitions as "natural" givens, wishful—Western—interpretations associate *femininity* with surrender, altruism, empathy, emotional expressivity, as well as masochism, depression, and the unspeakable. By contrast, *masculinity* depicts enlightenment goals of rationality, ambition, autonomy, and self-reliance. Even in Freud's sympathetic essay describing femininity in so far as women's "nature is determined by their sexual function", he notes their problematic, lesser functioning, adding that he did "not overlook the fact that an individual woman may be a human being in other respects as well" (1933, p. 135). He dispels the fallacious anthropomorphization of gametes as paradigm for masculine "activity" and coy feminine "passivity", likened to the nutrient-heavy ovum, patiently awaiting penetration by the competitive sperm. Correcting this "error of superimposition", Freud reminded us that "[W]omen can display great activity in various directions, [and] men are not able to live in company with their own kind unless they develop a large amount of passive adaptability" (1933, p. 115). Nonetheless, despite endorsing psychic bisexuality—"[E]very individual . . . displays a mixture of character-traits belonging to his own and to the opposite sex" (1905d: 220)—even in his theorizing, passivity continues to be feminized and libido masculinized. However, no longer caught up in an essentialist binary perspective, many of today's psychoanalysts tend to acknowledge gender multivocality rather than applauding oedipal renunciation of cross-sex identifications.

If femininity/masculinity may be said to represent self-evaluation of "*psychological* femaleness or maleness" (Person & Ovesey, 1983), theoretical positions have differed on the nature of manifestation—whether "womanliness" is a "masquerade" (Riviere, 1929), a series of stylised gestural enactments, "performative" in private as well as public (Butler, 1993a), or involuntary expressions of deep identificatory experiences (Benjamin, 1998; Chodorow, 1989) reflecting artificially constructed representations of distinct normative dichotomies (Bem, 1993) and/or, possibly, a different (female) value system (Gilligan, 1982).

Today, most theoreticians agree about the cultural loading. However, the *impetus* towards role differentiation is variously interpreted. Despite the lack of any consistent research findings of a single sex-linked trait, some analysts still stress an instinctual pathway. Object relational theories emphasize the psychosocial asymmetry of the sexes, treating gender-role identity as a process of acquisition that begins from differential permutations of mother–father boy–girl interactions.[9] As noted, metaphorization of the paternal function ignores the common practice of fathers involved in basic baby-care (especially in Scandinavia, with a year to 18 months' shared parental leave). In families where several generations of children now have been brought up by primary caregiver fathers, the reaction-formation view of femininity as failed masculinity is stemmed, and, conversely, paternal desire to nurture—often intensified by birth attendance—is regarded neither as "feminine" nor as "effeminate", eliminating the crucial necessity for sons to "disidentify" from mothers (Greenson, 1968; Stoller, 1985).

In sum, femininity and masculinity are acquired within a plurality of sexed and non-gendered identifications. *Gender identity as experienced today is but one age-linked facet of multiple aspects of our complex fluid self-representations.*

Subversive agency

> Unsex me
> I will fold up
> this my wrapper
> I will rise up
> and be a man.

Micere Mugo [militant African "matriot" poet], (1976: 14)

Representations of femininity and masculinity depict "collective" historically based features yet are also highly idiomatic, personalized psychic experiences. Similarly, gendered life-styles, appearances, roles, and achievements reflect both unconsciously internalized expectations and more conscious, affirmation-seeking, or challenging social gender-displays—which are not "essential" but are products of beliefs specific to time and place. Domestic violence is still as rife in the West as female infibulations in low-income societies. In our complacency, we tend to overlook the many countries where demure "femininity" is closely defined and disobedience, whether burning the food or undertaking unseemly activity, is severely punished by beating. Transgressions may have fatal consequences, inducing mutilation or "honour killings" by male family members or, as in Iran, public stoning to death of adulterous women while their lovers go free. Although accepted unquestioningly by many, some courageous women (like Anna O) do challenge oppressive gender restrictions. Currently, a female UN worker cum journalist in Sudan is insisting on an open trial while awaiting the humiliating judgement of public flogging, after having been arrested by the Morality Police for wearing trousers.

Radical changes have occurred in the Western world since Freud's writing of "Femininity". First- and second-wave feminists debunked many socio-political ideologies. Growing resistance to cultural stereotypies has led to greater liberalization of gender constituents for *both* sexes. Nonetheless—and despite greater educational parity, convergence in dress, and cross-over toys—career status and pay disparities prevail. Dual expectations of domestic and public involvement are similarly inequable as are emotional "literacy" *and* behavioural assertiveness in both sexes. Nonetheless, gendered self-images for little girls, boys, and their parents are more complex, leading to modifications of psychoanalytic theorizing, particularly in relation to optimal oedipal resolution and gender-role representations.

Erotic "desire"

> Every woman I have ever loved has left her print upon me, where I loved some invaluable piece of myself apart from me—so different that I had to stretch and grow in order to recognize her. And in that growing, we came to separation, that place where work begins.
>
> Audre Lorde [black lesbian mother, lover, poet, activist for feminist acknowledgement of class, race, age, sexuality, differences among women]

This component of gender identity traditionally signified "sexual partner orientation", regarded as the outcome of incestuous attractions honed within the context of a nuclear family's oedipal identifications. While some psychoanalysts assumed an innate heterosexual drive that need not be explained, Freud saw it as "a problem that needs elucidating" (1905d: 146 n), noting that—when mothers are primary carers—exogamic heterosexuality renders loss of the early erotic connection to the maternal body more complex for girls than for boys. Disavowal of primary female homosexual attachment, is an issue oft overlooked by Anglo-Saxon theorists (cf. O'Connor & Ryan, 1993) but prevalent among French psychoanalysts (e.g. Aisenstein, 2006).

Once again controversy reigns. There are those who treat homosexuality as a self-proclaimed preference on a spectrum of potentially infinite but discursively restricted marginalized sexual identities, identifications, and practices (Butler, 1993a; Irigaray, 1985a). Some decree it an "inversion" grounded in differing identifications within the context of universal human bisexuality, as did Freud. Yet others treat same-sex desire as perversion of a "natural" heterosexuality within a discrete reproductively defined binary system and, therefore, abnormal or pathological, utilizing primitive defence mechanisms (McDougall, 1979; Socarides, 1978). Unlike non-specific "queer" culture, after 1970 Radical Feminists politicized lesbianism, arguing for separatism, freedom from domination, and a multiplicity of representations.

It is noteworthy that the anatomical sex of a chosen partner does

not necessarily signify a corresponding identification (O'Connor
& Ryan, 1993)—a same-sex partner may represent otherness or
diverse identifications with masculine/feminine aspects of father
or mother, siblings, or others. Similarly, in sexual fantasy life many
entertain a variety of homoerotic yearnings, not necessarily expressed in practice. In psychoanalytic treatment, phobic avoidance
by heterosexual therapists of same-sex passion—possibly related
to a sense of transgression against oedipal prohibition of imaginative participation in an incestuous primal scene—may inhibit the
patient's expression of feelings and lead analysts to dissociation or
denial of homoerotic countertransference (Sherman, 2002). The
stigma has lessened with the decriminalizing and depatholgizing
of homosexuality, and many gay and lesbian therapists and analysts
contribute to reappraisals of sexual theory (cf. Domenici & Lesser,
1995).

"Excitation"

Contemporary psychoanalytic writers now tend to address eroticism
and object choice separately from gender identity. Importantly,
Freud made sex speakable. Post-1960s efficient female-based contraception decoupled sex, procreation, and marriage, further unbolt-
ing psychosexual "chastity belts". Women, previously the "objects"
of male desire, became desiring subjects. Subverting psychoanalytic
theory that advocated exchange of "polymorphously perverse" pleasures for penis-awakened vagina, women reclaimed clitoral orgasm
from Freud's "pine shavings" (1905d, p. 221). Asexual procreation
and areas of socio-political agency hitherto barred to women led
to a variety of new choices—childlessness, "pro-women" entrepre-
neurship, proud single motherhood, civil partnerships, same-sex
assisted reproduction (including lesbian egg-exchange and legal
adoption).

Previously seen as static or generalizable "sexual conditions",
both hetero- and homosexualities became pluralized (Chodorow,
1994b), viewed as changeable products of multiple conscious and
unconscious intersections of gender and sexuality and informed by
the wider social context of ideology, differential cultural/familial
values and asymmetries of sexual dominance. Indeed, the range

of sexualities today encompasses heterosexuality, homosexuality, bisexuality, pansexuality, polysexuality, and asexuality.

As with femininity, other approaches to sexuality are no longer posited as failed heterosexual pursuits or cross-sex male- or female-identified activity—in a dichotomized field (Burch, 1993). Even among "stone" butch femmes, it is woman-to-woman love that is emphasized rather than a "disguised" heterosexual couple (Creith, 1996). Similarly, gay men are assumed to experience a different kind of masculinity rather than feminine identifications.

Finally, celebration of non-reproductive sexuality and sensual intimacy has not eradicated the unconscious vulnerabilities, splitting, compromises, and anxieties inherent in all submission to passion. Subjective meanings of *embodiment, representations,* and *desire* interweave with unconscious fantasy, cultural imagery, and normative psychosocial underpinnings, feeding into *generative identity,* to which I now turn.

Generative identity

Despite their conceptual shortcomings, delineation of these three constituents of gender refines our understanding of gender. They highlight how manifestations of preconscious fantasies of sexed embodiment, gender representations, and sexual desire are formed dynamically, through subtle inter-psychic processes remoulded by interactive exchange. The constituents of gender identity demonstrate potential conflicts, synchrony, incongruities, or discordance between various facets that may be experienced by any one individual. Into this medley I have introduced a fourth gender component—the notion of "generative identity" (Raphael-Leff, 1997, 2000a)—as an explanatory model to accommodate the diversity of (female and male) responses to new reproductive choices and women's growing participation in cultural creativity.

Generative identity proposes that beyond one's core sense of *femaleness or maleness* and in addition to *feminine or masculine* role representations and articulation of *erotic desires,* there is a further post-oedipal psychic construction of oneself as a *potential (pro-)creator,* rooted in negotiation of basic reproductive facts.

Freud (1905d) posited the primal question as: *"Where do babies come from?"*

Interest in "anthropogeny" is crucial in initiating a process of acquiescence to a simple fact of origin: we are not self-made, but come of two others. Sexual difference confronts us with what we are not, instigating further awareness of what we are/do have. Re-examining this momentous psychological division into two sexes, I suggest that for the toddler sexual differentiation is bi-phased: earlier recognition of anatomical difference is re-evaluated *après coup* through an awareness of distinct *procreative capacities*. Generative identity is consolidated somewhere after 18 months when children with a psychic "bisexual disposition" who had unquestioningly identified with capacities of both sexes face four fundamental facts:

▷ of *sex* ("I am either female or male, not the other sex, neither or both.")
▷ of *generation* ("Adults make babies; children cannot.")
▷ of *genesis* ("I am not self-created but procreated by two sexes.")
▷ of *generativity* ("Males impregnate; females gestate, give birth, and lactate.")

These also link to other issues I have termed *"genitive"*: *finitude, arbitrariness,* and *irreversibility,* which take on greater significance when generative identity is reworked again during adolescence. These genitive issues deal with constraints—with chance (meeting of parents and gametes alike), the irreversibility of life's trajectory (once born, never returning to the womb); and a fact learned and disavowed throughout life: the inevitability and universality of ultimate death.[10]

Having to accept limitations involves undeniable pain. With the help of genital categorization, a little child who had previously regarded him/herself indiscriminately as having/being "everything" now has to become reconciled to implications of being restricted to a specific sex, and genitalia that will not magically transform. While linguistically and cognitively coherent, subjectivity now becomes fragmented when contradictions and discontinuities are dissociated. Generative facts of two-sex coupling defy theories of auto- or parthenogenesis. Reproductive facts highlight parental sexual difference from each other, and from the child who emerged from Mummy's (not Daddy's) "tummy".

The emotional meaning attributed to these discoveries will depend on specific psychodynamics and sexual hierarchies within each family. The oedipal parents' excluding sexual relationship is now also recognized as a *reproductive* one—a situation that differs with adoption, assisted conception, step- and same-sex parents. Studies show that in non-conventional families a toddler's recategorization of generative experience and discovery of a father's seminal role may be complicated by assisted reproduction (cf. Corbett, 2001). However, the crucial element is not the physical presence of both progenitors but their psychic significance in the minds of caregiver/s and child.

Furthermore, I argue that today's psychosocial conditions, such as lone parents, serial non-cohabiting relationships, increased geographical and social mobility, fragmented extended families, loss of traditional patterns, and contracted support networks, foster an extremely intense dyadic relationships between carer and child. A child in a possessive twosome may not find a "parental couple" to triangulate from. Rivalry, competitiveness, and counterphobic reassurances against "castration" anxiety may be compelled to seek extra-familial outlets. A further consequence of small families is the impeded working-through of primary experience during childhood. An only child has few opportunities for *active* processing of his/her own infantile feelings in the presence of a baby sibling/ cousin, thus rendering recent generations of parents unprepared for the emotional impact with the birth of their own baby and more susceptible to perinatal emotional disturbance (Raphael-Leff, 1991, 2000b, 2009).

To recapitulate

Sexual difference and gender classification commencing in late infancy are consolidated with the acquisition of language and supported or distorted within intense primary dyadic relationships in nuclear families. *Conscious* articulation of one's own gendered identity is retrospectively re-inaugurated in toddlerhood, arising out of the seedbed of a "bisexual disposition".[11] In the early stages categorization of sexual differences and gender representations are not only based on familial relationships but also highly dependent on peers (and story-books/dvd/media depictions).

Emotionally, for the child who has hitherto loosely identified with reproductive capacities of both sexes (Freud, 1909b) acquisition of generative identity threatens the previous "over-inclusiveness" (Fast, 1984), resulting in feelings of loss; penis-, womb-, and breast-envy; jealousy of the other sex; and curtailed omnipotence. In the post-"terrible-two" rebellion, compensation for losses entails strict adherence to sex-typed behaviours. Many 3-year-olds conceptualize gender roles as increasingly rule-bound and even stereotypical, with same-sex friendships and imitative enactments of "femininity" and "masculinity". Such concrete reliance on perceptual saliencies of gendered appearance and activities has been attributed to the young child's poor cognitive capacity to understand subcategories or exceptions to the rule (cf. Coates & Wolfe, 1995). However, loss, anxiety, and uncertainty temporarily increase the need for conformity and compliance with convention.

Moreover, limits of sex, generation, and generativity are bounded not only by difference but by *deferment*. For some little girls and boys, the realization that they are pre-potent and must wait to become parents in their own right induces feelings of impatience and generational envy. Eagerness to have a baby may escalate, especially when this is regarded as the culmination of feminine aspirations. Paradoxically, possibly as a result of a disillusionment with promised sex equality, US and UK rates for very young teenage mothers are the highest in the Western world, even though most adolescent pregnancies are not consciously intended and over half end in abortion. Conversely, an estimated 12–20% of European women decide to remain "childfree", expressing their generative agency in creative endeavours other than procreativity. Finally, career women who postpone childbearing until their late 30s often find that their reduced fertility necessitates treatment. Sexually transmitted diseases and the falling quality/motility of sperm render natural reproduction an impossibility for one in six adult couples who do wish to conceive. I argue that reactions to diagnosis of subfertility reveal a spectrum of generative identities—indicating that for some becoming parents is optional, while for others it feels desperately essential.

Adult reproductive decisions reflect the way oedipal and generative limitations were negotiated in childhood. Acceptance of limitations, militant resistance to or over-compliance with normative aspirations; retention of psychic bisexuality and multiple self-representations; and early uncoupling of creativity from procreative activity all influence future gender identity. Satisfaction in "love, work, and play", and decisions whether to reproduce, when, with whom, and how, reflect generative identity, as do acceptance of childlessness or determination to override infertility, should this arise. When formation of generative identity is troubled due to family dysfunction, traumatic events, or incestuous seduction, the child's play and creativity may be anxiety-driven or self-consciously inhibited (Raphael-Leff, 2010a). A child who disavows some or all of the basic facts of life may, in later life, utilize biotechnology to concretely enact their annulment.

In sum, generative identity does not instigate sexual dimorphism but arises from it and, to achieve agential sublimation, must transcend it. Personalized configurations of generative parameters underpin each man or woman's orientations to both procreativity and creative endeavour. These determine whether generative agency is expressed healthily or is inhibited, disregarded, or reversed by imaginary means; whether enacted concretely, compulsively, deviantly, or even psychotically due to the paralysing effects of breast, womb- or penis envy or overdependence on glorified parents or on the other sex. Or, conversely, oedipal triumph, the idealization of lawlessness, and refusal of prohibitions may take the form of psychosomatic expressions, sexual perversions or pathogenic pursuit of concrete bodily transformations—or the creativity of transgressive art. . . .

It has been suggested that creativity involves metaphorical assumption of *joint*—male/female—*generative capacities of fertile progenitors*: internal mental "intercourse" to create an intellectual "brainchild" or artistic baby of the mind (McDougall, 1995a; Money-Kyrle, 1971). In today's emancipated social climate, no longer exclusively tethered to childbearing, "femininity" can manifest in accomplishments other than, or in addition to, "*Kinder, Küche, Kirche*". In both men and women, creativity is facilitated by multiple coexistent identifications and simultaneously held cross-sex and age-varied representations of the self, expressing yet transcending limitations of anatomy.

I argue that once "reality principles" of generativity are

negotiated, a gendered child can make the imaginative leap to symbolically repossessing a medley of psychic potentialities, in narratives of imaginative play, daydreams, and creative endeavour made possible through receptivity to—rather than renunciation of—myriad ego-syntonic self-representations.

When creativity remains closely linked to future procreativity, generative agency often remains on hold while awaiting a real baby. This may manifest in devaluation of other achievements as second-rate; or in a sense of emotional emptiness and lack of agency, sometimes leading to premature testing out of fertility and/or devastating effects should infertility arise. For others, the creative capacity can be abstracted—articulated in vocational, artistic, intellectual, and innovative attainments. I suggest that a capacity to tolerate gender ambiguities and a belief in internal resources lies at the root of their generative agency.

In conclusion, the notion of "femininity" has undergone profound changes. Few analysts today would subscribe to Freud's declaration that a woman patient of 30—or even of 40 or 50— "often frightens us by her psychical rigidity and unchangeability . . . as though, indeed, the difficult development to femininity had exhausted the possibilities of the person concerned" (1933, pp. 134–135). Indeed, far from nihilistic "exhaustion", the majority of today's candidates and patients in psychoanalysis are women, actively invested in maximizing their generative capacities.

Notes

1. Already in Freud's day, this position was negated by assumptions that "woman is born not made" (Jones, 1927). Reluctant to voice his own "feminine intuitions"—possibly due to his own unanalysed early generative trauma (see Raphael-Leff, 2007)—Freud increasingly relegated authority to female colleagues and analysands—Lou Andreas-Salomé, Marie Bonaparte, Helene Deutsch, Ruth Mack Brunswick, Jeanne Lampl-de Groot, and so on. As the ensuing debate polarized, the concept of psychic bisexuality became submerged. Wish for a child based on preoedipal maternal identification (Horney, 1924, 1926; Jacobson, 1968; Jones, 1927) counterbalanced the baby as a "symbolic equation" consolation prize for switching from maternal love-object to the penis-endowed father (Freud, 1924d: 179). Conversely, countering Freud's phallic monism, seen as defensive for girls (Jones, 1935), "primary femininity" was postulated to negate the convoluted route to femininity from a little girl's origins as "a little man" engaging in clitoral (vestigial

penis) masturbation. *No longer adhering to bodily experience as interpreted through psychosexual fantasy, the debate now shifted away from mental representations to sensory (vaginal) sensations, ascribed a predetermined body-based female path with inherent heterosexual tendencies.* This position gradually assumed an *essentialist* quality, ascribing what we would now call "gender identity" to anatomical sex. Each gender became treated as a (fixed) *unitary construction* in itself and *polar complementary* to the other. Freud's pioneering concept of bisexual fluidity was superseded by reification of binary concepts that occluded both within-gender variation and between-sex similarities. When the controversy resurfaced decades later, pioneering French psychoanalysts of the "classical school" emphasized the centrality of the maternal imago in the little girl's developing sexuality, the "phallic meaning" of creation inducing "feminine guilt" and penis envy as a symbolic expression of the desire to detach from the mother (Chasseguet-Smirgel, ed, 1964/1981). Keen to dispel phallo-centric definitions of "femininity as lack", American counter-formulations valorized female—bodily—experience (Barnett, 1966; Elise, 1997; Lax, 1998; Richards, 1996; Tyson, 1994). Depictions of the seductive archaic mother, her "dark" female void and projected assumptions of her moral inferiority and anatomical deficiency, were counterbalanced by a focus on representations of presence rather than lack. Emphasis on "primary femininity", cathexis, and "the" girl's mental representation of her own sexed body, including labia, vulva, clitoris, vaginal opening, and, indeed, "inner" genitals (Kestenberg, 1982), decentralized the phallic stage—renamed "early genital". Specifically female anxieties were delineated as opposed to the "castrative" fantasy of the imagined lost penis (Bernstein, 1990; Dorsey, 1996; Mayer, 1985). However, here, too, essentialism and solipsistic psychology resurfaced as focus on corporeal origins of anxieties obfuscated *unconscious psychosocial influences and inter-subjectively charged psychic representations,* as attempts to redress the balance fostered a polarity of reversals with a tendency towards gender stereotyping and normative prescriptions of "femininity". The ideal persisted of a post-oedipal consolidation of mutually excluding dichotomies and repression of other-sex representations, although British Independents continued to posit an admixture of "male and female elements of the personality" (cf. Payne, 1935; Winnicott, 1966). It is only recently that normal gender identity has once again become recognized as a less than unified coherent entity. Relational therapists in particular now argue for a view of *gender as a multilayered, variable, and unstable interplay of fantasies, relational configurations, and identifications* (Benjamin, 1995; Dimen, 1991; Harris, 1991; Sweetnam, 1996), both "culturally mandated, but . . . individually crafted" (Goldner, 2005, p. 253), shot through with a fluid indeterminacy, which some still designate as pathological (see Chasseguet-Smirgel, 2005).

2. In this complex field, many researchers concede to "interactionism" between pre- and post-natal factors and between hormonal and environmental determinants of psychosexual differentiation, also recognizing sociocultural influences in male/female "dualism". Across a myriad studies, the only consistent finding of "inborn" sex differences relates to superior female verbal skills vs. better spatial cognitive processes in males. Yet even

these differences are a matter of degree rather than two distinct populations. Even constitutional sex-specific behavioural differences are found to be malleable and environmentally primed yet complex, as evidenced by a sex-reassignment of a male twin brought up as a girl after accidental "castration" during circumcision (Diamond & Sigmundson, 1997). Furthermore, neuroscientific research on neonatal orbito-frontal cortex activation during primary caregiving emphasizes selective enrichment or pruning of synaptic connections, demonstrating the interactional component of brain development itself (Schore, 2001).

3. In the early stages of embryonic development there is no sex distinction, with all embryos identified by the mother's genotype. Around the first six weeks of gestation the primary gonads begin to differentiate into ovaries or testicles. During this critical period decisive influences include both genetic markers and endocrinal factors, which affect sex-dimorphic structures. In the absence of hormonal changes in the prenatal environment, the embryo develops into a female. The "anatomical" bisexuality to which Freud referred now seems to apply to the male but not the female embryo. Rather than clitoris as "atrophied penis", testicals and male vestigial nipples act as reminder of proto-female origins. Finally, epidemiological studies indicate that maternal hormone production is affected by "stress", influencing the degree of prenatal masculinization.

4. This chapter draws on my psychoanalytic specialization in reproductive and early parenting issues over the past 35 years, in both clinical work and academia as a psychoanalyst and social psychologist. Clinical experience has included psychoanalysis/psychotherapy, with over 200 patients treated 1–5 times per week, individually, as couples, or in groups, sometimes spanning several pregnancies. In addition to clinical supervisions, I consult to perinatal projects on six continents, including psychodynamic exploratory workshops with thousands of primary health workers and/or parents. My small-scale in-depth qualitative studies have been replicated in large representative community samples conducted by independent researchers in different countries. My thrice-weekly longitudinal observation of a sample of 23 children in several cohorts over a period of 8 years extended from birth through toddlerhood to 40 months, involving 200 families in a large community play centre. This was supplemented by my weekly (filmed) observations of a troop of Orang-Utans focusing on three mother–baby pairs, from birth over a two-and-a-half-year period, to ascertain a common primate baseline.

5. Before laws prohibiting the use of technology to identify the gender of a foetus, almost all aborted foetuses in India were female; in China five decades of sex-selective abortion, abandonment, neglect, or infanticide of female babies have led to a sex-ratio imbalance of many million women (see Raphael-Leff, 2000a, 2002).

6. Historically, work with intersex children (Money, 1955) and research on vaginaless female babies (Stoller, 1968b) suggested that the intrapsychic sense of being male or female is determined by unequivocal parental assignment of the baby to one sex or the other at birth. Stoller coined the concept *"core"* gender identity to depict the child's affectively laden sense of being the

"right" sex, a confluence of both hedonic pleasure and a rudimentary sense of propriety in being male or female (see Coates & Wolfe, 1995) assumed to be more complex for boys as female primary care fosters "proto-femininity". The concept of "core gender" has been criticized for insufficiently taking into account more recent foetal research findings of constitutional sex-specific brain differences (Robbins, 1996). However, neuro-endocrinologically primed sex dimorphism is by no means clear-cut, raising complex issues regarding biogenetic determinism.

7. The impact of the archaic maternal is variously theorized. In contrast to the object relations view of feminine/masculine self-images ascribed to internalized sexual differences in the course of the formation of subjectivity, Lacanians assume construction of subjectivity by subjection *to* sexual difference through language acquisition in relation to the phallus (see Mitchell, 1982). Following Freud's emphasis on castration anxiety, Lacan assigned to the female child who cannot be what the mother desires a place within the phallic economy as *the feminine "Other"*—a negative standard by contrast with which masculinity is self-defined (Lacan, 1977), whose *jouissance* is "beyond" linguistic representation. Post-Lacanian feminists (Cixous & Clément, 1986; Irigaray, 1985a; Kristeva, 1984) negated his notion that, submitted to—male—unconscious structures in culture, a "woman" does not exist in language. Sharing Derrida's antagonism to dualistic hierarchies (of sex, and other dichotomies), these French theorists argue for multiple differences and subversive creativity by drawing on the archaic rhythmic raw material of the "semiotic" (Kristeva) to express shifting heterogeneous subjectivities through *"ecriture feminine"* (Cixous)—open to both female and male writers who share anarchic preoedipal forces. This project of weakening traditional gender divisions in which women are regarded as defective men and mothers are unsymbolized (Irigaray) is seen to require both women and men to find their "feminine" voices (from this primal maternally governed period).

8. Studies on anatomical self-concept demonstrate that genital awareness in very young children, including the ability to experience and label their own genitals, is *not* commensurate with a subjective sense of gender. Genital recognition indicates neither the child's capacity for *gender discrimination* (de Marneffe, 1997) nor its capacity for gender *conservation*—that is, "constancy" (sex recognized as independent of appearance/activity, and "stability"), understanding that these categories will remain unchanging (see Coates & Wolfe, 1995)].

9. In view of this, some aspects of theory are interrogated as specific repercussions of *same-sexed maternal primary care*, with implications for a girl's developing gender identity. These have included persecutory anxieties about retaliatory threats to her reproductive body integrity (Klein, 1945); bodily co-identification leading to greater female relatedness (Irigaray, 1985a); an ego marked by permeable boundaries as the mother's self-extension (Chodorow, 1989); and maternal pressure on the daughter's psyche to acquiesce or at least accommodate to the patriarchal social order (Mitchell, 1974; Orbach & Eichenbaum, 1982). However, such generalizations underplay differences of maternal subjectivity. Research on my model of parental orientations

finds that emotional cathexis of body sameness varies: whereas "facilitator" mothers tend to relish and foster primary identificatory fusion with their daughters, "regulator" mothers dread it, downplaying female-to-female symbiotic merger and handling their daughters at a greater distance than sons (Raphael-Leff, 1986, 1991).

10. "Finitude" is a philosophical concept utilized in psychoanalysis to replace "castrative" aspects of recognizing monosexuality and human constraints (see Moi, 2004). Here I stress that the transition from omnipotence is affected by new reproductive and medical biotechnologies, which alter "eternal" facts of life, seemingly eliminating finitude and constraints. Today sex and generative limitations can seem to be undone by an illusion—fast becoming reality—of infinite possibilities: sex-change; asexual conception; post-mortem cryation; egg-swapping and gamete donation; post-menopausal childbearing; grandmother surrogacy; prenatal surgery; cultivated aborted-embryo stem cells and eggs; projected extra-uterine male gestations, cloning and artificial-womb pregnancies; to name but a few that, along with medical procedures such as life-support machinery, organ transplants, hormonal supplements, breast implants, genetic engineering, prenatal selection, and so on, endeavour to remove arbitrariness, reverse time, or prolong life.

11. The period before psychic sexuation occurs has been variously described as non-discriminatingly "polymorphous" or pregenitally "multifarious" (Freud, 1905d), an "amphimyxis of eroticisms" at an age of "unconditional omnipotence" (Ferenczi, 1938), in which the "undifferentiated" child is narcissistically "overinclusive" (Fast, 1984). The common denominator among these terms points to an—unselfconscious—assumption that *all sex and gender possibilities are available.* If newly gendered sons are said to "disidentify" from female primary carers (Greenson, 1968), daughters too must recognize their pre-nubile difference from the fertile maternal body (Raphael-Leff, 1997). Inevitably, body image may be further affected by the persistence of a collaborative illusion of a phallic mother, or complicated by parental non-affirmation of the child's future fertility, or reinforcement of anxieties about her own unseen vagina and womb. Observers have long noted the depressive effect that discovery of sexual difference has on the jubilant toddler's "love affair with the world" (Galenson & Roiphe, 1976; Mahler, Pine, & Bergman, 1975). Since Money's and Stoller's early work, most researchers designate this sensitive period to the second and third years of life, when budding genitality and social markers of sexual distinctions and bodily configurations are consciously recategorized into male and female differences and gendered identifications. I argue that this sadness is hardly surprising when illusions of over-inclusivity are re-evaluated through the restricting lenses of "genderization". The humiliation of relinquishing the self-creational illusion of auto-genesis is coupled with accepting being not omnipotent or even potent but *pre*potent. And, to top it all, even the promise of eventual reproduction is disappointingly two-sex *inter-dependent* rather than autonomous/parthenogenic. Furthermore, disillusionment about spontaneous generation reduces the belief in parental omnipotence too, with recognition that it takes two to procreate.

3

The analyst's meta-theories concerning sexual difference and the feminine

Leticia Glocer Fiorini

This chapter aims to examine the analyst's meta-theories in relation to the various theories in circulation concerning the feminine and sexual difference—a logic and models of thought that have a great impact on interpretations and constructions, as well as on transference–countertransference and, consequently, on the entire process of the cure.

This inquiry implies taking up concepts that are usually affixed acritically to discourses regarding sexual difference and the feminine. It involves focusing on their epistemic sources as well as ideologies, prejudices, and fantasms, both personal and collective, that support theories and sustain clinical work and from which no analyst is exempt. It is also indispensable to consider how these categories acquire their status as beliefs and myths that infiltrate and become part of the language.

For this purpose, we need to focus on the meta-theories that support the theories—implicit or explicit, conscious, preconscious, or unconscious, private or shared—regarding sexual difference and the feminine. It is a question of bypassing unconditional acceptance of basic suppositions that have been considered immutable and advancing towards their necessary deconstruction.

The questions are: What theoretical and personal frames are available to each analyst for the investigation of these issues? What are their limits? To what extent do we have a "free choice" of theories? How does castration anxiety come into play in each male analyst? What role does penis envy play for women? How do the social norms of each period intersect with the fantasms, ideologies, and private theories of each analyst, and how do they self-perpetuate and potentiate each other? What logic is involved in each interpretation in relation to sexual and gender difference? To what extent do female analysts identify with male castration anxiety and try to appease it by occupying the place they are assigned by theory?

With these questions in mind, I will discuss concepts traditionally associated with women: the female enigma, "the dark continent", the foreign, as well as the implications and connotations of the castration complex described in women. Since all these concepts are intimately related, my aim is to focus on their connections with the concept of otherness, recalling that the feminine is too frequently equated with the other. We also need to underline that this equivalence is supported by binary polarities (subject–object, subject–other) and their close ties with the masculine–feminine polarity. This, of course, also involves the nature/nurture debate.

I would like to emphasize that, in this line of thought, bodies are not exempt. Our body is our own and is also an other. We need to point out that the woman's body quite frequently appears to be the incarnation and support of sexual difference. This attributes to it a quality of otherness that is superimposed on the condition of otherness that any subject's body always has for that subject.

My objective is, therefore, to analyse and deconstruct the feminine = other equation, with the intention of delving into its genealogies and meanings and consequently its effects in clinical practice. I began developing this analysis in other publications (Glocer Fiorini, 1994, 1996, 1998, 2001a, 2001b, 2006, 2007, 2008). In my view, the study of these genealogies contributes elements to the understanding of meta-theories and the epistemic and logical sources underlying the analyst's work, which may translate into ideologies, prejudices, or unshakeable convictions regarding the feminine and sexual difference.

A transdisciplinary view:
discourses and narratives

The equivalence of the feminine and the other refers us to an opposition—culture versus nature—which is supported by a notion that transcends epochs: that women are indissolubly linked to the biological and nature and men to culture and reason. In other words, that whatever is rational corresponds to men and whatever is emotional to women. We observe that the idea of the woman as a weak, incomplete, inferior being, or as incarnating demonic temptation, runs through the centuries and is evidenced by religious, philosophical, and medical discourses, as well as myths and customs; nor is psychoanalysis exempt from the force of these discourses.

We see some of these aspects in the Bible, where women appear either as devalued beings or as enchantresses—depositories of dangerous sexuality. In the Middle Ages, the figure of "the witch" demonstrates malignant and uncanny aspects associated with the feminine that, with seemingly more benevolent connotations, remain intact even today. This is the counter-figure of the woman–mother pure and idealized. By contrast, these aspects tend to emphasize women's natural–biological fate, mainly the reproductive one. We also recall that it was only at the Council of Trent that the Catholic Church decided that women have a soul.

We also find the feminine = other equation—this other generally having malignant and threatening characteristics—in other cultures. In some primitive peoples, menstruating women were excluded because of their supposedly evil influences. Others held ceremonies in which women were burned alive with their dead husbands. Israël (1979) describes the Native American legend of "vaginas with teeth", which roam about at harvest time and, when captured by men, are deprived of their teeth, put back in their place, and bolted down with a clitoral nail. This author considers that it embodies a fantasmatic of fear of women that echoes the clitoridectomy that is practiced on pubertal Muslim girls, among other reasons, as a means to control their *jouissance*.

Nineteenth-century medicine grounded women's inferiority on supposed scientific bases. Bouillaud considered that the uterus was not an essential organ in women, since it did not exist in men. This

type of analogical thinking, applied in different disciplines, reveals
the condition of otherness assigned to women by an investigative
masculine subject that analyses his object of study. It is well known
that Plato (Penguin edition, 2003) pondered whether to include
women among the rational animals or among the brutes, and Erasmus, in his *In Praise of Madness* (1511), considered that the woman
was like a stupid and crazy animal. Aristophanes, in his *Lysistrata*
(411 BC), mirrored ideas prevalent in antiquity that women were
unpredictable, mad, inferior beings, although at the same time
he depicted their skill at avoiding wars promoted by men. Spinoza
(1677) wondered whether women could have an ethical position.
Freud (1933) did not escape these ideas when he described female
characteristics: a small sense of justice, a weakly constituted superego, psychic rigidity after the age of 30, weaker social interests, and
a lower aptitude for sublimation.

The itinerary we have traced shows us that the feminine has
always been thought of in negative terms, either by devaluation or
by denying it representativeness. Confrontation with the difference
of the sexes traditionally attributed to the feminine a condition of
emptiness and silence necessarily demanding decoding. In other
words, *the feminine appears to be something strange, and as such is idealized or devaluated or else situated outside language and the symbolic order.
This aspect strongly infiltrates the fantasmatics about women and places
the woman as the other in contrast to a masculine subject. Hence, transdis-
ciplinary narratives and discourses have intradisciplinary effects on the
psychoanalytic field.*

We may also bear in mind that this is inserted in a context in
which two conceptions of sexual difference coexist in the field of
culture. On the one hand, two strictly differentiated spaces are
drawn: masculine and feminine, heavily accentuated in illustrated modernity, which support a radical difference. On the other
hand, the turn of the century has ushered in a multiplicity of
sexual and gender variants that question concepts of modernity
regarding sexual difference. These sexual migrations, which accompany the phenomenon of post-modernity, construct narratives
that, although they may add no new phenomena, acquire special
resonance with the advances of biotechnology as well as increased
social acceptance.

In this regard, we need to underline that various periods have questioned the classical binary dichotomy of sexual difference. A nearly infinite series of processes of mixtures, transformations, and identifications between the masculine and the feminine (Zolla, 1981) has been present throughout the history of culture: dual beings, the androgynous described by Plato; shamanic phenomena of trance and transformation into the other sex; the lamas who identify with their goddesses hallucinatorily; the frequent representation of mixed figures such as feminine or breast-feeding Christs in the Middle Ages, to mention just a few.

As we have said, these two tendencies coexist in the present: the strict separation of the sexes accentuated in modernity and sexual variants ushered in by post-modernity (which some authors term late modernity and others hyper-modernity). They are part of the consensus of significations of a period that supports a number of social practices and relations. But even though these sexual and gender variants tend to erase any strict masculine–feminine polarity, they have not, in spite of changes in the feminine condition in large sectors of Western society, substantially modified the persistence of the ancestral equivalence of the feminine, the other, the enigma. The two conditions coexist in today's societies.

We also need to point out that, although the feminine and woman are different categories, they also support necessary relations. It is on these inevitably ambiguous relations that we need to work.

We might remember that the fixation of the feminine and the woman in a condition of otherness has strong implications in the psychoanalytic field. Its impact is felt not only on the theoretical and epistemic plane but also on the empirical plane, where it may become a part of the analyst's position.

Genealogies of the feminine as the other in the psychoanalytic field

The structuring of the subject in the context of social bonds has been discussed from various angles. This issue has been examined by various disciplines in the field of human sciences: philosophy, anthropology, sociology, psychology, and psychoanalysis. In this context, Todorov (1995) states that we need to speak, not only as we commonly do, about the place of humans in society, but also about the opposite: about the place of society in humans.

One of the great debates in the psychoanalytic field focuses precisely on the following option: whether human beings are constituted fundamentally on the basis of their drive life or whether the processes of subjectivation inevitably include an other, essential for psychic structuring.

This issue has been addressed from different perspectives, beginning with Freud's works—the concept of fellow beings (1950 [1895]), the influence of culture (1930a [1929]). We may also recall, among others, the theories of object relations (Klein, 1945), the transitional object (Winnicott, 1959), the analytic field (Baranger & Baranger, 2009), the objectizing function (Green, 1995), and the concepts of intersubjectivity and trans-subjectivity (Ogden, 1994, Renik, 1993), the imaginary and the symbolic other (Lacan, 1966), the crisis of representation in the intersubjective frame (Puget, 2003)—all proposals with sometimes significantly divergent meanings, but which put forward the need to include the concept of otherness both in the study of processes of subjectivation and in clinical practice.

In other words, a broad range of current psychoanalytic publications take different perspectives to support the indispensable participation of an other in the production of a subject. The role of the other and others needs to be considered a necessary condition to cross boundaries of narcissism and recognize something outside the subject and the other's determining function in the construction of subjectivity.

Many of these proposals speak of the intersubjective or the other without considering their relation to sexual difference—in other words, as a neutral or asexual other. However, at the same time, whenever sexual difference is discussed in the psychoanalytic field, the concept of otherness inevitably arises and has strikingly often been equated with the feminine and women.

Freudian logic

This equivalence assigned to the feminine and the other is, in my opinion, rooted in several sources: (1) the feminine conceived as an object of desire and knowledge; (2) the feminine interpreted as equivalent to the enigma and lack; (3) the feminine equated with the maternal. All these sources are interrelated. In this chapter I focus mainly on Freud's positions concerning women and their subjacent logic, since I understand that they influence contemporary psychoanalysis in that they are either accepted or challenged by subsequent psychoanalytic developments.

1.   The subject–object issue

In Freud's works, subject–object polarity is operating in relation to sexual difference. Freud (1905d, 1923e) draws a sharp division between, on the one hand, masculine, subject, active, and possession of a penis, and on the other, the feminine as equivalent to object, passive, and non-possession of the penis. This defines the feminine in terms of the negative. He also points out that the vagina comes into consideration only at puberty as lodging for the penis—that is to say, in a passive position. In *Totem and Taboo*, Freud states (1912–13) that women are possessions of the Father of the horde and, as such, are objects of exchange. He also indicates their position as objects when he tells us, in "The Taboo of Virginity", that

> a generalized dread of women is expressed in all these rules of avoidance . . . woman is different from man, for ever incomprehensible and mysterious, strange and therefore apparently hostile. The man is afraid of being weakened by the woman, infected with her femininity and of then showing himself incapable. . . . In all this there is nothing obsolete, nothing which is not still alive among ourselves". [Freud, 1918a (1917), pp. 198–199]

Therefore, one cause of the taboo is that for men, women are strange, hostile, and foreign. We emphasize that in these developments the object is the woman and hence the other, in the sense that this other attacks the ego's certainties. *This brief mention of Freud's statements reveals an inevitable point of view: that of the masculine subject of knowledge, faced with an object yet to be known—a point of view also superimposed on the position of the masculine desiring subject faced with the feminine object of desire.* Freud implicitly recognizes this position when he tells his readers, in reference to the enigma of femininity: "Throughout history people have knocked their heads against the riddle of the nature of femininity . . . to those of you who are women this will not apply—you are yourselves the problem" (1933, p. 113). This is a clear reference to Freud's position as a masculine subject of knowledge, defining his object, and also to the given perspective that is the point of departure of this subject. Later he also says: "If you reject this idea as fantastic and regard my belief in the influence of lack of a penis on the configuration of femininity as an *idée fixe,* I am of course defenceless" (p. 132). It would not be overhasty to connect this idea with another of Freud's declarations in the same text: "A woman of [about thirty] . . . often frightens us by her psychical rigidity and unchangeability" (p. 134). Neither can we forget Freud's famous letter (15 November 1883) to Martha Bernays, his future wife, discouraging her from reading John Stuart Mill, who favoured women's liberation, and reminding her that women must dedicate themselves to home and children.

At this point in our discussion we need to recall that the position of women as objects of knowledge is akin to the place of the enigma, the dark continent, and therefore to otherness. In other words, the other and the object, even though they are not the same, are intimately connected in these sequences of thought.[1] Here we see a strong connection between the Freudian experience and hysterical patients. The hysteric's games of seduction, kindling desire and then refusing, remained connected to the concept of enigma and the "dark continent". In this context, hysteria is equated with the feminine. These equivalences tend to hystericize the field of the feminine and to universalize it as such, since they describe their connections but not their differences. This hystericizing of the feminine could also explain the origins of the concept of penis envy as well as theories that interpret the feminine position from an androcentric position and universalize it to all women. This implies, for example, the risk of over-interpreting phallic rivalry or misinterpreting it when other dimensions may be involved.

Now, if we consider the subject–object issue in the light of infantile sexual theories, we see in the case of Little Hans (1909b) that Freud establishes sexual difference on the basis of infantile sexual theories as described by two adults: Hans's father and Freud. The child is a young investigator whose discoveries are theorized and signified by these adults. This investigation encounters the theme of castration: the investigating subject discovers sexual difference and assigns a lack to girls. *However, it is still necessary to emphasize that this "lack" is placed into a previous frame that interprets this difference as a lack.* Thus, in the resulting sequences of thought, presence–absence, phallic–castrated, and masculine–feminine polarities are equated. These theories locate the "castrated" other in the girl, who is subject to penis envy, and contain what is disavowed by little Hans in reference to himself: castration. However, they also establish her as an object of desire in relation to a desiring subject. This presents an interesting paradox, since what is most desired is what also provokes "horror". . . .

From this point forward, we recall, psychoanalysis defines the subject–object relation in the field of sexuality. However, as we said, the same occurs concomitantly in the field of knowledge. We also recall that according to Laplanche (1980), adult sexual theories may replicate infantile theories. This certainly implies strong consequences when an analyst is unable to differentiate these planes and their metaphoric aspects; in this sense it is important to deconstruct psychoanalytic theories of sexual difference and their relation to infantile sexual theories.

However, we may also note that Freud's work is open and multi-centred. Thus, we see that the themes of psychic bisexuality, which Freud never abandoned, as well as subject–object permutations and crossed oedipal identifications and desires, add complexity to this issue. The feminine is thereby displaced from its forced equivalence to the object and from its inevitable localization in the woman. Also, Freud (1905d, 1933) always considered the masculine and the feminine to be categories with uncertain contents. This assumes the addition of other variables that de-centre the masculine–feminine polarity, although he never renounces this initial subject–object polarity, which he equates to masculine–feminine polarity on the levels of both knowledge and desire.

At this point, we need to stress that these polarities respond to binary logic. The anthropologist Françoise Héritier (2007) describes quite precisely how these and other equivalents of masculine and feminine (hot–cold, strong–weak, high–low, dry–humid) involve hierarchical and power relations. We may therefore conclude that binary logic is also inevitably the logic of power, since hierarchy is inevitably attributed to one pole over the other. On the basis of these slips, discourses, knowledge, and power concerning the masculine–feminine relation are structured. This concerns both sexual and gender differences. In my opinion, these discourses also affect the psychoanalytic field, the formulation of theories, and psychoanalysts themselves. For example, Freud states in "A Special Type of Choice of Object Made by Men": "In normal love the woman's value is measured by her sexual integrity, and is reduced by any approach to the characteristic of being like a prostitute" (1910h, p. 167). In this statement, power and knowledge about women intersect at the masculine pole of masculine–feminine binary polarity. This discourse may also be shared by women.

Now, from the girl's viewpoint, I believe that Freud presents two instances: on the one hand, he introduces the preoedipal phase, which increasingly emphasizes the difference between girls and boys as well as another important fact, which is that the feminine position is acquired through oedipal resolution and not given by nature, at which point the nature/nurture debate becomes important. However, on the other hand, with respect to the difference, the girl adopts Little Hans's viewpoint of her lack and "falls a victim to 'envy for the penis'" (1933, p. 125). That is to say, the girl is different, but her viewpoint, sustained by phallic monism, is the same. In the Freudian narrative, the girl again accepts the riddle and supports it. But why does the girl support this theory according to Freudian theory? Because what is visible (the penis) is a symbol of power and knowledge? Because it supports male narcissism?

We also need to bear in mind that, as Kristeva states (1984), when girls are confronted with castration theories, they may submit to them but not truly recognize themselves. This author considers that these theories shape fixations to *semblant* [appearance] to which the masculine fantasmatic is attached.

In this frame, we also recall that Monique David-Ménard (1997) emphasizes that in the field of knowledge there is no neutral subject. She underlines the inevitable fantasm involved in the person who constructs the theory (who for the issue of sexual difference is masculine, despite exceptions). She also points out that castration anxiety defines conceptualizations and theories on sexual difference. Derrida's (1987) concept of "phallogocentrism" also refers to this problem in that the phallus seems to be a transcendental element, re-introducing the metaphysics of presence.

For this reason, the subject of knowledge is not dissociable from the subject of desire, thereby contributing to the theory that there is no neutral knowledge, much less in the field of the humanistic disciplines, and least of all in the field of sexual and gender differences.

In this way, a *misunderstanding* is structured: *the riddle of sexual difference becomes localized in the girl. In this displacement the girl is also assigned to the place of lack and to the incarnation of otherness—that is to say, what is different to oneself—whereas self is assigned to the masculine. In my opinion, we need to relocalize the riddle, which does not mean cancelling the notion of difference but supporting it as such without displacing the riddle of sexual difference onto one of its polarities: the feminine. The riddle is the difference itself rather than the feminine.*

However, the thought sequences we are discussing tend to universalize the feminine as the other. For example, a male patient, a phobic with marked inhibitions in his relations with women, says in a session when referring to a failed love affair: ". . . well, as you know, with women you never know, you never know how women are going to react, they're unpredictable . . ." This is the patient's attempt to detach himself from any subjective involvement in the conflict, formulated via a statement that tends to circulate quite frequently. To do this, he resorts to a "truth" that he considers universal and consensual. If this comes up in a session, one of two things may occur: (1) The analyst may agree with his available theory and his fantasms in connection with this statement and share in them either consciously or unconsciously; consequently, the analyst will not interpret it. (2) The analyst may question it and not accept it as an unquestionable premise. In this case, the analyst may ask, investigate, connect, and differentiate a phobic position from beliefs and myths inherent in collective thought. It also presents an interesting aspect for female analysts: "I (a woman) also know that with women you never know." This identification with accepted knowledge and power is also a paradox worthy of analysis.

Therefore, various aspects of this statement may be analysed: (1) anxiety with regard to sexual difference; (2) anxiety about maternal power, placed in women; (3) the psychic interiorization of norms, ideologies, and prejudices concerning the relation between men and women so collective discourses and beliefs intersecting individual castration fantasms coincide; and (4) the epistemic sources attributing equivalence to the feminine and the enigmatic other, unknown and therefore threatening to the subject of knowledge and desire, whose castration fantasms operate effectively. *In other words, if these genealogies are not analysed, castration fantasms remain localized in the feminine other, rather than in the incompleteness that is common to both men and women.*

2. The woman = mother equation

This is another source supporting the feminine–other equation. We know that the maternal other is always a focus of both fascination and rejection. In "The Theme of the Three Caskets" (1913f), Freud states that the mother is always present in a man: first at his origin; then in the woman he loves, chosen for her similarity to his mother; and, finally, when he returns to Mother Earth. In other words, the mother is omnipresent throughout the stages of a man's life. In this sense, there is nostalgia for primordial *jouissance* supporting the emergence of the maternal other as the double: what is most familiar or *heimlich* is also *unheimlich*, strange, and uncanny (Freud, 1919h). This means that something radically familiar appears to be something foreign, which, I emphasize, leads to its becoming established as an enigma *par excellence. At this point we find a slip that supports another basic misunderstanding: the mother = woman equiva-lence. The enigma of the maternal other is displaced to the woman and the feminine in general and, again, we should be able to re-locate this enigma.* This is particularly significant in clinical practice.

In this context, one theoretical limit is to restrict, as Freud does (1931b), the outcome of girls' psychosexual development to inhibition, the complex of masculinity or motherhood. The last outcome, reached through the symbolic penis = child equation, is considered by Freud the ultimate goal of femininity. Following this theoretical line, a representation of femininity is successfully accessed only through maternity.[2] All non-hysterical and non-mater-nal feminine sexuality is thereby disavowed. More precisely, these three roads ignore the possibility of a desiring type of feminine subjectivity—which may eventually also include and support a posi-tion as an object of desire. But what operations might disrupt this strict equivalence of the feminine and the maternal? *A third func-tion is involved (not only in the sense of the exogamic symbolic separation of the child from the mother), which must also detach the feminine from the maternal other.* An operation of de-identification is needed in order to relaunch necessary symbolic identifications. In other words, we must consequently emphasize that although the two categories— woman and mother—are related, they also need to be detached from each other.

We show that there is a thin, porous line between the feminine as a principle, the feminine as a given identity, the feminine in terms of sexuality, the feminine as an identification ideal, the feminine as a quality and a role (femininity), the feminine equated with the maternal, and the feminine equated with the woman. This calls for unceasing work of deconstruction and construction.

In this regard I mean to say that the feminine is polysemic and covers complex concepts, whose roads are heterogeneous. Therefore they may diverge in one single woman. This requires us to take another look into sexual difference, with the consideration that this difference is inevitably historicized and interpreted. Since this difference is never neutral, it cannot be analysed from an objective position outside its context in discourse.

Post-Freudian and contemporary debates

Freud's proposals concerning women and the feminine have permeated psychoanalytic thought up to the present, either in consonance or dissonance. It would be impossible to list in this text the enormous number of contributions by post-Freudian and contemporary analysts, but we will mention some that are significant for our review. In doing so, we need to consider that in relation to this subject—and others as well—there is not just one psychoanalysis.

The concept of primary masculinity, one of the most widely discussed, was a subject of the well-known Freud–Jones debate. Jones (1927) considered that primary femininity was based on primordial knowledge of the vagina. This contribution did tend to re-locate the feminine in a position different from Freud's, but some aspects of the discussion were limited to purely anatomical–physiological aspects. Klein (1945) assigned primary value to the contents of the feminine body. The debate then broadened into proposals that emphasized the role of culture in the structuring of femininity (among others, Horney, 1924). It was also discussed whether penis envy was primary or secondary, and in this debate some analysts close to Freud raised arguments against his ideas on this issue. We recall that Freud told the female psychoanalysts who argued against his position that the masculine element predominated in them, thereby evading the problem with a tautology that allowed him to preserve the subject = masculine and object = feminine equations.

These debates centred on determining the entity to be given to women and considerations of the feminine in general. The waters parted. In the Anglo-Saxon world the issue of primary femininity was accepted by nearly everyone. In this way, an attempt was made to give femininity an entity of its own, albeit inevitably in comparison, and always in relation to a referent: the masculine model.

On the other hand, in French psychoanalysis, including its theoretical influences in other regions, the Freudian proposal was highlighted and developed with greater sophistication by the Lacanian School with the "mathemes of sexuation" (Lacan, 1972–73). In this case, the difference was emphasized, now on the basis of a lack localized in the feminine gender. Even though Lacan considered that a feminine position could be occupied by men as well as women, obviously by labelling it feminine the connotation was undeniable. For Lacan the feminine Other is the Other *par excellence*, so that the problem persists and even coexists with another of his propositions, stating that "there is no signifier for woman" (1955–56).

Elsewhere, Winnicott (1966) de-centres the problem. For him, femininity, in terms of primary identifications, is a category related to being. In this sense it concerns both sexes and derives from the initial relation with the mother. This unlinks femininity, in Winnicottian terms, from a direct relation with women. In other words, it may be part of processes of subjectivation in men as well as women.

As I pointed out, a review of the wide range of publications on the feminine in psychoanalysis and contributions from anthropology, linguistics, historiography, and so on, exceeds the limits of this text. However, we may say that many view the feminine as equivalent to the other: either due to absence or lack of a fundamental signifier (the phallus) or else as a depreciated other; in both cases, because they, implicitly or explicitly, postulate that the feminine is structured in terms of a masculine subject of knowledge and desire. *The Second Sex* (Beauvoir, 1949) enlightens many aspects of this topic.

In another group, these postures coexist with other currents of thought whose discussions of this issue take two roads. One road revalues the other by accentuating commonly deprecated feminine characteristics, the other questions the place of the other for women and the feminine and investigates causes and difficulties blocking the access of women to the position of subject in the theory, with inevitable consequences in clinical work and in the experiences of each woman. According to this line of thought, the implicit interrelation between experiences and theories cannot be dissociated.

Gender theories contribute other important elements. Although they have not been accepted unanimously in the psychoanalytic field, authors like Stoller (1968b), with his studies on transsexualism, have included different facets of these contributions. Sex–gender polarity (Rubin, 1975) postulated the disarticulation of sexuated anatomy and cultural determinations supporting gender identity. In this way, gender became a cultural construction. However, there is not just one gender theory; also, the role of sexuated anatomy continues to be a subject of discussion (Faure-Oppenheimer, 1980). Furthermore, for authors like Butler (1990) and Laqueur (1990), the body is not pure anatomy; in other words, it is not "natural". This means that it does not pre-date cultural norms but, rather, is a part of them.

Bourdieu (1998) also contributed interesting elements to the analysis of the role of the body in relation to gender difference. In ethnographic studies of the tribes of Cabilia, he describes women's bodily postures as indicators of submission and points out that the assimilation of domination is inscribed in the bodies—postures, disciplines, submission, and emotions. He emphasizes that domination is legitimized through its inscription in biological nature, so that it is naturalized. He calls this the "historical work of de-historization". In his study, we see how the quality of otherness for women—in this case a submissive other—may be inscribed in bodies and become "naturalized".

In this sense, we need to underline that the mother–child relation inevitably involves not only verbal, but also pre-verbal transmission, contacts, and vibrations that condition and mark the bodies

and assign meanings to sexual difference. However, at the same
time, we cannot ignore what the body proposes from the very moment of birth in relation to gender difference. The production of
subjectivity depends on the different ways in which these variables
intersect.

Reflections

Nowadays we are facing singular and collective experiences that
challenge psychoanalytic theories concerning gender and sexual
differences. There is also a gap between theories and clinical practice that makes it necessary for us to deconstruct classical theories.
Theories must accept changes, and psychoanalysts must too, if they
propose to deal with some degree of truth.

In this sense, I would like to emphasize that the focus of these
reflections aims at the proposal to deconstruct the concept of otherness as inseparable from the feminine. There are different ways
to conceive of otherness, which have consequences in our way of
thinking in relation to the feminine and sexual difference.

Foucault (1966) maintained that the episteme of modernity
was based on the self–other relation. In this sense we may recall
that for discourse of modernity the other is an other to the extent
that it may be included in the subject, thereby cancelling the difference; if this fails, the other is expelled or deprecated until it is
denied representation. This is one way to understand the feminine
as the other. In contrast, as Lévinas (1947) had already suggested
in his critique of the transcendental subject, one aspect of otherness aims at what is radically other, foreign, and totally alien to the
ego. This is another way to understand the feminine as the other.
In a different perspective, Castoriadis (2002) underlines that "Same
and Other are the two ultimate dimensions of the unfolding of being, interminably interwoven but for that reason not reducible to
each other". This involves two important consequences: on the one
hand, that it is possible to detach otherness from unchangeable attachments to the feminine; on the other, it implies that the other,
the radically other, is also included in each subject and that its equation with the feminine indicates a projection in defensive terms. It
also involves recognition that the other is a subject as well.

This way to understand the same and the other, constantly in processes of permutation and movement, detaches them from fixed positions or attributions as masculine or feminine.

Each of the psychoanalyst's interpretations is supported by some of these logics and epistemological sources. To recognize them implies an ability to bypass essentialist interpretations regarding the feminine condition. Examples of the latter are a rigid positioning of the feminine in place of the other, or the strong tendency to universalize the feminine, when in reality no category supports the notion of women as a "class" in psychoanalytic and psychological terms. These considerations are part of a broader critical review of modes of thinking that tend to universalize categories by means of "class logic", which was questioned by Deleuze (Deleuze & Guattari, 1980), Castoriadis (1998, 2002) and others.

The deconstruction of the equivalences described (subject = masculine, object = other = feminine, woman = mother) and the analysis of their genealogies require an ability to surmount the logic of the binary dichotomies at the root of these meta-theories. Since binary systems are part of language, we cannot simply cancel them. The point of inflection is the production of "lines of flight" to break up rigid dualistic schemes (Deleuze & Parnet, 1977) and their inclusion in larger complexities. This trend may generate another type of symbolic difference and enable us to surpass substantialist positions concerning the feminine.

As I proposed in other publications (Glocer Fiorini, 1994, 2001b, 2007), I consider that sexuated subjectivity is constructed beyond binary logic at the intersection of various categories: anatomical heterogeneity (always interpreted), gender diversity, plural identifications, and "productions" of desire. These categories are mutually heterogeneous[3] and, at the same time, cannot be dissociated from significations assigned by accepted discourses. Each is related to the other or others that are in operation from the very beginning of life and before. In this sense, assumption of sexuated subjectivity depends on the way symbolization is processed on the basis of continuities and discontinuities between these categories.[4] This de-centres subject = masculine and object = feminine = other polarities.

These processes of subjectivation also involve recognizing that in each subject there is an other, and that the other is also a subject. They lead us to think in terms of subjectivity "in process", as a "becoming" that is never the same, beyond rigid and fixed identities. In these movements, in which both subject–other and other–subject are interchangeable, meta-theories supporting theories on the feminine and sexual difference may be modified.

Notes

Parts of this chapter were first published in "Verso una deconstruzione del femminile inteso come altro", *Psicoterapia Psicoanalitica, 2* (July–December 2008).

1. The object, even with its relative foreignness, is always in a relational order with respect to the subject and the ego. No object is totally foreign to the subject or radically not–I. In contrast, according to Lévinas (1947), the concept of otherness implies something radically foreign to the subject.

2. In other publications (Glocer Fiorini, 2001a, 2001b, pp. 117–129, 2007, pp. 96–106), I proposed the idea of thinking about the desire for a child beyond the concept of symbolic equation considered a symbolic substitution for primary lack. For this purpose, I borrowed the concept of "desiring production" (Deleuze, 1995; Deleuze & Parnet, 1977), which surpasses the tendency in vogue to consider that desire originates only from lack.

3. For thinking about heterogeneous and contradictory categories, I have suggested (Glocer Fiorini, 1994, 1998, 2001b, 2007) working with models of the paradigm of complexity (Morin, 1990), which accepts the coexistence of heterogeneous variables and proposes to sustain not only their mutual connections and conjunctions but also their antagonisms and contradictions.

4. I consider that although processes of subjectivation in general encompass more variables, they cannot dispense with the above-mentioned points concerning sexuated subjectivity.

4

Vicissitudes of the feminine dimension in men and bisexuality in the analytic situation

Thierry Bokanowski

> At no other point in one's analytic work does one suffer more
> from an oppressive feeling that all one's repeated efforts
> have been in vain, and from a suspicion that one has been
> "preaching to the winds", than when one is trying to persuade
> a woman to abandon her wish for a penis on the ground of its
> being unrealizable or when one is seeking to convince a man
> that a passive attitude to men does not always signify castration
> and that it is indispensable in many relationships in life.
>
> Freud, "Analysis terminable and interminable" (1937c, p. 252)

In the closing paragraphs of "Analysis Terminable and Interminable"—a paper that can be regarded as part of his last will and
testament with respect to his long experience as a practitioner of
psychoanalysis—Freud (1937c) suggests that the "repudiation of
femininity", in both men and women, is one of the main obstacles
to the ending of psychoanalytic treatment and bringing about re-
covery by means of psychoanalysis.

The main factors of resistance that are met with at that point
have, in female patients, to do with their "envy for the penis" and,

in men, with their "struggle against [their] passive or feminine attitude" (1937c, p. 250)—in other words, for Freud, the common
denominator of these psychological difficulties in both sexes is
the capacity for psychic internalization of the feminine position or
feminine dimension. The refusal of that dimension—what Freud
calls the "repudiation of femininity"—constitutes a "bedrock" and
is "part of the great riddle of sex" (1937c).

Consequently, the refusal of the feminine dimension, or even
its "disavowal"—the "bedrock"—is, for Freud, one of the major issues at stake in psychoanalytic treatment, with its implications for
the more or less harmonious management of the patient's psychic
bisexuality.

Although we may implicitly understand what the feminine dimension in women involves—over and beyond the idea that it may
designate the non-sexualized sphere that is part of all human beings, male and female—what are we attempting to describe when,
following Freud, we talk of the feminine dimension in men? In
other words, what content are we to give to the idea of the feminine
sphere in men? Usually, when we talk of femininity or feminine
tendencies in men, we are referring to the passive aspect of their
drive-related aims, to their propensity for so-called "feminine" masochism, or to a mind-set that could be described as homosexual. In
the clinical practice of psychoanalysis, the elements that have to do
with the negative or inverted mode of the Oedipus complex linked
to castration anxiety are, more often than not, those that, via passivity and masochism, manifest a defensive organization described
as feminine in nature.

From time immemorial (cf. Plato's *Symposium*), it has been acknowledged that, just as women may have a significant phallic component, so men may manifest some feminine character traits that
are an integral part of bisexuality.[1] However, their phallic dimension
and the need to assert their masculinity mean that men often experience their feminine tendencies—their feminine dimension—as
a source of anxiety (castration anxiety and shame); these, in turn,
give rise to conflicting feelings that their mental apparatus may well
find impossible to overcome. Women,[2] on the other hand, seem to
have little difficulty in tolerating their phallic aspirations and possible masculine tendencies.

What, then, are the reasons that make men fall prey to such fears when they have to face up to their feminine dimension? Why, generally speaking, do they find that particular aspect so difficult to think about? By what kind of uncanny feelings (*Unheimlich*) are they afraid of being overwhelmed?

Again, why is it that the feminine dimension is perceived or defined only in negative terms—that is, based on its "repudiation" or "disavowal"? Does this have something to do with the fact that this dimension in men is too closely related to primary identification with the maternal feminine dimension? Or to what Winnicott called a primary non-instinctual identification with the breast, part of an element that he described as "pure female" (Winnicott, 1971a, p. 76), which is found in both sexes?

In other words, how are we to understand those fears and that shame, which sometimes lead to a hatred of all feminine aspects? Do they involve simply the invisible traces brought about by the loss of, and perhaps nostalgia for, the primary object, traces that the self fears to encounter later with a concomitant experience of being made passive? Or is there some additional factor involved?

Bisexuality and the feminine dimension in men: some hypotheses

Psychoanalysts do not deal with sexuality as such but with the complex forms that its representations adopt in their polysemous diversity. With regard to these representations in psychoanalysis, sexual identity and gender identity, masculine and feminine, have their roots in the schemata and bodily experiences that are reflected in an individual's genetic sex and anatomical sex.

The fact of being a girl implies that throughout life one's bodily and mental experiences will differ from those of a boy. (The opposite is, of course, equally true.) This goes some way towards explaining why the composite nature of bisexuality has to do both with the complex forms of these identifications and with the masculine and feminine components of the sexual and erotic fantasizing that is related to the emotional experiences specific to the reality of the child's sex. As such, these unconscious fantasy dynamics—

which, linked to the body image, govern each individual's psychic bisexuality—need not correspond entirely to the self's sexual reality: they depend to some extent on certain features that constitute the structure of the self, including the highly important factor of identification with the opposite sex.

If the analyst listening to his or her patient does not focus sufficiently on the transference modalities associated with the patient's bisexuality and on the countertransference modalities associated with the analyst's own bisexuality, the analysis may well founder on the "bedrock" represented by what Freud called "repudiation of femininity" on the part of both participants (Bokanowski, 1998).

All through one's childhood—and, therefore, throughout the development of the oedipal situation—differences related to anatomical sex, to bodily sensations, and to psychic experience (fantasy processing) widen between males and females. It follows logically that the masculine dimension in women is not of the same nature as that in men, just as the feminine dimension in men is not the same as that in women. However, as I mentioned at the outset, what is common to both sexes is their *rejection of the feminine dimension*—although the consequences are different for each sex, since this refusal affects women in the sex they have and men in the sex they do not have (Cournut-Janin & Cournut, 1993).

Before attempting to account for hypothetical factors that might hinder our attempt at identifying the feminine dimension in men, I shall briefly mention the main stages of a boy's mental development in this field, which facilitate this structuring of his bisexuality.

In the first months of life, the boy, in constant contact with his mother, quite naturally introjects her primary maternal and feminine components and identifies with them. In this first stage, which is crucial for the structuring of the mind, mother and son "nourish" each other: the mother feeds on her son's libido that establishes her as a mother, the son on the introjective components of his mother's maternal and feminine libido—n other words, her "maternal feminine dimension" (Bégoin-Guignard, 1988).

Nevertheless, even though this relationship is set up in terms of the primary feminine and maternal elements, it is one between two people who are not the same: who are in essence different because the mother cannot but acknowledge that her son is different, as regards both his sex and his masculinity. This stage is also the time when a psychic matrix is set up so as to lend support to auto-eroticism; it forms a prelude to the loss of the primary object—equivalent to what Green (1986) calls "cutting the psychic umbilical cord". This is when mourning for the primary object takes place, with the onset of the depressive position, which, in turn, generates awareness of the father as the object's Other; the father is thus established as the third party, both separating and remaining present as a love object.

From then on, the boy's feminine dimension is no longer a function simply of identification with the maternal feminine dimension; it is structured also with reference to the father. (This is a forerunner of the setting-up of a structuring homosexuality that is part of the boy's bisexuality as well as of the oedipal situation in which he finds himself.)

I shall now try to outline the possible reasons that often make it difficult for men to acknowledge and take on board their feminine tendencies.

My hypothesis is that, since it is linked to his relationship with the primary object, the young boy's feminine dimension contains traumatic traces of that relationship which have been repressed (due to primary repression). These traumatic traces are the mental consequences of the individual's primary identification with the maternal feminine dimension, which involves the mother's unconscious cathexis of her infant.[3]

As regards primary identification with the maternal feminine dimension, my hypothesis is that there are two phases at work in each individual; moving from one to the other could be a source of specific excitation for the infant, setting up a series of possibly traumatic markers in his or her mind (primary trauma). I would suggest that the initial phase of this primary identification with the maternal feminine dimension is more *maternal* in nature than *feminine*, given the fact that the mother is completely taken up with her "primary maternal preoccupation". During the second phase, in which the mother re-cathects the father sexually, the infant's primary identification with the maternal feminine dimension is modified, becoming more marked by the *feminine* aspect than by the maternal one.

Since the movement from primary identification with the maternal aspect to that with the feminine one brings the infant face
to face with the mother's feminine dimension, it is possible that, in
boys, the excitation to which this gives rise is less restrained than
in girls. There is another element here too: the modalities of the
mother's unconscious cathexis of her infant and the importance
that the latter takes on in comparison with her own primary object
and with the mourning process she had to go through with respect
to it.

Implicitly designated as representing the "lost memory" of the
object's primary object (i.e. the mother's mother), the individual
is to some extent identified with that object.

At the point where disengagement with respect to the object
takes place—the onset of the depressive position, which enables
the third party element to intervene—the self, faced with the need
to mourn the loss of the object, has then to contend with an additional element of mental work. This has to do with the need to
internalize the shadow of the object's primary object which, having
fallen on the object, tends to imprison the individual, at least to
some extent, in a mausoleum of nostalgia. Experienced from that
point on as a foreign body, linked to the identifications that are a
feature of the primary maternal feminine dimension, engraved in
the individual's feminine dimension, that shadow leaves in its trace
the painful mark of something traumatic.

In the case of girls—who are of the same sex as their primary
object, so that the relationship is *from similar to similar*—we could
argue that the mother sees in her daughter something that she can
identify as a possible renewal of ties with her own lost object. There
is thus it set up between them, via their nostalgia for the lost object,
the capacity to communicate and to integrate as part of their sense
of identity the various feminine components linked to the primary
maternal feminine dimension.

This is not the case for boys. Here the mother finds herself in
a quite different situation because she can convert some of her
nostalgia for the lost object into cathecting her son as a member
of the opposite sex. She can then smooth away or even rub out altogether those traces with the unspeakable pain that is forever part
of them. Faced with the object's tendency towards nostalgia, boys
have to experience—quietly and in the background—something

which, given the unconscious identifications that result from their relationship with the object—a relationship between two people who are not similar but different—makes for a much more painful feminine dimension than in girls.

To summarize, I would say that moving from primary maternal identification to one that involves the feminine dimension may lead in boys (and therefore for their future development as men) to identificatory modalities that are more traumatic than in girls. This factor may explain why that dimension is more difficult to grasp, since primary repression then turns it into something that cannot be represented ideationally, something that is unknowable—or quite simply something that is lost.

So-called "feminine" masochism in men

Elusive? Impossible to represent? Unknowable? Lost? Without a doubt, but only up to a certain point, because it would seem that the so-called feminine masochism in men (Freud, 1919e, 1924c) carries the trace, the memory and the scar of the pre-traumatic (and perhaps even traumatic) markings of primary maternal and feminine identifications. In addition, it is the function of this feminine masochism to make such identifications more tolerable, through binding them together and with the drives involved. For Freud, the pivotal fantasy of the child being beaten, linked to the Oedipus complex, is a replacement (in both boys and girls) for the incestuous relationship with the father. In girls, however, this is basically a heterosexual fantasy, whereas in boys it replaces a regressive incestuous relationship (homosexual, i.e. psychic homosexuality) with the father, based on "the inverted attitude, in which the father is taken as the object of love" (Freud, 1919e, p. 199).[4]

As far as boys are concerned, this position has to do not only with the father's strength but also with his violence, which are simultaneously dreaded, admired, and therefore envied. It is because the boy longs for these features that he tries to take them for himself in a regressive way. The "characteristically female situation", with its reference to "being castrated, or copulated with, or giving birth to a baby" (Freud, 1924c, p. 162), thus opens on to a fantasy of appropriation by introjecting an omnipotent paternal penis that cannot be castrated (non-castratable, as it were).

In boys, however, it is nonetheless possible to see in the fantasy of a child being beaten a metamorphosis that gives shape to a primal fantasy of seduction of a child by an adult—and, *inter alios,* by the mother. The boy has the experience of being the mother's sexual object and participates fully—though passively—in her pleasure, feeling himself to be the mother's privileged pleasure-giving instrument; recourse to this fantasy is a way for the boy actively to control and bind his excitation so as to disengage from the depths of "primary seduction" and the threat of making passive that it entails—a source of primary anxiety and terror. The fantasy of a child being beaten is not only an attempt to re-establish unity with the mother but also a way of protecting the child—and especially the boy, since the father beating the child comes between them in his role as third party—from the feminine dimension that the mother opens up . . . and from the threat of losing it forever.

The untenable and incredible desire
for the feminine dimension in men

With the help of a clinical illustration, I shall now attempt to highlight how important it may be for a male psychoanalyst to explore the resistances set up by the feminine dimension of his male patients. I shall show also how, thanks to interpretations concerning the feminine tendencies in both participants in the analytic process, it becomes possible to disengage from situations resembling an impasse in which they might find themselves, given the interplay between their respective unconscious feminine aspects.

Before doing so, however, I think it is important to remind the reader of the various levels—not in any particular order of priority—at which a male psychoanalyst will listen to his male patient in the course of their analytic work together.

At the most manifest level, the psychoanalyst, a man, will have to listen to the masculine traits of another man, in line with the patient's masculine (father, brother, son) identifications. He will also be confronted with the feminine (mother, sister, daughter) aspects of this man.

At a more latent level, he will be attentive to his patent's masculine tendencies directed towards the analyst as a feminine transference object; this, from the countertransference point of view, leads the analyst to function in terms of his own feminine identifications. His troubles are not yet over, however, because—*last, not least*—he will be confronted in the transference with a situation in which he will be functioning as a woman, in touch with the feminine tendencies of his male patient.

Clinical vignette: Mr M

Mr M is a young man who undertook psychoanalysis as a way of understanding the reasons behind his general feeling of malaise. From the outset, Mr M's analysis was characterized, in the transference, by depression linked to significant guilt feelings with respect to his oedipal objects; this was expressed through the need he felt to repair highly defective parental imagos (his father had more or less abandoned him at one point in his childhood after his mother's sudden death, which occurred in circumstances all the more traumatic in that they related to the consequences of an attempted abortion).

For some considerable time, the analysis was virtually at a standstill: it could even have been described as finding itself in an impasse. Mr M kept on complaining that he could not change anything in his life, claiming that he would just have to resign himself to the fate, based on his feelings of guilt, that awaited him because of his profoundly masochistic tendencies—that is, repeated failures in his love life and professional career. This attitude on his part gave me the impression that he suffered from a fate neurosis structured as an inevitability that would prove "abortive" as regards whatever projects he might have. In addition, the analytic space appeared to be all the more "saturated" (any comment or interpretation on my part seemed to have no effect whatsoever) in that for some time previously Mr M had stopped reporting any dreams.

In the sessions that preceded the material I am now about to report, Mr M had spoken (in a somewhat ambivalent and ironical manner) of the "incredible power" that patients have over their analyst, given that they can "think and talk about everything", whatever their analyst's state of mind and internal availability.

With respect to how the transference was developing, I felt that in bringing up these issues Mr M was referring in a negative manner to how he experienced the analyst's capacity to take in the patient's projections; this could make him think of the receptive qualities, both maternal and feminine, of the analyst: qualities that Mr M could both fear and envy.

I commented on the parallel between the "power" he feared that he could wield over me and what had previously been worked on in the analysis concerning his fantasy of domination/ submissiveness with respect to a mixed-race woman friend of his, whose skin colour obviously attracted him sexually.

Mr M and I both knew that the essential function of these fantasies was to protect him not only from his tender feelings towards this woman friend but also from those that he feared she might have for him.

As he became aware that, for him, there might be some analogy between his attitude towards me and that towards his woman friend, Mr M associated to the fact that he sometimes arranged to meet her either shortly before or shortly after his sessions. He added that he "never thought about the analysis, nor about [me], between sessions".

I then reminded him of a childhood memory he had often brought up during his sessions: whenever, as a schoolboy, he did drawings or made objects in class, he would destroy them on his way home. (We had analysed this in terms of a fantasy of the voluntary termination of pregnancy.) I commented that, just as he had at that time the wish to compartmentalize two spaces—that of his school (maternal space) and that of his home (paternal space)—so that they could not communicate, he seemed to be treating his sessions and perhaps even me in the same way.

After this comment, Mr M remained silent for several minutes.

He broke the silence to say, just before the end of the session, that he felt "blocked" by something he couldn't bring himself to tell me.

In the following session, Mr M said something about what had made him fall silent during the final part of his previous one (when he had felt "blocked"). Before that session, he had gone to see his woman friend and had had sex with her. After having intercourse, he had realized that his condom had burst; his first thought was of the risk of contamination by the Aids virus. His partner, who did not seem particularly worried, had tried to reassure him—but, ever since that moment, it had preyed on his mind.

I pointed out that his "blocking" seemed to have occurred after I had drawn a parallel between how he treated me in his thoughts and the way he used to destroy objects he had made in school.

Mr M agreed and went on to talk at some length about the sadness that used to overwhelm him as a child whenever his father gave him the impression that he (his father) was not particularly receptive to or even available for him.

Although Mr M and I had already discussed and tried to work through the theme of destruction/abortion of his objects, it seemed to me (though at the time, I did not say this to him) that, thanks to the various parallels that had previously been suggested, in the transference this theme also involved the following two aspects:

▷ first, his fear that deep inside himself he might suddenly feel both the wish to have tender feelings towards me and the wish that I might prove more receptive and available than his father had been in the past;

▷ second—and perhaps more importantly—his refusal to put himself in a feminine position with respect to me that might lead him to desire and to fear being "impregnated" by my interpretations, and therefore to fear that I might transmit a psychic Aids virus to him

In the following session, Mr M said that he would have liked to continue with what we had been discussing previously, but in the interval something had happened that had "amazed"[5] him.

The day before, one of his male friends had spoken very openly to him about an extramarital relationship that the friend's mother had kept up for some time because it had meant a great deal to her. Mr M was "flabbergasted" by the apparently natural manner in which his friend had talked of his mother's sentimental and sexual life.

I said: "In other words, that a mother can have feelings for a man and be sexually active?"

Mr M avoided all association to his own mother; instead, he spoke about *Lucy*, the Australopithecus female discovered in Tanzania: "The original mother, the African female with a capital 'A', the mother of all mankind", he said. The "African female" led him to associate to his mixed-race woman friend and to the fear of Aids that had haunted him since the episode of the burst condom.

I made a comment in relation to his earlier associations: "The fear of being contaminated by the Aids virus ('amazed') or that of having impregnated the woman he associated with the 'original mother'?"

Mr M replied that there was something else he had not mentioned. After the condom incident, his woman friend had said to him by way of a joke: "I hope you haven't given me twins." Deep down, he had been delighted by that remark. Why twins? Mr M did not know, but the idea pleased him, because he thought that he would therefore be more "powerful" than he felt his father to have been.

Mr M's thoughts then turned back to Lucy and to the idea that she seemed to be at the "origin" of all mankind.

With reference to the material in the two earlier sessions—the "incredible power patients have over their analysts" and the danger represented by the desire of and for the "original mother" (Lucy the African, his mixed-race friend, and me in the transference)—it seemed that Mr M was trying to get rid both of his feminine wish to be impregnated by me and of his fear of my feminine wish to be impregnated by him. I proposed an interpretation along these lines.

Thereupon Mr M fell silent for several minutes. When he came out of his silence, he said he had been thinking that he did indeed feel a need to destroy my comments and interpretations. I pointed out that he said this after the long comment I had made . . . adding that perhaps he was trying to destroy that one too.

Mr M laughed. The session ended at that point.

In the following session, Mr M reported a dream—something that had not happened for quite some time. In the dream, *he was sticking together two pieces of a broken plate*. He associated to the fact that, the previous evening, he had watched a television programme that had fascinated him: it was about the fall of the Berlin Wall (a reversal of splitting).

The work of bisexuality in psychoanalytic treatment

Given the history of an individual's unconscious identifications with his or her objects (both feminine and masculine), everything that derives from the instinctual drives must be more or less related to psychic bisexuality. The work of an analysis enables certain former identificatory tendencies to come to the fore, develop, and be re-sexualized thanks to their being "re-bisexualized" in the transference relationship underpinned by imaginary relationships with past objects (Bokanowski, 1998).

As a result, the psychoanalytic situation puts to the test the specific nature of sexual identity, of narcissism, and of bisexuality. This demands that work be done on the economics of the instinctual drives: on the one hand, regression of psychosexual uncertainty; on the other, a restructuring of identity and a greater degree of flexibility as to identificatory cathexes and counter-cathexes.

Due to the regressive modalities inherent in psychoanalysis, the treatment may turn out to be "de-constructing" and reveal painful narcissistic conflicts that bear witness to both a hatred for and deep-rooted attachment towards the object. Combined with primitive anxiety, these conflicts lead to confusion as to the patient's sense of identity, which, in turn, renders ineffective the genitalized use of his or her identificatory patterns and any prospect of a genuine reprocessing of psychosexuality.

This puts the analyst's capacity for listening to the patient severely to the test. Subjected to the patient's de-symbolizing manoeuvres, the analyst's sense of self-identity and countertransference are placed in a very difficult position. The analyst may be swept into a kind of confusion such that he or she loses all sense of the problem complex that the patient is dealing with as regards his or her wishes—with no idea any longer, perhaps, of the kind of transference pattern that is being addressed (narcissistic? maternal? paternal?), of whether he or she is treated as a masculine or feminine figure (man or woman?), or whether that image is, in each of the protagonists, adumbrated by their masculine or feminine dimension.

Faced with such transference situations—often nerve-racking because they go right to the heart of the analyst's gender identity (the "reality" of his or her sex)—the analyst must nevertheless structure the way in which he or she pays attention to what the patient says in a complex pattern that keeps both sexes simultaneously in mind. At the same time, the analyst has to try to conceptualize the specific features of each of those dimensions—masculine and feminine—in their mutual relationship; it is only by so doing that the analyst will be able to experience him- or herself as representing both sexes at the same time.

That being the case, if the male analyst listening to his male patient does not focus sufficiently on the transference modalities associated with the latter's bisexuality (and on the countertransference modalities associated with the analyst's own bisexuality), the analysis may well founder on the "bedrock" represented by what Freud (1937c, p. 250) called the "repudiation of femininity"; as Freud pointed out, the treatment may then culminate in a negative therapeutic reaction or, worse, turn into an interminable analysis, both of which bear witness to the failure of the treatment as a whole.

Notes

1. "[all] human individuals, as a result of their bisexual disposition and of cross-inheritance, combine in themselves both masculine and feminine characteristics" (Freud, 1925j, p. 258).

2. Women's identity is based on the specific features of their "inside": invisible, able to be penetrated, and productive.

3. According to Monique and Jean Cournut (Cournut-Janin & Cournut, 1993, p. 1547), the feminine dimension in men is a "lost knowledge"—"neglected, repressed, misunderstood, the mourning for which has probably not been worked through, it remains in the unconscious like a lost knowledge, something once known and therefore repressed (via primary repression)."

4. From the point of view of psychoanalytic treatment, the feminine dimension in men can similarly be approached as a function of the defensive modalities linked to variations in the negative Oedipus complex—that is, of the boy's psychic homosexuality. On the one hand, this is a defensive form of homosexuality by means of regression when faced with the normal Oedipus complex and the castration anxiety that is linked to it. It leads to passive submissiveness with respect to the father, some manifestations of which may take on a masochistic aspect ("feminine" masochism). On the other hand, there may be a more regressive form of homosexuality in which the erotic object does not participate in the oedipal scenario, given that this kind of homosexuality is a defence against a primitive maternal imago (phallic, narcissistic and omnipotent).

5. The French words *Sida* ["Aids"] and *sidéré* [staggered, "amazed"] share a certain resemblance as to their pronunciation.

5

The limitations of Freud's 1933 bisexual hypothesis to explain impediments to creativity in a woman

Barbara S. Rocah

> I have only been describing women in so far as their nature
> is determined by their sexual function. It is true that that
> influence extends very far but we do not overlook the fact that
> an individual woman may be human in other respects as well.
>
> Freud, "Femininity" (1933, p. 135)

In his paper on femininity, Freud approached the topic of the
"enigma of women" by conceptualizing how "a woman develops out
of a child with a bisexual disposition" (1933, p. 116). His purpose
was to elaborate universal bisexual conflicts that followed from a
girl understanding the duality of the sexes. Although he appreciated the ambiguity of this great antithesis in the mental life of adult
men and women, his bisexual hypothesis obscured the significance
of a woman's individually created psychological bisexual ambitions
derived from identification and fantasy.

In this chapter I critically reconsider Freud's 1933 application
of his bisexual hypothesis to explain impediments to creativity in a
woman. Freud theorized that women were creatively bereft secondary to infantile fixations on bisexual ambitions to overcome the

centrality of castration in their psychology. To that goal her "libido has take up final positions" (p. 135), maintaining repressed phallic preoedipal ambitions directed towards her mother, and/or oedipal eroticism fixed on her father that exhausted the possibilities of sublimation, a process he theorized was necessary for exchanging sexual aims for others of cultural value. In his view, a woman's development was dominated by shame that "has as its purpose . . . concealment of genital deficiency" (p. 132). Freud asserted that the necessity to maintain this concealment limited women to a single cultural achievement: "that of plaiting and weaving. . . . Nature herself would seem to have given the model which this achievement imitates by causing the growth at maturity of the pubic hair that conceals the genitals" (p. 132).

I present my ideas about creativity and the connections to bisexual fantasies by analysing a creative inhibition in a woman whose life was dominated by her unfulfilled wish to be an artist—a wish that had earned credibility earlier in her life. In contrast to Freud, I do not discuss her bisexual fantasies as a means to undo the centrality of castration in her mental life. Rather, I discuss her bisexual fantasies as shards of derailed and needed attributes of an intact, alive, mindful self *beyond* gender. Her movement into using her creative potential depended on her ability to gain an intact mindfulness that possessed qualities previously relegated to her bisexual fantasies: agency and freedom to access knowledge about her body, her passions, her individuality, and her expressiveness. This chapter provides a widening understanding of the significance of bisexual fantasies not in order to overcome castrated genitals, as Freud proposed, but to overcome the traumatically imposed necessity in her childhood to have a castrated mind free of intention and initiative.

Other psychoanalytic writers have also explored issues connected with the connections between creativity and bisexuality in a different way from that proposed by Freud (1933). Milner (1950) speaks about the tendency to focus on differences, like male and female, but then, having done that, it is necessary to bring the two halves together. "Art is not only a created fusion between what is and what might be, it is also a created way of giving the inner subjective reality an outer form that it may be shared" (p. 132). Winnicott (1971a) states that acts of self-initiation are thwarted when the environment demands compliance and adaptation, interfering with the first creative act: the creation of a transitional object. Gedo clinically observes women blocked in their quest for creativity by symbiotic attachments to intrusive mothers who perpetuate passivity and lack of initiative, or who relinquish self-assertion in favour of a commitment to the well-being of their mothers (1989, pp. 69–70). McDougall asserts that "creative acts may be conceptualized as a fusion of masculine and feminine elements in the psychic structure" (1993, p. 75), unconsciously experienced as a "theft of parental sexual organs and generative powers that can block creativity" (p. 77). Gedo conceptualizes the artist's need of a "secret sharer: the creative partnership in which an emotional bond is formed with someone who can serve as one's alter ego" that unconsciously supports psychological integration, relieves isolation, and shares a creative goal (1996, pp. 22–23). Kavaler-Adler, using biographic data, examines the lives of women authors where the role of the father in the author's creativity was not based on identification: it was an addictive attachment to a demon/father/lover "that lives through the woman's link to her creative work and defends against the preoedipal trauma with the mother" (2000, p. 80).

The clinical case

Poetry ought to have a mother as well as a father . . . since without some mixture of the kind the intellect seems to predominate and other faculties of the mind harden and become barren.

Virginia Woolf, *A Room Of One's Own* (1929)

My patient was a middle-aged married woman with two children. Born in Scandinavia and educated at Kings College, Cambridge, and the London School of Economics, after her marriage she had emigrated, to the United States and consulted with private foundations concerned with the advancement of global health and social care policy. Unfulfilled in her career, she sought analysis after her children were grown in order to explore the reasons she was blocked in satisfying her consuming ambition to become a creative artist.

A transference enactment

The patient began her initial contact with me by occupying my mind through scrutinizing me closely and commenting relentlessly on the significance of my every gesture and intonation. She confessed her obsessive preoccupation with "loving me". She said "You are in my head." She could not stop thinking about me. I eventually responded to her insistent declarations of love by telling her that I could not work under this pressure and that we had to find other ways to talk about her experience. She immediately restrained herself and soon dreamt about being "under plastic": a dream of living death that dismayed me more than it did her. She remained "under plastic" for years, relatively inaccessible, showing little emotion except copious tears of frustration that flowed only in her sessions.

The obsessive nature of what she expressed as "love" had aroused my countertransference, and I momentarily turned away from the pressure of her demands. From her perspective, her behaviour with me was a reversed expression of her mother's intrusive, controlling love that as a child had trapped her as an acolyte in what we came to call the "Church of Mary" (her mother's name). Her intrusiveness also had its roots in an early memory of her father. When she was 3, he came upon her in the bathroom absorbed in her play with watercolours under the running water of the sink. Harshly angry, he atypically enforced her submission to his will and made her stop playing. I felt ashamed that I had pushed her away and, for a long time, the incident remained in the air—a piece of unexplored experience that was closed off from understanding.

Understanding the enactment

Many years later, during a period in which she was mourning her father's death, she remembered a shared favourite adolescent activity of drawing house plans with him. This activity seemed to bridge the distance between them that had begun after the bathroom incident. What stood out for her was the calmness and serenity that accompanied this "parallel play" with her father. As an adult, my patient had obsessively continued drawing house plans while remaining emotionally isolated from everyone. Now, surprisingly, she thought of inviting someone to join her in a crafts project.

Simultaneously, in her mind, "she went out of the room" and began a prolonged silence.

I found myself in a reverie in response to her retreat and silence,
saying to myself the nursery rhyme about "little Miss Muffet" who
got scared away by a spider that sat down beside her. I remembered
our beginning, when I had responded to my patient in a way that
was similar to her memory of her overpowering father, and had
"scared her away". I thought about how she, initially, acted on me
and "scared me away". I inferred during my reverie that she had experienced shame when her father interfered with her pleasurable
self-absorption. In the transference, in identification with him, she
continued to interrupt her own associative process and lose access
to her thoughts. I inferred that my quiet reverie while she "went
out of the room" satisfied her transferential longing for me to sit
beside her reviving pleasurable memories of parallel play with her
calm and serene father.

My inferences, slowly communicated over time, were followed
by new memories. My patient had discovered and been recognized
for her artistic talent in her middle childhood. She had stopped
painting when she went to Cambridge. Never fully aware of her
resentment about deferring to the wishes of her admired parents,
she retrospectively realized that in her choice of university she had
frustrated her parents' hopes that she would become an artist.

One sustained remnant of her early pleasure with paints was
her habit of making patterns with the morning lights dancing on a
building on the way to her session. I said, "You use your artist eyes to
see things in a unique manner that changes my experience when I
join you in looking." She became anxious and disorganized, feeling
that I had exposed her as a person who was capable of acting on
the world in a way that didn't just reflect it as a mirror but actively
changed it. That alerted us to a danger inherent in her wish to
become an artist: a fear of her potential to see, to change what she
perceived and influence her world by acting on it (Milner, 1950).

We explored her fear of acknowledging her active intentions in
many ways. That is, her screen memory could be a reversal of what
had happened. Perhaps it was she who had intruded on her father
in the bathroom, saw him urinating, and he got angry and pushed
her away. This would make sense of her intrusive beginning with
me. But what grew out of our transference discovery of her "artist

eyes" was our impression that shameful anxiety, connected to her absorption in her intentions, motivated her to hide her intentions. She inferred as a child that she must not reveal she had a "mind of her own".

She remembered that before she went to university, she vowed, "I will not paint until my father is blind." He loved looking at art. She thought retrospectively that this was a vindictive attack on her father, who had seen her "artist eyes" when she was a child. In her vengeful dismissal of her father—in her blinding him—she blinded herself as well. She could not use her "artist eyes" to create or play, and she automatically closed off her imagination to herself and to me in the transference.

First formulation of her inhibition: "I will come, but nothing will happen here"

Our work shifted to understanding her relationship with her mother. My patient grew up thinking, after she learned of her mother's renunciation of her promising career as a musician and her multiple miscarriages before my patient was conceived, that she owed her mother her life to make up for mother's losses. In addition, at 6 months of age, her mother had toilet-trained her. Compliance with her mother's "velvet aggression", which took control of my patient's body, was associated with life-long constipation because she "didn't know the signals" and waited for something to happen. In like manner, she depended upon her husband to initiate sexual intimacy, finding that she could respond to him without having to learn her body's arousal patterns. "Mother gave up playing music when I was born, and the promise of her talent was passed on to me. But mother robbed me of my insides and my power to act independently. I will not fulfil mother's ambitions. I have lived in a fantasy bubble in my head. Mother couldn't intrude there. You did in the beginning: you aroused my hopes that I could live in the world and be somebody, yet I resented that you were in my head and I wanted you out."

We discovered that another dimension of her inhibition, secondary to traumatic interference by her mother, was loss of agency and lack of knowledge about her body's signals. At one point, she proposed that she wanted to meditate to "clear her mind" of confusion. She read my exploration about the meaning of her meditation as my refusing her permission. "You want to know the content of my mind in order to control me." She knew she could meditate without my permission, but she did not. She associated to wanting to go barefoot into town when she was an adolescent and her mother telling her that it was not proper; my patient had given in without protest. "I know the rules", she said. She spoke of "diving-board decisions": ideas you acted on because you got so far out, you could not change your mind. "I stayed with you after our stormy beginning because I could not change my mind once we started. If I had changed my mind, I would have exhibited independent thinking, and that is not allowed in the 'Church of Mary'. I decided I would come, knowing that nothing will happen here."

Loosening the inhibition: exploring what was under plastic

Much later, in spite of her vows to remain vengefully under plastic, she began to take art classes. We saw the tenacity of her inhibition against any form of spontaneous exploration as opposed to being able to work creatively when she was given abstract but discrete assignments. The following dream linked her repressed passion to her inhibition.

> I was in a store buying an item from a woman sales clerk. I put my red purse down on the counter, paid for it, and then left. Then I was on a road that seemed perilously cut into the rock of a mountain. I looked on the seat beside me and discovered that my purse was not there. I retraced my steps and found my purse, which was empty of its contents.

She thought the purse represented her mind, which she defensively and vengefully emptied, as part of "living under plastic". She revealed that her mind had been turned over to me now that it was emptied of passion in the stormy beginning of our work, and again in response to my questioning her initiating meditation. She began to refer to me as "the keeper of the flame": expressing both anger that I wanted to control her flame and hope that I would keep her passion and agency safe for her until she could reclaim it in her own way.

Bisexual fantasies: The "boy/girl" doll

Her earliest memories of passion and agency were linked to a childhood androgynous doll she had called "boy/girl", which was given to her when she was a toddler "tomboy", assertive and independent. At the time of her menarche she had thrown away the doll and had become a decorous, inhibited, intellectually achieving, attractive young woman. She fantasized she could be aggressive, assertive, and competitive *if* she could recover "boy/girl" within herself.

Multiple meanings that had become attached to this concrete representation of her psychological bisexuality throughout her development emerged over the course of her analysis. "Boy/girl" was transformed into "best boy companion" to her father as an aspect of her oedipal resolution. Longing for her father but thwarted by his sole submissive commitment to her mother, she accompanied him on his sporadic "quirky" exploits and joined him in making architectural drawings—an activity her mother ignored. She believed being his "best boy" would lessen the psychological distance between them. In college, she fantasized she would produce paintings under her maiden name, so that her father's lineage would stay intact. Secretly, accompanied by guilt, she believed she was a "hot shot" who could autogenously produce many live painting/babies and outdo her parents. In her analysis, she reconstructed that her mother competitively sought her daughter's creative flame after mother confided, "I do things competently, I am always busy, but I have no fire in my life." Unable to act on her "hot shot" fantasy, my patient consoled herself that her talent was "inherent, intact, waiting to be used".

"Boy/girl" was also an early forerunner of her later omnipotent self-sufficiency. In her late adolescence, she had developed "the dragon lady": a bisexual costume, worn to a college dance, portraying her "hot shot" fantasy as charismatic invulnerability. As the dragon lady, she was free of distraction by sexual desires. She thought: "If I were singly gendered, there would be sexual tension with men or women that would interfere with my being complete within myself."

The third version of "boy/girl" emerged in connection with her longings for "mythic women": actual women whom she had

idealized in childhood as she was growing up for their free thinking, sensuality, ambitiousness, aggression, and competitiveness.
These women were so different from her mother, who lived in a
beautiful but "genteel void". She confessed that she had "fallen
in love with me" when she met me, only to be disappointed by
my backing off from her, because I seemed to her to be a mythic
woman: confident, secure in my career, surrounded by tasteful objects in my office. She believed that if she were fully in touch with
"boy/girl", she would take the risk of accomplishment and not
protect her mother—nor me in the transference—from envy or
competition by hiding under plastic.

She began to understand the significance to her of her
mother's renunciation of her early career as a musician in favour
of ambitions to become pregnant. In connection with a dream
image of "*levitating but tethered by huge rubber bands*", she remembered having gone alone, before leaving for Cambridge, to a
cabin in the mountains that the family owned. She was frightened, unable to sleep, when her parents left her at the cabin.
At dawn, looking up at the soaring trees, she tried to paint what
she saw. Her "artist eyes" failed. She felt momentarily suicidal and
ashamed when she returned home. She never painted again. We
reconstructed that her unconscious guilt, connected to her fantasy of soaring with her talent and creating multiple painting/
babies rather than sacrifice her ambitions as her mother did, tethered her to renunciation and self-negation. "I will get older, but
nothing will happen."

Searching for a fertilized mind

My patient experienced some measure of freedom when we considered "boy/girl" as a composite of what Virginia Woolf (1929)
termed a "fertilized mind". She reported a dream at the time of
her mother's gradual physical deterioration.

> *I was wearing a beautiful crinoline ethnic skirt, feminine and blos-
> soming.*

In her associations, she felt it was dangerous to want beautiful
feminine things because it would make her stand out as "full of

life" in contrast to her dying and fatigued mother. I asked what she was representing in the dream about herself as a woman. She said: "Emotions are feminine, like the skirt. I need to be able to access my emotions. Mother emphasized control over emotions like she emphasized control over my faeces." For my patient, the essential contrast in "boy/girl" was not gendered. The contrast was between being alive, "full-skirted", blossoming, or being dead under plastic, as her father was in his bondage to her mother. We now understood her deadness to be an accommodation to strain traumas (Sandler, 1967) re-experienced in her analysis, where accommodation took the place of living. Deadness was also the result of repression of oedipal longings to be father's intimate in order to remain committed to compensating her mother for what she had relinquished.

Coming out of hiding

As she witnessed her mother's failing health, she announced her retirement and her decision to "come out of hiding". What she planned for her retirement was to realize her dream of painting full time. The blossoming skirt that covered her body in her dream also hid concerns associated with a planned colonoscopy. The colonoscopy stirred up fears of being penetrated again by a composite parent and losing control of her faeces. Once again she experienced anxieties connected to her hope that she was intact, and she became temporarily dissociated in the session.

We further explored her anxieties concerning the intactness of her mind and body. Intactness signified to her that she was capable of being absorbed in her own intentions. This capacity would separate her from her internalized commitments to her mother and from me in the transference. However, for the first time she acknowledged that she still needed my support of her "full-skirted mind", even if she was intact and absorbed in her own intentions.

My patient reflected that each act of renunciation of intention had brought her closer to sainthood in the "Church of Mary". Each act of renunciation brought her safety from the possibility of being shamed over ambitions that interfered with her requirement to fix the life of her mother who had sacrificed her early ambitions.

Each assertion of omnipotent self-sufficiency brought her protection from being taken over by others. Each refusal to symbolically take off her sandals kept her distant from desire and a fertilized, rather than frozen, mind. She explained: "There is a fine line between reason and imagination. I am afraid to break the rules because I will go crazy, like I felt in the cabin." In this way, she realized that she clung to her mother as much as her mother clung to her. Mother was the voice of affect management, conventionality, and rationality that kept her sane.

Her analytic work constantly tempted her to gain access into her internal world and to let go of her mother as an internalized controlling agent. Renunciation of intention, desire, and ambition exposed her to a perilous existence under plastic in which she would force herself to be content with fantasy, remaining isolated and dead. Affectively, she realized that continued adherence to goals to make up for maternal losses aroused her ambivalence and her unconscious guilt over her wishes to "kill the angel in the house" (Woolf, 1929) and "blind" her father to her passions—potentially revealed in her paintings. For a long time, she oscillated between wish, action, and anxiety about pursuing her own intentions.

Re-finding "boy/girl"

Eventually she made a decision to meditate, even though she was certain that I disapproved. She came in, saying that she had "broken the rules". She reported an unusual dream:

> *There was a woman on the couch in your office. You and I were sitting beside the couch, watching her. There was a huge phallic-shaped object on top of the woman. This huge phallus was raping the woman, and she seemed unafraid—in fact, she looked liberated. You said nothing. You just watched and let it happen. I asked the woman, "do you need help?" She said "no". After the rape was consummated, the phallic shape collapsed, and the woman went to sleep.*

My patient felt she had liberated herself by "breaking the rule" and meditating. She commented, "You let the rape happen." I said, "It looks like in your dream you re-found 'boy/girl'. In your dream you represent yourself both as girl: penetrated yet triumphant; and boy: powerful, and phallic as your father seemed to you in your screen memory." My patient replied: "Those two aspects were split in the dream, but both belong to me. The phallic shape is both big and powerful and then it becomes flaccid and small. I have kept my talent small so that it won't hurt anyone. I don't use it, I don't show it, but I know it is there, fragile, invisible to everyone. You know it is there; maybe you think that it is big. You sat back and let something happen. That was comforting to me. You didn't panic, you weren't a worry mother."

Her phallic imagery was dramatic. One could certainly interpret this dream as a wish-fulfilling illusion of finding a hidden fertilizing phallus, or a sadomasochistic primal scene in which she pictured her father as a raping phallus that she revelled in and tamed for her own purposes. I inferred that in this dream she represented her talent as the narcissistically intact "boy/girl". In her past, she had yielded her talent to her father, who made accommodation to him more important than her expressiveness. In her dream, she felt liberated, triumphant, not raped as the phallus grew small. I interpreted that her power, projected onto him in the bathroom scene, was reclaimed by her in her dream. Her dream, I felt, was an imaginative integration of externalized phallic power and restored internal attributes of her mind. In her dream, I was neither afraid nor restraining. I did not repeat the trauma of our beginning and prohibit rather than let something blossom in her "full-skirted mind".

Working through insight

A pivotal transference dream helped us think further about her oscillations about pursuing her artistic intentions without destroying other people.

There was a storm, a wave, and you were with me. We sought safety and shelter in a cave that was filled with blonde wood furniture and art objects. One piece of furniture was a three-legged stool that was next to a desk like yours.

She thought the dream cave represented our psychoanalytic work. The cave filled with artefacts represented her new attempts to get closer to me without fearing my taking over the contents of her mind. Reflectively, she said: "I can't remain in touch with my passion only in my head. I need another person to love and hate, to long for and push away. You have been that person. I have learned about what we share and how we are different. I created that stool that is beside your desk in my dream. My mother interfered with my giving 'my stool' freely to the world and taking things in from the world that I could use rather than fear as a takeover. Each leg of the stool stands for something I kept buried from my parents: aggression, competition, and ambition. You and I have joined forces in our search for the truth about my deadness. For so long I insisted on my self-sufficiency. I couldn't take in anything that you said. Now I wonder if I can keep this process going on my own." This was the beginning of a long termination phase and the beginning of her use of her creativity.

Discussion

Creative sterility and bisexual fixations in women

Freud (1910a [1909]) held that artistic activity did not use instinctual energy directly, but made use of sublimations that transformed instinctual aims for creative and scientific work (pp. 53–54). Was Freud (1933) correct that a gifted child was destined by her "bisexual disposition" to be caught in instinctual conflicts that interfered with the plasticity of the sexual drive and sublimation of sexual aims? A broader question, which I cannot discuss, is Freud's assertion that creativity is dependent upon instinctual vicissitudes.

My patient, in her early pleasurable investigative play with paints, had sublimated forbidden knowledge about her body to a new avenue of investigation to overcome the impact of her early restrictive toilet training. As a child, battling between adherence to parental demands and preserving her endangered intentional self, she demonstrated that attempts to escape the imposed strictures through sublimations were unsupported by the environment, leading to repression of attributes of herself needed for creativity. She felt that her mother interfered with her, giving her stool freely to the world and taking things in from the world that she could use, rather than fear as a takeover. She felt restrained by shaming from using her "artist eyes" to see, to change what she perceived, and influence her world by acting on it. As Freud described, shame and humiliation were dominant affects in her development. As I have demonstrated, the origin of shame was not about her "castrated genitals" but about the imposed necessity to have a "castrated mind" free of intention and initiative, and desire

What were the conditions that contributed to her creative inhibition?

This woman's creative inhibition was secondary to trauma, not a developmental vicissitude of an inherent bisexual constitution. The initial trauma centred on maternal insistence on control of her daughter's body and mind, rather than supporting agency. As a child, she learned that she must remain passive, developing somatic apraxias such as constipation, and remain attentive to others at the price of forgoing her own aspirations (Gedo, 1988, 1989). Her childhood solution was to "live in a fantasy bubble" in her head, where mother couldn't intrude, and to live "under plastic" for a long time in her analysis. She submitted to her mother's "velvet aggression" out of her unconscious preoedipal guilt, which perpetuated obligations to offer her "aliveness" to her mother to make up for what mother had lost, and oedipal guilt, which perpetuated obligations to avoid the creative domain that had once been her mother's. In an early transference repetition she submitted to me because she could not "break the rule" and demonstrate to me that she could rethink her commitment to start analysis.

Second, following the bathroom scene, where her father "stole her flame", she experienced lasting disillusionment in her father's failure to support her attempt to circumvent her mother's repressive intrusions. Her adolescent vow, "I will not paint until my father is blind", expressed her rage that her father was also "under plastic", too merged with her mother to stand up independently and carry my patient's flame. She sacrificed artistic creation out of guilt over her vengeful wish to deprive her father of seeing *in her art* a disguised expression of her need of his support, erotized in oedipal longings. In the transference, she revealed that her mind, emptied of passion in the stormy beginning of our work and when I explored her meditating, had been turned over to me. In an ambivalent father transference she referred to me as "the keeper of the flame": expressing both anger that I wanted to control her flame and hope that I would keep her passion and agency safe for her until she could reclaim it in her own way (Tessman, 1989).

What special role did her father play in her capacity to be creative?

To be an artist, she had to access her passion, which was complexly linked to her father. Did her disillusionment in her father following the bathroom scene also function as a defensive veil that hid an essential truth, "I am nothing without a powerful male to fertilize my mind"? (Kavaler-Adler, 2000; McDougall, 1993). Her "giant phallus" dream seemed to address this issue: she represented her father as an omnipotent raping phallus that she revelled in and triumphed over. At the time of her analysis, I understood the giant phallus as an externalization of her disclaimed power, projected and split off onto this persecutory image of her father who, in the "primal" bathroom scene, insisted on her submission rather than freedom to explore. In her dream, power is returned to her in the form of a fantasy merger—her talent that is big and hidden—that protects her against the consequences of a maternal transference risk: "I broke the rules." This fantasy merger, in which she regains access to her projected power, constituted for her a merged "secret sharer" (Gedo, 1996) that fertilized her creative ambitions. This act of dream violence dramatizes multiple ideas: she could use rational self-determination to overcome her mother's life of renunciation of desire, her mother's prohibition of meaningful contact with her father, and transference rules against meditation. In addition, she felt empowered within her bisexual self to generatively create her own art/babies (McDougall, 1995b).

What was the significance of her bisexual fantasies to her creativity?

My work with this patient revealed an adaptive aspect to her bisexual fantasies. Analytic work demonstrated that her evolving boy/girl fantasies carried the shards of derailed self-determining emotional and motivational attributes needed for maintenance of her intact mindfulness and creative expression. From her assertiveness as a toddler, to the "best boy" companion to her father on his intermittent "quirky exploits" or, when he was occasionally free of his bondage to her mother, in joining him in making architectural drawings, she was attempting to rediscover her initiative and absorption she lost in the bathroom scene. In her androgynous fantasies of being a dragon lady she felt invulnerable, self-sufficient, and free from distractions by sexual desire. As a "hot-shot" she retained competitiveness, free of paralysing commitments to her parents. In mythic women she found sensual, ambitious, free-thinking women who were not afraid to go after what they needed. Although disillusioned in me as a mythic woman when we began, in the dream of the phallus where I let the scene unfold she felt reassured that I was self-confident and secure, able to let her be fertile and creative.

For my patient, the essential contrast in "boy/girl" was not about masculine or feminine attributes. The contrast, *derived from her individual experience with her parents*, was between being alive, "full-skirted, blossoming", free of irrational commitments to her mother, or being dead, under plastic, identified with her father merged with her mother.

Conclusion:
what were the conditions of creativity for this woman?

My patient's movement into making use of her creative potential depended on her ability to gain, within the analytic process, an intact, alive self that possessed qualities previously relegated to her bisexual fantasies: agency and freedom to access knowledge about her body, her passions, her individuality, and her expressiveness. Equally important to her entry into creative work was the significance of new growth-promoting experience in the transference as she allowed herself to become emotionally connected to me as a "secret sharer". Gedo states: "Analysands will cast their therapist as a secret sharer [a catalyst for creative efforts] only if the analyst's conscious and unconscious attitudes are congruent with sharing a creative goal" (1996, p. 23). She eventually accepted me as a catalyst when she experienced me as a differentiated person whom she acknowledged she needed to decipher the mysteries of her inhibition. She realized that she had fought against her dependency on me thinking that she would need me forever as she secretly needed her mother: the voice of affect management, conventionality, and rationality that kept her sane. As an alternative to this addictive dependency, she could contemplate an independent existence through learning the "truth about her deadness" and understanding that her creativity required both attachment and solitude, not isolation (Winnicott, 1971a). Thus, I became a person with whom she could interact affectively, not just imagine engagement in her fantasies. Ultimately, I became a person who could let her go and allow her to initiate actions on her own, such as planning the termination of analysis.

In my view, her creativity was not a sublimation of her bisexual ambitions. Rather, her capacity to be creative was dependent upon having access to the attributes that were condensed in her bisexual fantasies. Important in this regard was regaining access to her projected power, which she dramatized in her giant-phallus dream. The dual significance of work with transference repetitions of her traumatic past and new growth-promoting experience in the transference permitted entry into creative originality.

6

The riddle of the repudiation of femininity: the scandal of the feminine dimension

Jacqueline Schaeffer

According to Freud, "the repudiation of femininity [is] part of the great riddle of sex" (1937c, p. 252). It is a "bedrock", the ultimate stumbling-block that brings all therapeutic activity to an end.

I would like first of all to define what I mean by "feminine". My definition—and the same is true of the way in which I use the word "masculine"—has nothing to do with gender. Gender is not a psychoanalytic concept, since the purpose of any analysis is not to accept it as such but to call it into question in terms either of narcissistic or object-related cathexes or of identifications. I therefore define the feminine dimension in its conceptual sense as one of the elements of a specific difference that has to be constructed, a difference that is paradigmatic of all differences: that between the sexes.

I shall therefore not explore the feminine dimension as dissociated from its masculine counterpart.

I do not use the word in the sense of a "primal feminine dimension" of sexuality (André, 1995), of a "primary feminine dimension" (Guignard, 1997), or of a "pure female element" (Winnicott, 1971b, p. 76). These all refer to a "primal" factor that as such has nothing to do with the advent, in the individual, of the difference between the sexes, male–female: it refers to the identificatory phase with the mother's maternal or sexual female aspect. My use of the word "feminine" here has to do with the test of otherness that is part of the difference between the sexes. I draw a distinction between the feminine sphere—which is internal and invisible—and femininity—which is visible, goes hand-in-hand with the phallic dimension, involves illusion and masquerade, and is a reassurance against castration anxiety for both men and women.

Why introduce the feminine dimension?

When Freud came up against certain difficulties and failures in his psychoanalytic work, he spoke of a "bedrock"—that of the "repudiation of femininity", which formed a stumbling block. This Scylla coming after the Charybdis of the death drive was, to my mind, his way of reintroducing the sexual element, of restoring to the sexual drive the diabolical capacity that he had taken away from it—thereby acknowledging that it has just as much potential for disruption as the death drive itself.

But why the *feminine* dimension?

In an attempt to answer that question, I examined several hypotheses in my book *Le Refus du Féminin* (Schaeffer, 1997).

The feminine dimension and the difference between the sexes

One hypothesis could be that this famous bedrock is the refusal of what seems to be the most bizarre feature of the difference between the sexes, the element that is particularly difficult to express in terms of anal or phallic factors: the female sex organ.

Freud described the development of psychosexuality in terms of three pairings: active/passive at the anal sadistic stage; universal penis/castrated penis at the phallic stage; and masculine/feminine at puberty—that is, the so-called "genital" stage.

The active/passive pairing denotes two opposite polarities, while the phallic/castrated pairing functions in an all-or-nothing manner. Only the masculine/feminine pairing denotes a true difference: the difference between the sexes.

That said, the way in which Freud expressed these ideas does tend to show how difficult it is for the "genital" aspect to break free of its pre-genital forerunners. Lou Andreas-Salomé spoke of the vagina being "taken on lease" from the rectum, and that phase was adopted by Freud (1917c, p. 133). The penis is seen as a "faecal stick". The female sex organ is defined with respect to the penis, as an annex to it: the value of the vagina is that it functions as an abode for the penis. Freud refers to the male partner in sexual intercourse as "an appendage to the penis" (1917c, p. 129).

However, after defining the importance of the difference between the sexes, Freud went on to call it into question. In 1937, a fourth pairing was evoked: bisexuality/repudiation of femininity in both sexes. He did not describe any forerunners of that element but saw it as having biological origins—this was Freud's usual way of circumventing something that he found problematic: treat it as predetermined.

It is interesting to note that this new pairing—as well as each of the polarities that go to make it up—have to do with denial of the difference between the sexes.

▷ Repudiation of femininity (what I call refusing the feminine dimension) is a refusal of what turns out to be well-nigh impossible to express in terms of anal or phallic logic: a female sex organ that is invisible, secret, strange, and which carries with it all kinds of dangerous fantasies. It makes men uneasy not only because it gives them an image of their own sex organ castrated, so that they become anxious as regards their own genital organ, but also, and above all, because the opening-up of the female body, its quest for sexual enjoyment and its ability to accept great quantities of the constant thrust of the libido, are sources of anxiety.

▷ In addition, although psychic bisexuality plays an organizing role as regards identifications—and in particular the crossed identifications of the oedipal conflict—the fantasy of bisexuality, like bisexuality that is acted out, constitutes a defence against cathecting and processing the difference between the sexes.

It would therefore seem to be the case that access to the difference between the sexes does not guarantee stability or security;

what Freud called the bedrock may well be that of the difference
between the sexes.

I have argued that it is "the work of the feminine sphere"—in
both men and women—that ensures access to the difference between the sexes and enables that difference to be preserved, however conflict-ridden it may turn out to be. This contribution to
building up psychosexual identity nonetheless remains unstable,
because it requires work to be done on it constantly; it is always
threatened by regression to the active/passive antagonism or the
phallic/castrated pairing, both of which afford some relief to an
ego that "needs some work to be done" when faced with the constant thrust of the sexual drive.

Simone de Beauvoir wrote that "one is not born a woman, one
becomes one" (1949). I would argue that on the genital level the
feminine dimension, like its masculine counterpart, is not something that goes without saying once puberty has been reached,
as Freud would have it, and sexual intercourse begins; it has to
be fought for over and over again, linked as it is to the constant
thrust of the libido. As far as the mental apparatus is concerned,
neither the physical changes nor the sexual excitation experienced at puberty can process the difference between the sexes.
One has to wait, as the woman waits, for the "lover-for-ecstatic-
pleasure" to come along before the genital feminine dimension
can be wrenched from the woman's body. At that point there is
an experience of a true sexual differentiation, the creation of a
feminine dimension that at last makes it possible for the ego to
introject in accordance with the constant thrust of the drives in
sexuality.

The feminine sphere
and great quantities of drive energy

Another hypothesis: what inevitably defines the sexual drive in
a contradictory manner belongs to the feminine sphere—those
drives both nourish the mind and erupt into it.

The Freudian theory to which I refer is a drive-related one: that
of the libido and of the conflict that the latter creates for the ego's
defences. Here, a trajectory is involved: an unavoidable internal

excitation that, from its source in the body to its aim, the quest for satisfaction, takes on a mental dimension as it becomes a drive. "On its path from its source to its aim, the [drive] becomes operative psychically" (Freud, 1933a, Lecture XXXII, p. 96). If that excitation does not succeed in becoming mentalized as a drive, or if the drive degenerates back towards excitation, what may then emerge is what we call "psychosomatic" disorders, pathologies of addiction, of acting-out, of out-and-out frigidity, and so on.

Sexual drives—libido—have one fundamental predicate, which gives them their true distinctiveness: constant thrust. That thrust derives from and is in opposition to the periodical impulses of the sexual instinct. Freud wrote: "An instinct [*Trieb*] is a stimulus applied to the mind. [It] never operates as a force giving a *momentary* impact but always as a *constant* one" (1915c, p. 118). In 1933 he added: "it operates as a constant force [that] the subject cannot avoid by flight. . . . It is from this pressing that it derives its name of *Trieb*" (1933a, Lecture XXXII, p. 96).

Jacques Lacan (1964) emphasized that point too when he wrote that the constant nature of that thrust implied that a drive cannot be looked upon merely as a biological function, since the latter always has a periodic rhythm to it. Drives do not ebb and flow: they are a constant force.

It is because drives are constantly exerting pressure while the ego is periodic and temporal in nature that, according to Freud (1915c, p. 122), there is a "demand made upon the mind for work". In this way, the ego differentiates from the id, mere excitation becomes drive-oriented, genitality in human beings moves away from sexuality in animals, which is operational only when they are in heat and dependent on *oestrus*, and is transformed into psycho-sexuality with a constant pressure: this is a major characteristic of human beings.

The signal that the constant thrust of the sexual drives has reached the ego is the anxiety that is then experienced. The ego is not "master in its own house". Overwhelmed by the libido, the ego experiences it as an internal foreign body. From the very beginning of life, the ego is indebted to anxiety, because it has no choice in the matter: what bursts through is what in fact nourishes the ego.

Unlike need, which can be satisfied by some specific action or other, the libido, given its very nature, can never be gratified in

that way. As Freud put it, we "must reckon with the possibility that
something in the nature of the sexual instinct itself is unfavourable
to the realization of complete satisfaction" (1912d, pp. 188–189).
It is up to the ego to say whether it is satisfied by a love object or
by sublimation.

The constant thrust of the libido defines desire in human beings. If the drive were ever to be fully satisfied, why would the libido
go on pressing and what would become of desire?

It was his difficulty in theorizing the feminine sexual dimension
in terms of the unavoidable constant pressure of great quantities
of libido that led Freud to the idea of what he called the "repudiation of femininity", beyond which it was impossible to go; its characteristic features were penis envy and the refusal of homosexual
passivity.

What Freud did not theorize was what happened to the vast
quantities of unbound excitation that are allowed entry into the
ego without causing any traumatic break-in or complete paraly-
sis—a nourishing break-through, in other words. This is the point
at which great quantities of libido are introjected, and one of the
ways in which this is accomplished is via the genital feminine libido. Here, too, we find "anxiety concerning the feminine sphere":
Freud's theory of anxiety does not help us to think about that
feminine dimension.

Nevertheless, Freud, who was always extremely intuitive, wrote
to Fliess on 5 November 1899: "I do not yet have the slightest idea
what to do with the ††† female aspect, and that makes me distrust
the whole thing" (Masson, 1985, pp. 381–382).

The feminine sphere
and the genital dimension

A third hypothesis would be that, in employing the term "bedrock",
Freud was bringing a pessimistic note into his views on sexuality; it
is as though, without saying so explicitly, he was thinking of impo-
tence—both directly sexual and that of the analyst who tries to do
something about it.

For Freud, women would remain absorbed by their penis

envy—that, to some extent at least, is not a false premise—and men would focus exclusively on their homosexual anxiety about being penetrated. I would argue that, in both cases, we are faced with a pre-genital defence against anxiety about genital penetration—that of a vagina that has to let itself be penetrated, or which has to be penetrated by a libidinal penis. The difference between the sexes has to do with the sexual relationship as such.

The erotic feminine dimension and the sexual relationship providing ecstatic pleasure are without a doubt the most repressed and "taboo" of representations, even among psychoanalysts—who are much more comfortable with infantile sexuality, no matter how scandalous that may seem.

> Although psychoanalytic writings are full of matters to do with infantile sexuality or the drives, very much less has been written about how to define the part played by these factors in sexuality itself, in the kind of sexuality that is expressed in adult sexual intercourse. As long as the latter is not dissociated from the rest of mental life, it reveals an essential and fundamental feature of mental life as such. [Roussillon, 2008]

In 1915, Freud himself wrote: "Sexual love is undoubtedly one of the chief things in life, and the union of mental and bodily satisfaction in the enjoyment of love is one of its culminating peaks. . . . *Science alone is too delicate to admit it*" (Freud, 1915a [1914], pp. 169–170; italics added).

It is through sexual intercourse with its ecstatic pleasure that are co-created both the erotic genital feminine dimension, the most accomplished aspect of all in a woman's feminine sphere, and the masculine dimension in men.

If there is one way in which the entry of that constant thrust into the ego can be perceived, developed, and experienced as an enhancement, it is undoubtedly through sexual intercourse, which leads to that kind of enjoyment. The co-creation of the adult feminine and masculine dimensions, together with sexual pleasure, participate in those mutative experiences that lead to rearrangements of psychic economy and enrich the ego with affect-laden representations.

The "enigma of masochism"

It is therefore not by chance that Freud drew a parallel between what he called "the riddle of femininity" and the enigma of the "mysterious masochistic trends of the ego" (1920g, p. 14).

As regards transmission from mother to daughter, the fairy-tale *The Sleeping Beauty* comes to mind. The mother, as the harbinger of castration, says to the little boy as he charges straight ahead, his penis proudly at the ready: "Be careful, otherwise you'll get into trouble!" To the little girl, she will say: "Wait: you'll see, one day your Prince will come along!" The good-enough mother is thus the harbinger of waiting expectantly.

This consists in putting the erotogenic nature of the little girl's vagina in a safe place, under the tender maternal blanket of primary repression of the vagina (Braunschweig & Fain, 1975); the lover will one day come along and awaken it, reveal it. Her body will then develop various kinds of erotic capacity.

Waiting, however, is a painful kind of excitation; cathecting it will lead to the advent of that organizing nucleus we call primary erotogenic masochism. That primary form of masochism makes for an erotic cathexis of painful tension, gives sustenance to the non-gratification of a drive which by its very nature is impossible to satisfy, and constitutes a fixation point and a buffer as regards a disorganization that otherwise could be fatal.

The link between erotic excitation, the violence done to the ego, and the pain of the intermittent loss of the primary maternal object means that sexual desire necessarily implies a cathexis of the relationship between ecstasy and pain, the gap between hallucinatory wish-fulfilment and waiting for actual satisfaction, stamped with the seal of primary masochism.

> When this masochistic tendency turns towards the father, it implies that everything that happens to the girl's sexual body can be anticipated as coming from and attributed to a man's penis. The change of object transforms primary erotogenic masochism—a necessary element in differentiating from the maternal body—into a secondary erotogenic masochism that will lead the girl to want to be penetrated by the father's penis. The guilt attached to that oedipal desire means that the young girl expresses it in a regressive manner, in terms of the fantasy "A child is being beaten". [Freud, 1919e]

Freud did not deny the wound suffered by the ego, nor the sexual wound. He theorized such events as the fantasy of the female sex organ being mutilated, feelings of prejudice, penis envy, the wound caused by deflowering—all of these from the point of view of castration anxiety and the castration complex. He did not, however, consider masochism as part of the experience of sexual relationships and of the pleasure thereby obtained.

I myself have suggested that there exists a feminine erotogenic masochism that is part of the genital feminine sphere.

Feminine erotogenic masochism

I would distance myself from any conception of the feminine dimension that could be likened to "castrated" or "infantile". I see feminine erotogenic masochism as a genital dimension contributing to the pleasure that sexual relationships can offer adult masculine and feminine elements.

This is a mental form of erotogenic masochism that is neither perverse nor enacted. It is strengthened by primary erotogenic masochism and counter-cathexes moral masochism. When unbinding occurs, it guarantees the linking that is needed to give the ego cohesion so that it can deconstruct itself and let in a considerable amount of unbound excitation. Thanks to this erotogenic masochism, the woman's ego can take on board the irruption of ecstatic pleasure.

In women, this form of masochism involves submission to the sexual object. It has nothing to do with enacted sadism within a sado-masochistic relationship, nor with a preliminary ritual; it is the ability to open oneself up, to let oneself be taken over by a considerable quantity of libido and to accept being possessed by the sexual object.

As long as the lover's ego has managed to submit itself to the constant thrust of the libido, he will carry this into the woman's body in order to open up and create the "feminine dimension" by wresting it from her. In order to do this, he will have to confront her conflict between her libido and the resistances of her ego.

The dissymmetry in the difference between the sexes is enhanced by identifications.

Women submit out of love. They cannot give their all without love. That is why, as Freud pointed out, they are more exposed to the loss of love. That is what ensures her dependence and submissiveness towards men in sexual intercourse. However, the fact that a woman can appropriate her sex organ through the experience of sexual ecstasy mingled with tenderness brings her the significant benefit of pleasure.

A twofold change of object

From a psychoanalytic point of view, male domination—an undeniable fact of the organization of every society—has to do with the necessary paternal phallic function; this is a symbolic function that establishes law, enabling the father to separate his child from the mother and thereby give him or her access to the social structures of the world in which they live.

I would say that the lover-for-ecstatic-pleasure is also in the position of the separating third party, wrenching the woman from her primitive relationship with her mother. The mother did not provide her daughter with a penis—hence, as Freud pointed out, a great deal of aggressiveness towards her—but nor did she provide her with a vagina. It is through creating and revealing her vagina that a man will be able to wrench her away from her pre-genital mother. That change of object is a change in submissiveness: anal submission to the mother, from which the young girl tried to escape via penis envy, is transformed into libidinal submission to the lover.

There is therefore a twofold change of object: from pre-genital mother to the oedipal father (i.e. to the genital mother), and from oedipal father to the lover-for-ecstatic-pleasure.

The work of the feminine dimension

The "work of the feminine dimension" that a woman has to accomplish—a never-ending task—has to do with overcoming the conflict that constitutes, whether or not she denies it, female sexuality: "*Che vuoi?*" (Schaeffer, 1998). Well, a woman wants two contradictory things: her ego detests being defeated, but her sex organ demands just that. It wants to yield, to be defeated; it wants the "masculine dimension" of a man, which is the direct opposite of his "phallic dimension", an infantile sexual theory that exists simply to enable the difference between the sexes to be ignored, and therefore it wants the "feminine dimension" of the woman. It wants vast quantities of libido and erotogenic masochism. That is the scandal of the feminine sphere.

In the social, political, and economic fields, the struggle to ensure equality between the sexes is indeed a necessary one and must constantly be pursued. In the sexual field, however, such a struggle is harmful if it tends to become confused with the abolition of the difference between the sexes—a difference that has to be upheld. This is because of the antagonism between the ego's defences and the libido.

Everything that the ego finds intolerable may contribute to sexual enjoyment: breaking-in, sexual misuse of power, loss of control, abolition of limits, possession, submissiveness—in other words, "defeat" with all of its polysemy.

The feminine enigma can therefore be defined thus: the more she is wounded, the more she needs to feel desired; the more she falls, the more she makes her lover powerful; the more submissive she is, the more power she wields over her lover. And the more she is defeated, the more pleasure she takes and the more she feels loved.

The work of the feminine dimension in men consists in allowing their penis to be taken over by the constant thrust of their libido, whereas the pleasure principle may incite them to function quite happily according to a periodic rhythm of tension and discharge. It is the capacity in a man to desire a woman constantly with his libidinal penis; the capacity not to allow the fear of his own primitive mother, the fear of his own ecstatic pleasure or that of the woman to lead simply to discharge or to a return to the confines of his ego rather than to the discovery and creation of the "feminine dimension" in the woman. In other words, he has, at least for a certain period of time, to disconnect himself from the control of his ego, to overcome fantasies about his penis that have as their main aim that of verifying its solidity in sexual intercourse, and to ensure that he is not frightened by fantasies involving the danger represented by the body of the woman-as-mother.

The underlying terror in both sexes is their proximity to the sex organ of the mother from whose body they came. The avidity of drive-related pressure, never satisfied, cannot but be terrifying if all it implies is being devoured, swallowed up in the mother's body— an object of terror, but at the same time the lost paradise of fusion/ confusion. Yet sexual enjoyment is created precisely through facing up to these terrors and overcoming them. As Freud put it: "Anyone who is to be really free and happy in love must have surmounted his respect for women and have come to terms with the idea of incest with his mother or sister" [*sic!*] (1912d, p. 186).

Beyond the phallic dimension:
the female sex organ

Both sexes have to come to terms with the phallic structure. That narcissistic hyper-cathexis of the penis works towards breaking free of the pre-genital imago and the mother's ascendancy. Thanks to their castration anxiety, boys can symbolize the part for the whole, taking support from their paternal identification. But how are girls to negotiate an internal component that is a whole in itself, and how are they to separate their own from that of their mother? Can the female sex organ be symbolized and brought into the mental sphere (Schaeffer, 2008)?

For both sexes, the great discovery of puberty is that of the vagina. Of course, little girls are well aware of the fact that they have a hollowed-out part, and they have internal feelings, triggered not only by their oedipal emotions but also by primitive traces of their physical contact with and seduction by their archaic mother-figure. Nonetheless, the true revelation of the erotic vagina—the deep-seated erotogenic character of the female organ—can be accomplished only in the course of sexual intercourse giving ecstatic pleasure. For both men and women, the "other" sex is always the female one, because for everybody the phallic dimension is the same.

For how could that narcissistic phallic being, who can be paired only with a "castrated" being, avoid lapsing into fear of, contempt for, or hatred towards the feminine dimension?

The adult "genital" libidinal component is the most difficult and violent of all: it mobilizes the entire strength of those anal and phallic defences that we could call the "refusal of the feminine dimension". It demands that the ego do some work of processing when dealing with the constant thrust of the libido in sexuality. It is the violent nature of that test that can confront and oppose the violence of the primitive mother-figure's regressive capturing as well as the violence attributed to the death drive, both of which have non-differentiation as their aim.

Opposed to phallic logic, impelled by castration anxiety, the existence of which is limited to denying, dominating, destroying, or avoiding the feminine dimension, the masculine/feminine pairing is set up by means of a co-creation through the discovery of the female sex organ; this can come about only through the masculine dimension of the man conquering and tearing away the woman's anal and phallic defences. This is the masculine dimension of the lover-for-ecstatic-pleasure, on condition that he manages to discard his own phallic defences and lets himself be dominated by the constant thrust of his libido, carrying it into the woman's body. It is only thus that men can succeed in losing their fear of women (Cournut, 2001). From time immemorial, men have had to tear women away from the night of their mothers, the queens of the night.

Why drive-related violence? Let me dare to say it: because the scandalous aspect of the feminine dimension is erotogenic masochism. It makes the little oedipal girl say "Daddy, hurt me, beat me, rape me!" (the second phase—strongly repressed—of the fantasy that Freud theorized in his paper "A child is being beaten" [1919e]). And the woman in love says to her lover: "Do what you want with me, take me, defeat me!" Everything that the ego and the superego find intolerable can contribute to sexual enjoyment. The price to pay is for the ego, in both men and women, to consent to letting go of its defences when faced with genitality.

Nowadays, women know or at least feel that their anxiety about their feminine aspect cannot be soothed or resolved in any satisfactory manner by any kind of "phallic" manoeuvre. Above all, they know and feel that the fact of not being desired—or of no longer being desired—by a man brings them face-to-face with a painful feeling of not having a sex organ or of having it denied;

that rekindles the hurt they felt as young girls forced to structure themselves in a phallic manner when faced with the ordeal of perceiving the difference between the sexes. That is where their "castration anxiety" lies.

By way of conclusion

It was in his twilight years that Freud (1937c), after describing the Charybdis of the death drive, opposed to those of life and of love, theorized the Scylla of "repudiation of femininity" in both sexes.

It is somewhat disturbing to note the extent to which the refusal of the feminine dimension constitutes a characteristic feature of human behaviour and participates in its genesis in the mind—to such an extent, indeed, that Freud built up a theory of psychosexual development centred on the phallus; for Lacan, the phallus is the central signifier of sexuation, desire, and sexual enjoyment. That infantile sexual theory, in which there is only one sex organ, the phallic penis, must have represented a defensive manoeuvre against the irruption of the discovery of the difference between the sexes at the oedipal phase.

How are we to understand the sheer scope of the ongoing impact of this refusal of the feminine sphere? Are we to draw the conclusion that what has always threatened the political, social, and religious order of things is not only the power women have to procreate but also—and to an even greater extent—their erotic capacity, as well as the fact that the maternal dimension interpenetrates that of the woman, and the feminine dimension that of the mother? That said, we all know that the maternal dimension can contribute, in both sexes, to counter-cathecting the erotic feminine dimension.

Contrary to the phallic/castrated pairing, which upholds social structures and the balance of power, the masculine/feminine relationship is a mental creation that implies acknowledging and facing up to otherness in the difference between the sexes. The ability to transform a phallic/castrated pairing into a masculine/feminine relationship determines the manner and quality of the sexual, affective, and social relationship that is set up between a man and a woman and bears witness to a "work of civilization" [*Kulturarbeit*].

The status of women reflects the structure and history of any given civilization; it is the pivot and revealer of the changes that take place in society, the symptom of the crises and issues concerning the balance of power between the sexes, and the symbol of equality. That equality must of course be conquered and preserved in the political, social, and economic spheres—but it is extremely important not to see this as the abolition of the difference between the sexes; that difference is enhanced when it comes into play in sexuality, given the antagonism between the ego's defences and the libido.

In a society that is less and less "oedipal", one that tends to deny the difference between generations and between the sexes, perhaps psychoanalysts ought to feel that they have a particularly important role to play: that of guaranteeing a kind of sexuality that enhances the work of processing, the co-creation of couples in the true sense of the word, and sexual enjoyment or its positive forms of sublimation. At present, certain other elements are becoming more and more prevalent: instrumentalist or perverse forms of sexuality, pleasure in destructive violence, dehumanization and "faecalization" of people, and the unbridled development of power. Manoeuvres that aim to abolish differences—and in particular that between the sexes—are perhaps, as André Green (1997) has pointed out, the ultimate resting-place of the death drive in its work of doing away with any and all differences.

7

Are women still in danger of being misunderstood?

Graciela Abelin-Sas Rose

At the end of his lecture on "Femininity", Freud writes:

> If you want to know more about femininity, enquire from your own experiences of life, or turn to the poets, or wait until science can give you deeper and more coherent information. [1933, p. 135]

This chapter will try to honour that final paragraph. Our thoughts have been enriched by the many years that have elapsed since Freud presented his ideas, the unexpected cultural changes that have taken place, and the careful work of numerous authors. Thus facilitated, my own experience with a variety of clinical encounters guides me to consider possible ways of re-thinking femininity.

Although Freud offered a fascinating view of the development of the girl and its differences from that of the boy, some of his inferences are questionable, as are his conclusions. I am referring, specifically, to the idea of the girl developing first as a little boy (a theory questioned, among many, by Greenacre, 1950; Jones, 1935; Kleeman, 1976; and Klein, 1928) which led Freud to propose that the girl turns angrily against her mother, who has not granted her a penis or a baby and betrays her with the birth of a sibling (see

Dio Bleichmar, chapter 9, this volume). Others have contended that the girl's sense of femaleness is present early on, including early experiences of vaginal sensations (Richards, 1996). In my view each patient's babyhood experiences, the quality of her sensuous relationship with her own mother, father and others, her parents' emotional investment in her gender through their own personal histories as unconsciously conveyed to their offspring, early life traumas, early losses and disappointments, family life, the birth and characteristics of siblings—all these contribute to the unique way in which a girl will experience her body and gender (see Galenson & Roiphe, 1974; Mahler, 1963; Stoller, 1968b).

We can thus ponder whether the passage of attachment from mother to father is more subtle and complex; less centred on the lack of a penis, and more responsive instead to those other variables. Besides, the little child might feel attached to both parents equally since variations intrinsic to the family constellation and the models presented to the little girl differ not only in the character of each parent and from one culture to another, but also from one decade to the next.

The connection between the fear of castration in boys and superego development might also be put into question since castration doesn't promote the girl's sense of morality. Moral values might be present long before this particular phase of development takes place. In this regard, either sex might be influenced from the start by the quality of parental mirroring, so important in the development of empathy; by the first triangulation, the relationship established between the infant and both parents, linked to a foundation of a sense of otherness (Abelin, 1980); and by the identifications with available models—all of which may take a different turn in relations to the oedipal triangulation, where gender differentiation assumes such an important role (in terms of the relationship between child and either parent, and between the parents, see Herzog, 2005).[1]

Today, in our consulting rooms, we observe different female patients from those Freud conjectured about in Vienna in 1932. Let us hear his impressions:

The fact that women must be regarded as having little sense of justice is no doubt related to the predominance of envy in their

mental life; for the demand for justice is a modification of envy
and lays down the condition subject to which one can put envy
aside. We also regard women as weaker in their social interests
and as having less capacity for sublimating their instincts than
men. The former is no doubt derived from the dissocial quality
which unquestionably characterizes all sexual relations. . . . The
aptitude for sublimation is subject to the greatest individual
variations. On the other hand I cannot help mentioning an
impression that we are constantly receiving during analytic practice. A man of about thirty strikes us as a youthful, somewhat
unformed individual, whom we expect to make powerful use of
the possibilities for development opened up to him by analysis.
A woman of the same age, however, often frightens us by her
psychical rigidity and unchangeability. Her libido has taken up
final positions and seems incapable of exchanging them for
others. There are no paths open to further development; it
is as though the whole process had already run its course and
remains thenceforward insusceptible to influence—as though,
indeed, the difficult development to femininity had exhausted
the possibilities of the person concerned. As therapists we lament this state of things, even if we succeed in putting an end to
our patient's ailment by doing away with her neurotic conflict.
[1933, pp. 134–135]

Our clinical data

Some clinical illustrations might clarify the issues I am trying to
address. They contradict three major statements made by Freud
in relation to women—namely, that their superego development
was poor, that they were unable to change, set rigidly in their ways
quite early in life, and that they were more self-involved than men.
I found my patients to be capable of intense moral and noble
judgement, in great part to the detriment of their self-esteem. Ap-
proaching menopause, they were able to change: in fact, they were
eager to look into their internal worlds. Besides, all of them felt
responsible for the well-being of their partners and other members
of their families—to a greater extent than their partners, who were
more self-involved.

Their masochistic stance did not appear to be innate—that is,
an instinctual vicissitude inherent in women—but a solution to

complex infantile object relations that were later on reproduced in adulthood and were, thus, acquired and treatable.

I illustrate through four short vignettes.

Clinical vignette 1: "Monique"

Monique, a talented writer, had set her partner up in the role of a castigating presence. As an idealized authority, he was the only one who could claim authorship and creativity. Her assessment of his limitations was denied consciousness in the name of her love for him, while her own creative force was denied importance. Would we consider this a situation of primary masochism? We learned that she had felt guilty for being a well sibling of a younger disturbed brother. We couldn't find sadistic trends in her relationship to him but the sense that she shouldn't have been so much his superior. This made her feel undesirable as a woman. Her tragic surrender was based on *guilt about her endowment,* in a culture that would have preferred the male to be the intellectual.

Clinical vignette 2: "Jacqueline"

Jacqueline, who had lost a revered father soon after her marriage, established, with the willing participation of her husband, a relationship where the father/child dynamic was kept alive. She was enslaved to an authoritarian man, unable to find expansiveness, locked in an unconscious contract where the loss of her father was made less real. Here, *her masochistic relationship seemed based on a desire, as a young woman, to re-find a loved object more devotedly related to her than her often sick and self-involved mother,* by marrying an older controlling man. She mistook his need to control her as his devotion and interest.

Clinical vignette 3: "Debra"

In Debra, a successful art lawyer, the existential knot was one in which the *loyalty to her mother's limitations pre-empted her from a creative life of her own.* She could only improve and protect the creativity of others while she felt stilted in her own life. Her mother, who had been physically ill and addicted to alcohol since Debra had left home for studies abroad, had died shortly after Debra's marriage.

Clinical vignette 4: "Heidi"

As for Heidi, a highly qualified professional, *her role, in her family of origin, as regulator of the passionate feelings of others had impeded any fruitful development of her own.* At the time of her first consultation, her working conditions betrayed her unconscious contract: her office had doors that communicated with the offices of two older editors on each side, a man and a woman, who often asked her for help. Unable to limit their demands, she was left with no time for her own work.

In reviewing these vignettes, I observed certain common elements: all of these women, upon realization of the unconscious conflicts that kept them uncreative and therefore depressed, were able to make great leaps in their development, towards improving the quality of their lives and their emotional contract with their partners.

We should keep in mind the great variety of expressions of each woman's concept of femaleness and how that experience evolves in the course of her life, depending on her age and surrounding circumstances. For instance, as women approach the end of their reproductive years, having fulfilled an important biological and psychological task, they are often propelled to seek newer horizons. Freud vaguely referred to it in the same article:

But do not forget that I have only been describing women in so far as their nature is determined by their sexual function. It is true that that influence extends very far; but we don't overlook the fact that an individual woman might be a human being in other respects as well. [1933, p. 135]

Objectification of what defines femininity may be founded in prejudice unless we take into account the historical and cultural context in which our patient exists. Many women seek treatment for depression. As I have observed, this situation is often linked to a limitation in the expansiveness of their talents, also and consequently in the poor quality of their intimate relationships.

The following further underlines issues of the 1980s noticeable in the United States in the course of the years that separate us from Freud's last paper on femininity. It also puts the accent on changes that we have observed since the 1980s, compared to the female patients who consult us today, to which I refer later on in this chapter.

Some issues observed in the 1980s

The overall picture suggested that, *once committed to a relationship*, these women lost their concept of an independent other and insidiously became more and more insecure about their values and wishes, amalgamating them with those of their loved one.

Thus, in relation to their partners, these women acted as though they had surrendered their judgement, their values, and their sense of identity—in all, their autonomy. Intimidated by their partners' authority, they tolerated inconsiderate, irritable, and critical behaviours, which devalued and limited their autonomy. Even though outside their marital relationship they were active, productive, and efficient, their self-images did not integrate these qualities with their domestic worlds. Instead, the affect state of their significant other determined their own sense of value and well-being. Intimidated and submissive, they were nonetheless also aware of their partners' vulnerabilities. However, they acted as though it was their responsibility to justify those vulnerabilities by avoiding all confrontations. They experienced intense guilt if they failed to provide their partners with the expected support. A more assertive, reality-oriented, and demanding attitude made them question their own femininity and inspired concerns about being abandoned by their partners.

This constellation showed the woman investing her partner with the qualities of an ego-ideal to which she showed great deference. However, the so idealized character appeared to be envious and to covet her talents, her autonomy, and her possessions. In an apparent misplaced maternal empathy and dedication, she treated him as a vulnerable and rivalrous little child.

These observations pointed to an underlying concept the woman had of her role: to be the tamer of her partner's irritability, vengefulness, and attacks of rage. We saw her trying to justify his moods, to "understand" him, while bringing him back to reason. In other words, *she considered her responsibility to regulate his affects.*

None of these women could articulate their needs and disillusionment in a meaningful way, either to themselves or to their partners. Disappointment and the experience of emotional sterility in the relationship could only be expressed through symbolic performances, such as forgetfulness, losing objects, fleeting inattentiveness.

Why this barrier to awareness of her thoughts? For the woman, the man was seen in two different roles: the despotic frustrating master and the vulnerable child in need of protection and care. It took some time to realize that her turning from her first perception of her partner to the second seemed to happen when his irritation and anger made her aware of her disdain for him, an awareness that she feared. At that precise instant, in a reversal of roles, she attributed his irrational reaction to her supposed wrongdoing, invalidating her perception by acting guilty and solicitous. *Therefore, what was unacceptable was a conscious knowledge of her devalued image of her partner.*

Having in mind the fate of the beautiful maiden who was companion to the king at night but lived in fear of being beheaded every dawn, years ago I named this constellation of symptoms the "Scheherazade syndrome" (Abelin-Sas, 1994). Scheherazade, a mythical creature, lived in fear every day of losing her head. King Schahriar, who had been betrayed by his wife, overcame his humiliation by every morning killing a young virgin with whom he had spent the night.[2] Obsessed by the image of woman-as-betrayer, able to humiliate him before his court, King Schahriar finds no solution to his defeat other than to exterminate all women, lest one of them ever again expose him to his helplessness, his castration. Through her thousand and one stories, her voice, and her wisdom, Scheherazade manages to escape the inevitable death sentence, obtaining one more day of life so that, at the end of each day, she can provide an ending to the story she had left unfinished the night before.

In our own reading we see her eliciting the curiosity of this child–man, whose compulsion to kill does not differentiate between one woman and the next. As a loving mother would do in order to alleviate her child's insecurity at bedtime, she creates a world of fantasy and art. She succeeds in differentiating herself from the witchlike castrator and finds a way to lead this child/king out of his monothematic nightmare. And so, in a dreamlike process, the king's propensity for action is translated into words, as Scheherazade's stories replace his narrow reality with hundreds of fictional characters. Through their experiences, wisdom, and humanity, the king, a sanguinary baby grown omnipotent, relearns laughter and sorrow and begins once again to perceive the value of life, words, poetry, and love.

Through a thousand and one "sessions", Scheherazade performs the miracle of interrupting the repeated killings. She uses her creativity not only to win over the master–baby, but to uncover the potent man hidden under the castrated master: a man now able to love, create, and procreate. In the end she becomes the king's wife, and we learn that they had conceived three children during the thousand and one nights.

But let us keep in mind that Scheherazade herself was in an impossible situation. Her creativity was forced to be totally *invested* in placating the king's vengeance; at the same time, she was constantly threatened by his power over her.

Looking into the lives of these women, or into this fictional story created more than ten centuries ago, we find a woman who believes that she will be sentenced to death—metaphorically no longer loved, abandoned—unless she cures her partner's sense of humiliation and castration.

The psychodynamics of this constellation

As we just mentioned, the woman, unable to accept her feelings, did not verbally confront her partner. Instead, inattentiveness, indifference, or neglect became symbolic expressions of her dissatisfaction and disillusionment. Unable to read the latent message, question it, and self-reflect, her mate responded in a similar modality. His attempt to cancel out an intolerable image of failing as her ego-ideal (a narcissistic castration)resulted in a symbolic act: impotent rage.

The woman's difficulty in confronting him perpetuated his omnipotence. In fact, instead of bringing the problem to a fully conscious level of awareness, she fearfully altered the scene: her man became her distressed child while she became his concerned and guilty mother, as though she had indeed injured him.

Offering her man the promise of undoing his sense of failure through the sacrifice of her awareness contributed to his illusion that strength is obtained by "beheading" her. It could be argued that becoming the victim of an omnipotent, unruly child puts the woman in a special position of power: a unique moderator of his human aspects. In this master-and-slave concept of relating, each of them is an equal participant in a state of affairs that leads to tragedy. *This situation cannot change unless the woman overcomes her terror of seeming to be intensely aggressive by accepting her own power, realizing that she is entitled to be an assertive, creative, autonomous adult.*

Of course, the outcomes of a woman's difficulty to assume power in relation to her partner and/or indeed in relation to her public life can be many and varied. Sometimes she will react resentfully or with open anger to her partner's assertiveness. At other times, feeling utterly dejected in her own self-devaluation and envious of his more fulfilled position, she will become devaluating and disrespectful. When envious of her partner's display of joy, she may even become severely authoritarian, *expecting a similar destiny for her partner.*

Determinants of the concept of assertion as immoral and dangerous

We have noted that the woman fears that if she grows, she will appropriate a function that does not belong to her—one that might even hurt her partner. She feels intensely guilty and anticipates punishment (abandonment, loss of feminine identity) if she becomes independent and is seen as assertive and potent.

It is as though the woman unconsciously connects being influential and in command with being a castrating witch. This taboo can lead her to think of herself as immoral. In consequence, she may at times negate her own power, relinquishing knowledge of her abilities, judgement, expertise, and status. (In one such situation, a wife unknowingly provided her husband with the main ideas that permitted him to graduate with honours from a prestigious university. In another, a candidate's wife completely rewrote her husband's doctoral thesis, she told me this months after beginning her treatment.)

We have found that for many women, the anatomical differences destine her to submission and to a sense of responsibility. Her concern with appropriating masculine traits leads her to equate her power with immorality. Although in some cases this could be the result of an unconscious, envious wish to destroy maleness, it betrays her failure to believe that both sexes are entitled to creativity and power. This may explain the sense of shame that overcomes her when there is no man in her life, or the sense of utter despair at imagining herself alone (without love, home, or the ability to survive).

We will now briefly explore this aspect of the dynamic between the partners. In this, I will again quote Freud's lecture on femininity, as he refers to the transference of the woman's maternal relationship to her husband.

> The determinants of women's choice of an object are often made unrecognizable by social conditions. Where the choice is able to show itself freely, it is often made in accordance with the narcissistic ideal of the man whom the girl has wished to become. If the girl has remained in her attachment to her father—that is, in the Oedipus complex—her choice is made according to the paternal type. Since, when she turned form her mother to her father, the hostility of her ambivalent relation remained with her mother, a choice of this kind should guarantee a happy marriage. But very often the outcome is of a kind that presents a general threat to such a settlement of the conflict due to ambivalence. The hostility that has been left behind follows in the train of the positive attachment and spreads over on to the new object. The woman's husband, who to begin with inherited form her father, becomes after a time her mother's heir as well. So it may easily happen that the second half of a woman's life may be filled by the struggle against her husband, just a as the shorter first half was filled by her rebellion against her mother. [Freud, 1933, p. 133]

Certainly the woman might transfer her hostility from mother to husband. In a marital regression, both partners might transfer

experiences of early childhood, with either parent, to their partner. There is also a singular way in which a woman may remain
linked harmfully to her mother. Depending on the quality of
their relationship and on the mother's personality, as well as her
unconscious and overt relationship to the other gender, the girl
might even fear that her own growth may put her mother's power
and strength at risk. This may be an obligatory passage for many
women and one that poses many problems for them.[3]

Clinical vignette: "Cher"

I present here a dream brought by Cher, who in the course of a
difficult process of differentiation from her ailing mother demonstrates some of the anxieties to which I am referring:

*I dreamt that I was in a place like my country house. There was a large
mirror on the wall. I could see a crack beginning in the lower right-hand
corner. I was frightened, because I could foresee that the whole wall,
which was made out of glass, was going to shatter into pieces and come
tumbling down. I started to scream for my husband.*

Through analysis, we began to uncover a fundamental unconscious situation with her mother like the one present in her
fantasies with men.

She had consulted after the miscarriage of her second pregnancy, which had precipitated a serious state of depression: she
reproached herself for having been unable to keep her baby
alive. We learned that her self-reproach somehow corresponded
with the guilt she had felt on reproaching her mother for having
left the family for a few weeks with no explanation when she,
the daughter, was about 3 years old. Due to Cher's hospitaliza-
tion for her miscarriage, she had been forced to leave her own
3-year-old daughter at home, the way she had been left at that
same age. But, most important, the walls tumbling down in her
dream led the way to an unconscious fantasy: that as long as
she and her mother were one, she could keep her mother alive.
This woman disregarded her own intellectual achievements and
the depth of her emotional attachment to others as though she

judged herself by the extent to which she and her mother were alike. This confusion of identities is not unusual.

This is an internal mother whose life and power depends on the daughter's immature mirroring. It might demonstrate the unconscious interchangeability of concepts such as "big", "powerful", "mother", and "phallic". Their equation would lead the woman towards this particular mirroring, where she must remain small in relation to a powerful adult whose strength depends on her smallness. Any commitment to a man would threaten this mother–daughter system, replicated later on with her partner.[4] This particular situation:

▷ demands that the woman remain a submissive daughter to complete her mother's strong image;

▷ promotes the repetition of the same situation with her partner;

▷ defines her own womanhood as necessitating "completion" through her partner.

A new generation

Considering in this way the female patients whom I have observed in the prime of life over the last 30 years (I am referring here to white middle-class American and South American women living in New York City), they presented—unlike the women who seek my help today—the following central issues that impeded attaining contentment:

1. being unable to give up the feeling that a social assertive stance was robbing the man of his central role, as well as their own mother of a role of authority;

2. considering that their partner was the one to carry out their own de-centred, displaced ambition;

3. feeling more and more troubled and disappointed in their idealization of their partner and, as a result, turning into his fiercest critic.

But culture has evolved and has had an intense impact on the ways in which women experience their femininity, and the same pertains to men. Today's young woman in America has had sexual experiences that have permitted her to be aware of her patterns of sexual excitement, her conditions for obtaining pleasure, and her demands for the achievements of her partner, be the relationship heterosexual or homosexual. She has ambitions of her own that don't centre on her acquiring them through her partner.

The last four decades have witnessed great cultural changes that impact on the roles of women and men, with new challenges and possibilities. Legalized abortion permits the woman to influence the timing of pregnancy, or to surmount obstacles to pregnancy by means of donor eggs and surrogate motherhood, to mention only two. These revolutionary changes demand corresponding changes in gender theory.

The concept of gender relationship has profoundly changed for both sexes. Roles are easily interchangeable in the household, and both sexes show a multiplicity of expressions of their masculine and feminine tendencies that are far from being categorically established.

In the newer generations conflicts are based less on gender-expected behaviours and more on the appreciation and tolerance of complementarities and differences between the partners' temperaments.

Those marked changes do create a conflict between the woman's career and her wish to establish a family. She might find herself in the terrifying situation of having compromised herself by delaying motherhood while searching for achievement. We now find issues of a different order, such as:

1. the struggle to settle the uncertainty of roles that has resulted from the woman entertaining wishes different from those of previous generations, for which she has few models, mainly in terms of gender roles;

2. differentiating her maternal role from her ambivalent identifications with her own mother, mainly in relation to her mother's concept of gender roles;

3. putting into perspective her fantasized expectations of gender

roles and ideals, learning to tolerate her disappointments, and regulating her demands for power and her aggression towards her partner.

Autonomy and self-definition have been acquired by this younger generation. No longer dependent on their men, these women think that commitment and maternity could affect their self-sufficiency. They often feel overwhelmed by the tasks they have taken on. No longer idealizing their partner, they demand equality—a demand that is at times inappropriate in relation to their partner's potential.

Summary

It has been suggested (Glocer Fiorini, 2007) that the intersection of femininity, sexuality, and maternity is the locus of women's subjectivity. I would only add that as a result, female identity evolves throughout the life span. This constant redefinition takes place in relation to both genders as well as to changing life, personal, and social circumstances—biological changes, levels of desire, power relations, love, maternity, and work.

In thinking about Freud's opinions about women—leaving aside the historical constraints of the times—I wonder whether he succeeded in describing and adopting women's own defensive positions. Rather than uncovering and analysing the unconscious infantile principles that promoted those fixed masochistic defences, was "the dark continent" possibly the name he gave to the blind spot he shared with his female patients?

In that sense, we have learned that analytic listening requires a constantly open and adventurous mind. We analysts have a responsibility to stimulate a woman's curiosity and acquaint her with the principles and unconscious narratives that guide her relationship to her body, her gender, her sexuality. We may help her to become aware of the singular creative organization of her experiences and fantasies, her unknown theories, and their genesis and, in this way, offer her the potential freedom to undo forced identifications due to circumstantial events in her life and thus clarify her "dark continent" for herself and her analyst. We could help her centre on the problems that she encounters negotiating with the norms and expectations of her immediate intimate and cultural surroundings, the way she feels about being a woman and a mother, her theories and expectations about men, about what attracts her and what ignites her desire. We might thus help her gain the knowledge that may lead her to greater satisfaction with herself and others, independently of gender.

Notes

1. I am indebted to the many authors whose work has profoundly influenced my thinking (Abraham, 1966; Bergmann, 2000; Cornell, 1991; Fliegel, 1982; Galenson, 1971; Galenson & Roiphe, 1971; Greenacre, 1958; Grossman & Kaplan, 1988; Herzog, 2001; Horney, 1933; Irigaray, 1985b; L. J. Kaplan, 1991; M. Kaplan, 1990; Kestenberg, 1956, 1968; Kubie, 1975; Lax, 1990; Lichtenstein, 1961; Reich, 1940, 1953; Rocah, 2009; Spitz, 1962).

2. It seems that multiple sources contributed to the emergence of this extraordinary compendium of stories, which, under the title *The Thousand and One Nights*, first reached Europe through a French translation (Galland) at the beginning of the eighteenth century. Yet the book had actually acquired most of its elements as early as the tenth century. From India, from the Arab world, from Persia, and from Judaic tradition, stories were absorbed into the book the way a long, deep river embraces many tributaries. Multiple authors from multiple cultures gave birth to this Muslim production.

3. Through different methodologies, researchers in other fields have found data that help us in this inquiry. Carol Gilligan, in her 1982 study on college students, found that women's sense of obligation and sacrifice overrides the ideal of equality. Women measure their own value by the amounts of responsibility and caring they feel, while defining their sense of identity in relation to their connection with other people. They avoid causing pain and are keenly aware of their own sense of vulnerability, dependency, and fear of abandonment. Some years earlier, Jean Baker Miller (1976) had demonstrated that for women the total loss of a relationship was experienced as a total loss of self, and that this reaction was consistent with their putting greater value on their affiliations with others than on their own self-enhancement.

4. Julia Kristeva (1989) alerted women to this identification with mother—mother as the symbol of the absence of the phallus. In order for her to become a "subject" ("person") rather than an "object" ("thing"), the woman must identify with her mother's desire for a man. Only a "primary

identification" with her father might enable the woman to undo her attachment to the mother as the representation of a loss or of a lack.

Kristeva, in a Lacanian framework, and Jessica Benjamin (1991), in an object relations one, both come to a similar conclusion: in the pre-symbol of phallic presence. For Benjamin, girls need to identify with their fathers not only in order to deny the helplessness of the rapprochement crisis, but also in order to confirm that she is the subject of desire. Benjamin feels that the idealization of the phallus and the wish for missed love identification with father inspire adult women's fantasies about loving men who represent their ideals.

Identificatory love with father is indeed important but might not be sufficient to interrupt the phallus = penis confusion to which I referred earlier. On the other hand, according to Kristeva, if the female sees "mother" as a representation of "lack", it may be due to her failure to integrate the concepts of generativity and strength into her concept of "mother".

8

Autonomy and womanhood

Mary Kay O'Neil

Freud's views on women's psychosexual development were based on two premises: (1) Human beings are psychologically bisexual and develop predominantly feminine or masculine identity during two developmental stages: the oedipal and puberty. (2) All women as girls experience "penis envy" when they discover that males possess something they lack. Unable to revise his theory of female development in the light of metapsychological theory and to integrate his later insights into his early formulations, Freud held fast to these basic premises.

"Femininity" (1933) is a restatement of Freud's earlier papers on women: "Some Psychical Consequences of the Anatomical Differences Between the Sexes" (1925j) and "Female Sexuality" (1931b). By 1933, Freud realized that "the development of a little girl into a normal woman is more difficult and more complicated" (1933, p. 117) than that of a boy. Despite doubts, he could not allow that women's development followed a course separate from that of men, perhaps because of his awareness that psychoanalytic knowledge was not yet sufficient "to pursue the behaviour of femininity through puberty to the period of maturity" (p. 131). However, Freud's new acknowledgment of the vicissitudes of the mother–daughter relationship opened the door for understanding the impact of mothers and motherhood on a girl's development of her womanhood: "we knew, of course, that there had been a preliminary stage of attachment to the mother, but we did not know that it could be so rich in content and so *long-lasting* and could leave behind so many opportunities for fixations and dispositions" (p. 119, italics added). Recognizing that knowledge about femininity was incomplete, Freud challenged analysts "to enquire from your own experiences of life, or turn to the poets, or wait until science can give you deeper and more coherent information" (p. 135).

Beyond Freud, psychoanalytic theory of the psychology of women progressed with the well-documented historical controversy over primary and secondary femininity, which raged in the 1920s, was silenced for a time, and reawakened five decades later (1960s and 1970s) in the light of new scientific evidence and the emerging voices of feminism. This controversy centred around the questions: Is a woman born a woman psychologically, or is she made a woman when she discovers she is not a man? And "is anatomy destiny"? By the mid 1920s this controversy resulted in two differing theoretical positions: (1) Freud, Helene Deutsch, and Jeanne Lampl de Groot subscribed to the theory that until the oedipal period the development of both sexes is essentially identical (masculine), and only with the discovery of her lack of a penis does the identity and personality of the girl diverge. (2) Karen Horney, Ernest Jones, and Otto Fenichel subscribed to the point of view that gender identity—that is, femaleness—is an inborn phenomenon and that conscious awareness and pleasure in feminine identity—in being a girl—is present from the earliest awareness of one's sense of self.

By the mid 1960s psychoanalysts had become aware of new research into the biological underpinnings of sexual functioning (Sherfey, 1966). There followed a resurgence of interest in revising the psychoanalytic theory of female development. By the 1970s many analysts maintained that core gender identity belongs to the first year of life, penis envy is more often to be considered a defensive manoeuvre, and the capacity for orgasm is not dependent on emotional maturity. Ticho (1976) summarized much of the profession's acceptance of primary femininity: "There seems to be little doubt that girls do not want to become men but want to develop into independent autonomous women." The notion, "anatomy is destiny" had been put to rest. That is, psychoanalytic theory no longer held that a woman becomes a woman only when she discovers she is not a man—that is, does not have a penis. Nor does she become complete only when she has a baby—preferably a boy—with a man. Freud's phallic centrism—the Achilles heel of psychoanalysis—had become seriously challenged. As Easser (1975) asserted: "A woman is a complete individual even when she is not involved in heterosexual relationships or in a pregnant state or in the act of mothering",

With the recognition of primary femininity, the mother–daughter relationship was given a primary position in psychoanalytic thought. Primary femininity, however, "is no longer a unitary concept, but rather encompasses a related group of ideas about the female body and mind" (Kulish, 2000). Psychoanalytic theory eventually incorporated a balanced view of separate preoedipal development for both sexes. Gender theory recognized the independence and interdependence of gender and sexual identity. Gender role identity grew out of core gender identity influenced by gender differences in object relations and the context of social norms. The oedipal myth was questioned as the paradigm for women's psychosexuality. It was asserted that other myths provide a better paradigm (e.g. the Persephone myth, Holtzman & Kulish, 2000, 2003). Femininity and masculinity are considered parallel constructs: neither is the single natural state. The notion of universal bisexuality remains relevant, only the balance differs for each gender (see Elise, 1997).

Each woman, in her development as both subject and object, as Chodorow asserts, "creates her own psychological gender through emotionally and conflictually charged unconscious fantasies that help construct her inner world, that projectively imbue cultural conceptions, and that interpret her sexual anatomy. By making some unconscious fantasies and interpretations more salient than others, each woman creates her own prevalent animation of gender" (1996, p. 215). The rise of object relations theory, studies of infants and children, developmental research, gender research, and the role of psychosocial factors and life events coalesced with analysts' clinical observations to further understanding of women's development. According to Tyson: "a generally accepted, comprehensive, and integrated theory of female development, psychology, and sexuality has yet to emerge. Important controversies remain unresolved" (2003, p. 119). Early controversies within female psychology have shifted to (among others) the complex process by which girls develop into *independent autonomous women*.

This chapter highlights what single case studies from the author's clinical and research experience can contribute to the psychoanalytic understanding of the development of a woman's autonomous self. Clinical experience is illustrated by the psychoanalysis of a middle-aged married woman (Gwen): specifically, her progress from a false to a true autonomy. Research experience is derived from psychoanalytically oriented interviews for a study of sole-support mothers in a programme that provides safe, affordable housing for them and their children while the mothers pursue post-secondary education.[1] One woman's story (Jenny) provides an example of contributors (other than psychoanalysis) to a woman's autonomous self.

The concept of the autonomous self is not discretely defined within psychoanalytic theory. Autonomy, one attribute of the self, includes the partially overlapping concepts of sense of identity, separation–individuation, narcissism, attachment, and object relations. The term "autonomous self" was borrowed from Scharff's 1994 book on John D. Sutherland's work.

> Sutherland believed that a distinct self is present from birth, and that an innate organizing principle guiding development of the self is present from the beginning. And . . . effective development of the self rests on a joyful, empathic responsiveness from the mother. The infant can readily tolerate various limited frustrations of particular behaviours if the overall feelings communicated by the mother, and later the father, come from their genuine unqualified joy in the baby as it is. [Scharff, 1994, p. 303]

True and false autonomy are similar but not synonymous with Winnicott's "True and False Self":

> The True Self develops in an adequately empathic and caring maternal environment, but in its absence a False Self evolves to protect the True Self from adverse maternal influence. The True Self is first present at the inception of primitive mental organization simply as "the summation of sensory-motor aliveness (Winnicott, 1960, p. 149). It then becomes the psychological sense of the several ways in which a particular individual

experiences himself as being alive and real—authentic. [Bacal
& Newman, 1990, pp. 191–192]

Further theoretically exciting and clinically stimulating ideas about
autonomy have emerged in more recent psychoanalytic literature.
Kramer-Richards (1996) reviewed nine books (including the work
of European analysts) about the analysis of women and the interface between intrapsychic and social issues. These issues (such
as sexuality, motherhood, achievement in work, and relational
interdependence) reflect on women's autonomous development
and fulfilment. Psychoanalytic notions about autonomy seem particularly pertinent when considering women's dependence/inde-
pendence or attachment/separation tensions to which Freud had
alluded in his emerging awareness of the girl's rich and long-lasting
preoedipal attachment to her mother and its sequelae in her own
mothering capacity.

    The development of autonomy is only part of self develop-
ment. Freud, having described "women [only] in so far as their
nature is determined by their sexual function", commented
that "an individual woman may be a human being in other respects" (1933, p. 135). This chapter takes up Freud's challenge
to try to understand women beyond their sexual function by
addressing key aspects of autonomy: motherhood and womanhood.[2] Gwen illustrates how unresolved identity conflicts lead to
a false autonomy. Resolution of these conflicts, especially within
the mother–daughter relationship, as played out in the transfer-
ence/countertransference, led to a truer autonomous self.[3] Jenny
provides support for an hypothesis about sole-support mothers: a
sense of responsibility for a child can be a woman's *prime* psychological growth stimulator; other influences, such as personal history, maternal identifications, relationship patterns, coping styles,
and social supports, are, for these women, *secondary* contributors
to the growth of their autonomy.

Clinical vignette: "Gwen"

Gwen[4] had achieved all external manifestations of separation–
individuation, maturity, and autonomy.[5] She was a 52-year-old
professional woman with two young-adult sons; she had recently

separated after 29 years of marriage. For three months she told no one that her husband had left. Neurotic denial was her defence against shock and shame. Outrage as she acknowledged the identity of the other woman, immense anger at her husband's betrayal, and a brother's advice precipitated her call for help.

Trauma had reactivated Gwen's characteristic disavowal (denial of what she knew). An exceptionally well-organized woman, she "forgot" to attend her sixth session. In her next session, shocked that her mind could play such tricks, she wondered whether she wanted to keep talking to me. Interpretation of her fear of dependency and wish to avoid painful feelings allowed her to continue. In tears, she poured out her distress about her difficulty in acknowledging her needs, even to herself: she was always the caretaker. Tracing the major hurts of the marriage, she recognized that her denial of painful perceptions and affects had developed within her early assigned role of dutiful daughter. She then articulated the central motif of the analysis—the fantasy that symbolized her ego ideal and primary character defence: "As a young child, I memorized the story, "The Little Red Hen", and "so she did it herself" became my motto."[6] The unconscious fantasy underlying the Little Red Hen motto was enacted within her attachment pattern as well as the analytic relationship.

Gwen was the second child and first daughter of a self-made professional father and an upper-middle-class "at home" mother. Mother's gradually debilitating and eventually fatal illness and father's reactive addiction contributed to loss of parental nurturing and was adapted to by pseudo independence—"so she did it herself". A second type of loss—of opportunity for self-development and restriction of self-assertiveness—was also experienced. As the eldest daughter, Gwen became companion to mother and rescuer of father—a caretaking role that superseded personal aspirations. Gwen's unconscious fantasy was that if she dutifully "did it herself", she would compensate for the denied and painful real losses and prevent feared future loss (mother would not die). This self-sufficient role protected Gwen from the helplessness, passivity, and emotional isolation of depression and maintained her self-esteem. However, these character defences disintegrated with marital loss: being dutiful no longer prevented or compensated for real loss. Her depression, reactive to the current loss of her husband, was intensified by the unresolved depression due to earlier losses.

Gwen's first experience of loss of parental nurturing occurred just before age 3, when mother became depressed after a still-birth and father's addiction began. A curious, gregarious, and verbal child, she coped with parental unavailability by meeting her own needs and conforming to expectation. Lack of parental attunement to her emotional needs continued into adolescence. Although she identified with positive parental aspects to develop ego strengths and object constancy, expression of these strengths was restricted by her dutiful role and internalization of a critically exacting mother and shame about father.

Brilliant academically, she gave up her professional goals to care for mother. At 22, she married a man who had achieved her own thwarted educational aspirations. In spite of external multifaceted compatibility, the marriage was difficult. Her husband's narcissistic hunger led her to adapt her lifestyle to his needs: to stop her studies and work while creating a stable family and raising emotionally mature and successful sons. She "chose" to ignore what she knew intuitively—that her husband's emotional hunger was insatiable and that because of marked character problems related to early deprivation, he could not be there for her. Psychic/physical costs of her denial and obsessive defences were great: abandonment of her needs for husband's respect and support, and laparotomy for a spastic bowel.

Gwen's analysis, lasting seven years, initially focused on her incapacitating depression over her marital breakdown. Her self-esteem somewhat restored within the analytic relationship, she divorced her husband. When she was less devastated and more empowered, focus shifted to intrapsychic conflicts. Her first dream revealed her central conflict:

My husband returned to our bed, he had his arm around me, I felt his weight on me increasing, I felt protected and held yet extremely frightened; I awoke in panic.

She wished to be protectively held yet feared suffocation by duty and helplessness. She connected her panic to the facts that despite her own efforts as a dutiful daughter and wife, her mother had literally suffocated to death, and her husband's emotional neglect and self-absorption had suffocated her needs and their marriage. Being able to trust and depend upon her analyst (she did not have to analyse herself), she gradually allowed herself to trust her perceptions and reveal her feelings. Grief poured out in almost daily tears; feelings of rage, helplessness and self-blame were articulated.

After several years, Gwen interrupted her analysis to retool professionally. This was interpreted as the act of a young adult leaving home to find herself; the secure base was there to return to. Within the positive transference the analyst was a healthy mother/loyal husband whom she could leave for her needs without damaging either of us. This year of separation contributed to working through her Little Red Hen defence. She came to understand that being dutiful meant doggedly and cheerfully persisting, with no option of separation from mother (who might die) or husband (marriage would fail) to meet her own needs. Returning to analysis, usual breaks aroused separation anxiety and provided opportunity for interpretative work, which facilitated self-sufficiency, assertiveness, and capacity to bear the sadness of loss.

Readiness for termination gradually became evident. With grief over loss now resolved, she was no longer depressed. With decreased disavowal and denial, her ability to find words for her perceptions and ways of meeting her needs increased. When she actively divorced her husband, her capacity for self-assertion and self-esteem increased. At her son's wedding, she spoke movingly about her understanding that separation need not mean loss, and attention to one's needs within a relationship is possible. Understanding her contribution to the marital break-down (passive–aggressive dutiful victim role) led to increased mutual dependency gratification with significant others. ("My marriage had to be wrecked, I couldn't afford the price of keeping up a false front, and there was a solid basic self somewhere."). She now competed comfortably (in a dream, she *"twisted the nose of that other woman"*, defacing and rendering her powerless). More accepting of limitations and less critical with a decrease in guilt, shame, and rage, she felt ready to separate by ending her analysis.

Nevertheless, planning termination evoked anxiety, sadness, and tears over impending loss. Competitive impulses, passive aggressive anger, and envy were interpreted during the termination phase. For example: she expressed anger at my challenging her passivity about completing a goal ("how dare you upset me, you should be making me feel better"). Uncharacteristic delay in payment was interpreted: "Maybe you can feel freer to leave me if you put into words your anger at my need to be paid (like mother's need to be cared for) rather than expressing this non-verbally by not paying my bill". Eventually, she expressed feelings of loss of the analyst, "This has been one of the closest relationships I have ever had, we reached a depth of communication unknown to me before", and to acknowledge previously inhibited empathy; "as I realized my feelings about ending, I thought it must be hard for you also to let go of a long-term close relationship like we have had. I hope you feel a sense of pride and satisfaction that you helped me". With the reworking of central issues, especially conflicts around the dutiful daughter role, Gwen's analysis terminated well.

Yet it was not until the post-termination enactment of the Little Red Hen motto that the depth and strength of this unconscious fantasy became clear. She had had a good holiday but "felt very alone with no one just for me. At times I felt resentful you weren't there." I interpreted, "You feared I would not be available to you if you are not ill and that you must handle feelings alone." She was proud about talking over problems with family and friends, but "I never told anyone how I felt about finishing analysis". Astonished, "I can't believe I did it again", she had reacted to our separation as she had reacted to her husband's leaving: she spoke about it to no one for three months. This enactment enabled us to track incidents in relation to her mother, husband and now analyst in which Gwen felt hope and excitement in asserting or enjoying herself followed by an illness or reversion to a self restrictive dutiful role.

The last part of the Little Red Hen analogy, "She ate it all herself" became understandable. The Little Red Hen was angry for having been left to do it all herself. She had acknowledged that my final bill was the only one she had not paid before her vacation. I commented that she "had eaten my bread for 3 months". Gwen was also able to tolerate an understanding that her behaviour could evoke negative reactions in others (I was not without annoyance at the delay in payment). Acceptance with impunity of angry envy consolidated awareness of the passive-aggressive side of her dutiful daughter role. She commented, "I know I've changed, I feel this movement in me. OK life, here I am!"

Research vignette: "Jenny"

Jenny, 23, had a 3-year-old daughter and was in the second year of studies towards a Bachelor's Degree. She had been in the sole-support mothers' programme for two years and was interviewed on three occasions.[7] On an objective research scale, Jenny rated high on autonomy. Through the "research" interviews it became clear how her autonomy had developed. In her first interview, she spoke about herself in a matter-of-fact, emotionally integrated way. Living with her "irresponsible" boyfriend while pursuing education and working full-time to support them, she had become pregnant. With difficulty but with characteristic resiliency she stopped school and she had her baby, whom she breast-fed. Within four months, she was raising her baby alone while living on welfare. During her daughter's first year, she thought, "I don't see my life or my child's going anywhere". She found the facilitating programme for single mothers and returned to her studies.

Throughout her second interview, Jenny wept because: "I don't know to what extent I have grown as a woman. I spent the year pushing myself to meet academic demands, but the better I do academically, the less well I do at home. An 'A' means my daughter goes to grandparents or a babysitter. With me she watches TV, without the stability and cuddling she needs, so I can study. I tell myself I am right providing for the future, but I completely miss the present." Jenny experienced intense conflict between motherhood and her own advancement.

By the third interview, Jenny empathetically discussed her own and her daughter's advancement, despite ambivalent conflict. Obviously intelligent (straight 'A's) persistent, and resourceful, with well-developed coping skills, she aims for a Masters degree to teach underprivileged children. How did Jenny get to be this way, and what facilitated her growth?

Jenny described her personal history of abuse, neglect, and loss as "consistently—inconsistent". The home of her early childhood was violent and lacked basic necessities. Her parents, both substance abusers, separated when she was 3. She didn't see her father again until age 7. Within the year, she was placed in foster care, and from age 7 to 18 attended seven schools and moved 13 times between mother and foster parents.

Mother had a first son at 15, Jenny at 21, and then three other boys from different fathers. The children were in foster care during the week and with mother (described as totally self absorbed and unable to nurture) on weekends. Locked in or out of the house, Jenny often followed mother to bars, to get the house keys to look after the family. Her foster parents were described as loving, caring, good listeners, but strict and very firm believers in a fundamentalist religion. Central to Jenny's story is her caretaker role of herself, brothers, boyfriend, daughter, and the other women in the programme. Currently, this role has culminated in her founding a successful summer camp for foster children.

Jenny has a negative identification with her birth mother, who deeply hurt her, physically and psychologically. She asks, "Am I angry? No, because I also learned what not to do and I learned a lot by taking care of my brothers. I am sad for my mother and for children like myself and my siblings. So I have a soft spot for foster children." Although separated from her father, she later developed an emotionally distant relationship with some positive identification with him. As she says, "I admire what he did—it is very difficult to leave your wife and child to quit drugs. If he had stayed, bad things could have happened to me given the state he was in." Her foster mother—a nurturing stay-at-home mother with constraining rules—taught the value of structure and loving support. Her foster father was also strict but accepting. They were "very religious and consequently controlling without intending to be, but their intentions were good". She realized that she "needed to separate herself from the beliefs of her parents to become an individual. Between my two sets of parents I found a balance as to where I would like to be as a parent." Jenny used both positive and negative identifications to differentiate herself from her parental models and seems to have achieved a degree of autonomy.

Jenny has a "secure" internal working model (as measured on an attachment scale) that was hard-won because of her "consistently inconsistent" background. As a foster child, she wondered why she wasn't adopted—was something wrong with her? She pushed hard at school and in sports, music, and art, to make herself accepted, loved, and loveable. She feels guilt, remorse, and anger over her nurturing/academic conflict yet struggles rather than denies ambivalent feelings about raising a child while pursuing her education. She also struggles with meeting her womanly needs in a relationship with a man. Her ability to establish relationships with more responsible men and to manage hurtful break-ups has been growing, but she is not yet ready for commitment. She maintains mutually supportive friends. Both giving and receiving in our interviews, she used the semi-interpretative comments offered to self reflect.

To understand Jenny's development from a psychoanalytic perspective, it is useful to consider her psychological make-up as it affected her progress towards autonomy. Jenny had the constellation of strengths that enabled her to be research-categorized as a resilient woman with a secure internal model of attachment. Freud (1924c) believed that anxiety appears as fear of loss of the object and fear of loss of the object's love; he later recognized the importance of the mother–child bond for subsequent object relations. Jenny experienced parental loss and maternal rejection. She experienced anxiety and depression reactive to external circumstances (stress that was too severe for her adaptive defences). She had supportive substitute parents within a structured environment, and, to prove her worth and lovability, she used her intelligence to succeed at school, thereby developing a resourcefulness and resilience early on. She had both positive (foster mother) and negative (birth mother) maternal models.

Balsam (2000) described the subjective experience of internalizations, focusing on the daughter's inner world as she confronts the challenges of herself becoming a mother. Jenny learned maternal care taking by identifying with her foster mother and, unlike her birth mother, took responsibility to care for others. She lost her father early on, but he was not abusive and she realized that constructive relationships with men, though difficult, are possible. Jenny's capacity to deal with her ambivalence towards her child demonstrates the growth in her capacity for motherhood and womanhood. Despite a difficult year of her own physical illness, her daughter's severe asthma, the break-up of a love relationship, and marked conflict between mothering and her drive for achievement, Jenny has decreased her exacting standards (less rigid superego) and identified more realistic goals without losing her sense of self worth.

Discussion

Vaillant (2005) among many others, stresses that defences can be either adaptive or maladaptive. This is well illustrated in the two cases presented here. As with Gwen, Jenny's initial maladaptive defence was, superficially, adaptive to the situation. Through reaction formation (caring for someone else as one wishes to be cared for), she put aside her own needs to mother her siblings. Remnants of this defence are expressed in her conflict between caring for her daughter and achieving her academic goals. As her capacity for mothering grows, her maladaptive defence is becoming transformed to sublimation (summer camp for foster children). For Jenny, as with many of the 60 other women in the study, motherhood did catapult her into internal turmoil yet at the same time offered transformative opportunity. Given their traumatic backgrounds and difficult socio-economic circumstances, most of these women are, to varying degrees and using different defences, developing autonomous selves through motherhood to womanhood. Trad drew attention to this process:

> Parenthood, particularly motherhood, is one of the most common and powerful transformations in human experience. Recent clinical evidence suggests that the physiological and psychological transformations experienced by women while pregnant exert a significant impact on the relationship forged with the infant after birth. After childbirth, the new mother undergoes further transformation as the infant begins to manifest developmental autonomy. [Trad, 1990, p. 341]

The autonomous selves of these two women gradually emerged.[8] Gwen, through the analytic relationship (transference interpretation and identification with her woman analyst), grew from characteristic pseudo-independence to eventual recognition that her own needs and wishes are as important as those of others. Jenny grew through acceptance of maternal responsibility and recognition of her own and her child's individual needs. Gwen, in her middle years, emerged from a false to a true autonomy through analysis of her maladaptive defences (disavowal, intellectualization, reaction formation), to make room for the emergence of adaptive self-fulfilling strategies (affiliation, self-observation). Jenny did not—and probably will not—have the opportunity to have an analysis, but, given that her maladaptive defences at 23 were less solidified than Gwen's at 53, she was nevertheless able to grow when provided with a facilitating opportunity for self-development through education.

How does a woman's development of an independent autonomous self fit in with Freud's notion of 'Femininity"?

Freud's focus in 1933 was still on psychosexual development. His only nod to other aspects of development was his comment that "an individual woman may be a human being in other respects" (p. 135). Suffice it to say that both Gwen and Jenny were heterosexual with respect to gender identity, gender role identity, object choices, and behaviour. The autonomous self is not dependent on the orientation or nature of a person's psychosexual development. Just as sexuality and gender have a paradoxical and multidimensional structure (Harris, 1991), autonomy is complex, individualized, and relevant to men and women of all sexualities. Autonomy, like psychosexual development, is influenced by parental identifications and dis-identifications. As Chodorow (2000, p. 338) maintains, "The internal world and sense of self are formed developmentally, mainly through unconscious communications between mother and child." Despite positive maternal identifications, Gwen's and Jenny's problems stemmed from early life trauma and deprivations in the mother–daughter relationship. In keeping with Freud's recognition of the long-lasting effects of a girl's attachment to mother and, recalling the views of Sutherland and Winnicott regarding the deprivation of needed empathic responsiveness, both women developed similar character defences—care-taking at personal expense. As defensive aspects of care-taking gave way, both women began to relish their active and maternal potentials and were freed to find enjoyment in fulfilling their fantasies: travel (Gwen) and education (Jenny). Both were unlike their mothers—Gwen's mother was passive, dependent, and ill, and Jenny's was neglectful and abusive. Problems in relationships stemmed from subservience to needy men (emotionally hungry husband and irresponsible boyfriend), but positive paternal identifications promoted self-assertion. Freud, despite his inability to "pursue the behaviour of femininity through puberty to the period of maturity" (1933, p. 131), opened windows to reveal other aspects of femininity—here, autonomy.

In what way does the linking of "autonomy and womanhood" add to contemporary psychoanalytic thinking about women's development?

Often, within psychoanalytic thinking, independence and autonomy are conflated, and dependency is excluded as a facet of autonomy. The challenge is to further develop psychoanalytic thinking with regard to these concepts and to recognize that dependency is not necessarily incompatible with autonomy, nor is independence equivalent to autonomy. Undesirable circumstances forced Gwen and Jenny to live independently. True autonomy has to do with an inner sense of independence, a sense of wholeness—a woman's capacity to grow in self-confidence as a person, whether or not she is in a relationship or desirable circumstances. Akhtar (1999) refers to basic psychological needs that include the need for identity, recognition, and affirmation, for interpersonal and intrapsychic boundaries, optimal availability, and resilient responsiveness by one's love objects. These needs bring to the fore an essential facet of autonomy that has to do with mutual dependency within a relationship.

Autonomy is both intrapsychic and inter-subjective. As a final note, true autonomy eventually must include reciprocal relationships: the capacity to love in individualized form. Gwen having loved and raised a family and now hoping for a second more fulfilling relationship was finding generativity with sons, students, and younger persons fulfilling. Jenny, as her capacity to care for herself and her child increased, was defining and beginning to seek a responsible man. Benjamin's (1995) ideas on autonomy provide further support for the belief that true autonomy is not achieved without reciprocal attachment: recognition of one's own needs in relation to the needs of others:

> The concept of mutual recognition includes autonomy—or, rather, preserves and transforms it as a pole of the necessary tension of independence/dependence between subjects, of differentiation. To oppose the idea of recognition to that of autonomy would be misleading or self-contradictory, for it would deny the fact that recognition requires acceptance of the other's independence and unknowability. [Benjamin, 1995, p. 22]

Notes

1. This study, just completed, evaluated the Montreal Program "Project Chance". To achieve a psychoanalytic objective, the question "What can be learned (at conscious and unconscious levels) from these mothers about women's development: their motherhood, their womanhood and their autonomous selves?" was explored through an examination of the 100 author-conducted interviews with 60 of the mothers (40 current residents and 20 alumnae).

2. Freud uses the term "femininity" to discuss women's psychosexual development. Here, "womanhood" replaces "femininity" so that understanding of another aspect of a woman's development as a human being—the autonomous self—can be highlighted. "Motherhood", an aspect of womanhood, refers to the two sides of the mother–child relationship: being mothered and mothering.

3. Both parents play a vital role in the development of autonomy for boys and girls, as Ticho (1976), Benjamin (1995), and others have

emphasized. Although the importance of the father will become blatantly evident for both Gwen and Jenny, the role he plays in the development of his daughter's autonomy is less the focus of this chapter than is the role of the mother.

4. Pseudonyms are used for the two cases, and identifying information has been disguised as much as possible without distorting important elements of the history.

5. In the psychoanalytic literature, separation–individuation, maturity, and autonomy are often used interchangeably. An example of this is Clower's 1990 article.

6. The Little Red Hen found a grain of wheat and thriftily set out to make a loaf of bread. At each step she asked for help and was selfishly refused—"So she did it herself", efficiently and without complaint. When it came time to eat the bread, those who refused to help were then willing to participate. However, she ate the bread herself.

7. Using an essentially analytic interviewing approach to the personal and family history, I listened for underlying motivation, attachment patterns, especially maternal relationship, characteristic defences, and coping styles. Semi-interpretative comments attempted to further both mine and Jenny's understanding of her inner self. This approach was akin to what Cartwright (2004) described as a "psychoanalytic research interview". Participants are told the specific subject of the interview to provide the central context around which they are urged to associate (consciously and unconsciously). Stuart, in her research on "Work and Motherhood: A Psychoanalytic Study" (2007), used a similar approach, as did Kantrowitz in her work on patient–analyst match (1997).

8. Psychoanalytic understanding was based on object relations theory, with emphasis on attachment theory issues.

9

The psychoanalyst's implicit theories of gender

Emilce Dio Bleichmar

There is a great deal in the psychoanalytic literature about gender, spanning two decades. However, we find that, even today, neither its conceptual aspect nor its clinical application is clear. Whereas Freud wondered "What do women want?", femininity and feminine sexuality continue to be a riddle even now, in the twenty-first century.

There are several problematic issues related to the concept of gender: primary femininity, the place of the castration complex or penis envy and the importance of maternity in the subjectivity of many women, which have been much discussed and debated (Benjamin, 2004; Elise, 1997,1998a; Fast, 1990; Fritsch et al., 2001; Kulish, 2000; Lasky, 2000; Mayer, 1995; Richards, 1996; Torok, 1979; Tyson, 1982). Meissner (2005) states that our thinking about these matters has undergone significant change and that we may be drawing closer to a more comprehensive and meaningful understanding. However, despite intellectual acceptance of contemporary views of female development, many authors have found it difficult to assimilate these ideas fully in the clinical situation (Fritsch et al., 2001; Lax, 1995).

I have been working on the relation between the Freudian concept of primary femininity and contemporary views of gender (Dio Bleichmar, 1991, 1992, 1995, 1997, 2002, 2006, 2008), and in this endeavour have also encountered many difficulties for the acceptance of this close relation. One of these is the question whether the term primary femininity refers to a construct of self as female and feminine or to a sense of self specifically derived from the female body. Elise suggests that we should derive the term "sense of femaleness" from the female body and reserve the term "primary femininity" for feminine gender identifications and identity. However, she observes, "a primary sense of femaleness can never in reality be separated from social meanings of gender" (1997, p. 514). By introducing the idea of "social meanings of gender", I believe I can identify one of the difficulties in psychoanalysis for fully understanding and clinically applying this construct, which is so contemporary and important for female subjectivity. I refer to the implicit theory of a large part of the psychoanalytic community, which thinks that to speak in terms of "social meanings of gender" is foreign to psychoanalytic theories of development and, of course, to female development.

At this time, I consider that in order to clarify the relations between gender and female sexuality we should take into account contemporary psychoanalytic developments concerning the intersubjective structure of the self and sexuality in both Anglo-Saxon and French literature. This implies a major change in dichotomous thinking: sex and gender, femininity/masculinity, the rigid binary code of castration, the phallic logic of yes/no, have/have not, as described by Jean Laplanche in "Gender, Sex and Sexuality" (2007).

In this chapter I first briefly review theoretical proposals of several authors who maintain a perspective of development as an intersubjective (Beebe, Rustin, Sorter, & Knoublauch, 2005; Lyons-Ruth, 1999; Siegel, 2001) rather than a mono-personal process; I describe in greater detail the multiplicity and diversity of representations of the mother in the constitution of femininity, and I offer some clinical examples that illustrate the difference between the little girl's maternal representations as conscious and unconscious models of the self in contrast to her representations of her mother as an oedipal rival. By supporting a complex and multiple model of both self and sexuality, all clinical examples refer to a specific subjectivity that may find points of contact with others; even though they may be very general examples in our culture, they are not intended to be at all universal.

Sex, gender, and sexuality

I will open my theoretical review by borrowing the words with which Ruth Stein introduces one of the last works by Jean Laplanche:

> In a meditation that illuminates significant issues in American feminist and psychoanalytic theory, Laplanche's essay analyzes and distinguishes three interrelated terms, gender, sex and "the sexual ("*le sexuel*") or so-called "infantile sexuality".... What stands out in this paper no less than "*le sexuel*" is the use of the term "gender" by a French psychoanalyst, who is at once nodding in acknowledgment to contemporary American thinking. [Stein, 2007, p. 177]

Laplanche (2007) starts his paper with the following statement: "Gender is plural. It is usually twofold, masculine/feminine, but it is not so by nature. It is often plural, as in the history of languages and in social evolution" (p. 201); he then traces a chronological sequence, moving between adult and child: gender comes first, preceding sexuality; for him, the social unmistakably precedes the biological. What does this mean? What led John Money to propose the term "gender" in 1955 to designate the process of assignment made by doctors, parents, the town hall, the church, a declaration with assignment of the given name, assignment of parentage, and so on. "It is a boy! It is a girl!" This announcement, in turn, sets in motion a chain of dimorphous responses, beginning with the blue or pink colours in the crib and the baby's clothing, the use of pronouns, and the whole universe of varied behaviours that is transmitted from person to person and embraces all the people the subject encounters, day after day, from birth to death (Money & Ehrhardt, 1972). This conception of the role of others in the constitution of gender identity, highlighted by a neonatologist, was introduced into psychoanalysis by Robert Stoller (1968a). Laplanche, four decades later, also wants to stress that this assignment does not occur point by point, nor is it limited to a single act: it is a complex set of acts that extends into the significant language and behaviour of the family environment. The primacy of the other, the adult and language, are elements common to the conception of gender in both Money and Laplanche. The latter expresses it this way: "We can speak of an ongoing assignment or of an actual prescription. Prescription in the sense in which we speak of so-called "prescriptive" messages: in the order, then, of the message, indeed of the bombardment of messages" (2007, p. 213). And what I consider the most important consequence of this: "the precedence of assignment over symbolization" (p. 219).

This perspective on the structuring of human offspring places the child in the presence of adults, receiving all sorts of definitions from them about the self, all kinds of wishes, expectations, and demands about—among many others—how to be or not to be a feminine girl or a masculine boy. In Laplanche's words, "To speak of the small human being in this order is to put gender first" (2007, p. 212). He also highlights that the child/adult couple is to be conceived essentially not as one succeeding the other, but as one actually finding itself in the presence of the other.

In this text Laplanche (1992, 1997) adds gender to his theory on the primacy of the other in human development and draws close to positions and theories of American relational psychoanalysis when he states not only that gender is structured in the exchange of messages in the midst of the attachment relation and caregiving, but that gender is plural and not subject to any rigid code of oppositions such as passive/active, and raises the urgent need to find "models of symbolization which are more flexible, more multiple, more ambivalent thereby echoing contemporary interrogation" (p. 218). Jessica Benjamin (1988, 2004), Muriel Dimen (1991), Virginia Goldner (1991), and Adrienne Harris (1991), among other American analysts, have provided complex insights regarding the non-transparency, dense weave, and ambiguity of gender, as well as the dangers of its binary, divisive distributions.

A review of the literature shows that quite a number of authors understand that gender identity includes well-differentiated representations of the mother's and the father's body before the child comes to terms with the difference between sexes (Dio Bleichmar, 1991, 1997; Elise, 1997; Fast, 1979; Mayer, 1995; Person & Ovesey, 1983; Stoller, 1976; Tyson, 1982, 1994). These papers are joined by others based on direct observation of early development (Coates, 2006; de Marneffe, 1997; Roiphe & Galenson, 1981). Subjectively, nothing allows us to state that biological sex is intimately perceived, apprehended, and experienced by the child in any fashion that is separate or independent of gender, so that doubts and discussions on whether primary femininity is a construct of self as a female and feminine or a sense of self specifically derived from the girl's female body seem to be clarified. The little girl knows that her body is the same as her mother's and different from her father's—that is to say, she has representations of her female body, representations that have been formed through primary identification (Dio Bleichmar, 1997).

In the paradigm of intersubjectivity in human development (Lyons-Ruth, 1999, 2006), the concept of identification in development becomes more complex, since it takes place in the midst of an intimate relationship. Laplanche also joins this theoretical turn when he states that "assignment or 'identification as' completely changes the vector of identification" and suggests that if we understand primary identification as something generated in the adult towards the child, "Here I think there is a way to get out of the aporia of that 'beautiful' formulation of Freud's that has led to so much cogitation and commentary." With a fine irony, Laplanche (2007) proposes a solution to the riddle of primary identification with the father of personal prehistory, which is outstanding for its clarity and simplicity: "instead of 'identification with', 'identification by'" (p. 214). Thus, the girl not only identifies with the mother but is identified by the mother as a girl and hears herself referred to as "she", just as she is heard as referring to her mother and will be identified and referred to as "she" by her father, which is different from the person referred to as "he". Money (1988) accentuates this two-way process by adding another key piece: that simultaneously with the mutual recognition of sameness—mother and daughter— differentiation from those who are different also takes place: the girl is different from her father and the father identifies the girl as someone different from him.

The core of the idea of gender is that boys as much as girls recognize and identify with the father and mother, respectively, and are recognized and identified by the father and mother as a boy or girl who is the same as—or different from—themselves. This idea is based on the intersubjective structure that configures femininity and masculinity from birth to adulthood, since male and female traits are psychologically open and identity changes throughout life, as we have observed over the last century. The process of identification occurs very early, as Freud formulated it in his conception of primary identification, but it is a process initiated and maintained by adults before the human offspring, in turn, initiates the active process of identifying with the mother's femininity. And what is the mother's femininity? Her gender: her gestures, figure, and ways of relating. Therefore, what is important to emphasize is not to try to separate representations of the body and identifications as different processes, since communication occurs within the attachment relation.

> For communication does not only pass through the language of the body; also the social code, and these messages are especially messages of gender assignments, all those provided by the adults close to the child: parents, grandparents, brothers and sisters. Their fantasies, their unconscious or preconscious expectations. This domain has ultimately been very poorly explored, the domain of the unconscious relation of parents to their children. [Laplanche, 2007, p. 215]

The intersubjective aspect—the social meanings of gender—is constant throughout development, since the mother's and father's conscious and unconscious representations of the female or male are included in their modalities of interaction and in the way the couple relates to each other. The nucleus depends on the child's incorporation of a relationship rather than a figure, so that when children identify with their mother, the nucleus of identity they internalize is their mother's relationship with their father (Diamond, 2004).

Thus, the girl's identifications with her father or mother pertain not only to the Oedipus complex—that is to say, to the father as a sexual object and the mother as a rival—or to the parental couple as a sexual couple, but to their performance in general as a man and a woman—that is, their gender, in a much broader and general sense of masculinity and femininity.

One last comment in this brief theoretical review is that a large number of authors share intellectual acceptance and appreciate the importance of the contemporary psychoanalytic view of gender from an intersubjective perspective, but there is still a lag in relation to technical interventions in our clinical work. Laplanche says:

> In clinical psychoanalysis, generally speaking of "observations" that posit from the outset and without reflection: "the patient was a 30-year-old man or 19-year-old-woman, and so forth. Is the gender supposed to be nonconflictual to the point of being an unthought issue from the beginning? [Laplanche, 2007, p. 210]

The many mothers of the feminine self and intra-systemic conflict

Reproduced by permission

Frame 1. [Mafalda's little brother]:   "Hey, there's a guy here."

Frame 2. [Salesman]:   "Good afternoon, little girl, is your mother in?"
[Mafalda]:   "That depends. Which one?"

Frame 3. [Salesman]:   "What do you mean 'which one'? Just how many mommies have you got?"

Frame 4. [Mafalda]:   "One that I adore with all my heart . . . another that harasses me with her soup . . . another that protects me . . . another that yells at me . . . another that's happy at home . . . another that's enslaved for life to the house . . . another that . . ."

Frame 5. [Mother]:   "Mafalda, who was that?"

Frame 6. [Mafalda]:   "A salesman that was sold on that thing about that you've only got one mother."

The Mafalda comic strip points up humorously one of the most universal paradoxes concerning the mother: the same person and the multiple changes of meaning and value that take place in the course of the life of any human being, but especially the woman. From the mother of primary dependence to whom all the powers of the world are granted—and with good reason, since her function is the hetero-conservation of the child, with whom the attachment is developed that forms the basis of the child's emotional life—is the same person who, through the relation of intimacy, transmits most of the "enigmatic" messages of sexuality, establishing the rules of communal living that structure the superego, will be admired/envied for her privileged relationship with the father, valued positively or negatively depending on how she has been able to exert, broaden, and reconcile her different functions and roles with her maternity.

Different relationships with the same person and multiple identifications having different valences in the girl's and the woman's subjectivity—all representations of the mother that will have structured the woman's self when she begins an analysis, which will be displayed for us in the transference. When we speak of the mother's image, even in its Kleinian version of the good or bad breast, what mother are we talking about—or, rather, what aspects or qualities of the multiple relationships with the mother have been distilled as organizers of the self, and how can we distinguish and analyse them for their optimal transformation during treatment? How do we view aspects of the mother's gender in the configuration not only of the gender of her daughter but also of her sexuality? To what extent do we take into account messages the mother has given her daughter in relation to caregiving and the adult's identifications with this girl or woman? Again, this domain—that of the parents' unconscious relation to their child—has been very poorly explored.

The mother as oedipal rival

Clinical vignette 1

A married and professionally successful woman, 35 years old, who had requested analysis because of many and varied hypochondriac problems, had until recently expressed little concern with having a baby. She always expressed severe criticism of colleagues who were inefficient in their work, with the exception of one woman, who had no children. While she was at a party, she had seen this woman and her husband deeply engrossed in one another. She thought that this woman was pregnant and felt envious, jealous, betrayed, and outraged but could not understand why. In the session she finally said that she was going to be the last one left, and that for the first time she felt badly that she hadn't thought about maternity until that moment.

If we view this fragment of analysis from a classic perspective, a 35-year-old married woman with no thoughts about becoming a mother, envious, jealous, and feeling betrayed when she sees a couple very much in love, we would think in terms of unresolved oedipal conflicts (Glocer Fiorini, 2001b). If we look at it from the point of view of a theory that contemplates inherent conflicts of femininity as a gender, difficulties to develop and maintain a professional career with maternity, we would understand problems associated with intra-systemic conflicts of the ego ideal. This means that the conflict is with the mother as a model of woman rather than the mother as a rival in a triangular oedipal configuration. She had many memories of her as a woman who had no life other than her house and her daughter, her complaints, and several somatic problems, and she wondered whether she too was locked into a "sickbed grip". The patient felt great relief when she could understand how and why she had been rejecting maternity and had been denying the experience of other women, as for example her own analyst.

If the figure of the mother as a sick mother is understood as a representation resulting from her destructive rivalry, this may lead women who do not wish to reproduce this model of the feminine gender to feel guilty about abandoning the mother, as the clinical material provided by this patient seems to express through her memories that she could not leave the house while her mother was there in bed. This overlap in the same unconscious representation—"you've only got one mother"—of different relations—infantile attachment, self-preservative dependence, affective and emotional bonds, rivalry and competence, and consequently, different internal objects or representations of the same person, generates undesirable effects when the time comes to differentiate herself from the models of femininity represented by this mother, since differentiation is considered separation and rupture.

If the maternal representation is always understood as an oedipal rival, the mother as a member of the same gender and a model of femininity is left aside, a representation which cuts out multiple cognitive, instrumental or hedonic capacities or limits identification with the maternal figure (Lombardi, 1998).

The mother as a representation of restrictions on sexuality

The understanding of the mother as being admired, envied, and hated for being the father's sexual partner is only an infantile scenario that is often not supported when the adolescent or woman discovers how unreal or fragmentary this evaluation was, given the anxieties, difficulties, and restrictions of the sexual life of many married women, even in our generation. Reflections on the restrictive aspect of maternity on the woman's personal and sexual life were common in the memory of this same patient: "I always felt indebted to her when I went out; at other times I felt, how could she go out dancing, or with friends, now that I'm sick and she should take care of me?" It is understood that the patient might not fervently desire to be a mother and might also express relief that the analyst had a life apart from her, unlike her mother, who had no life other than her daughter and her complaints.

Greek and Roman myths, and today's publicity and films as modern factories of them, place women as the main symbol of sexual pleasure. Women are used as the most powerful symbol of masculine sexual stimulation, whereas the reality in female subjectivity is quite another matter. Nothing allows us to take for granted that the primal scene has remained unchanged in women's unconscious in adult life when, in our clinical work, we listen to the complaints of so many women about the lack of pleasure or of opportunities to have sexual experiences without side-effects such as guilt, persecution, or physical problems, and the long, long periods without any sexual experience in their lives. "I don't remember having seen my mother approach my father, or any other man, erotically." "She shared her suffering in bed with my father with me." "My father always had other women for love and sex; my mother was just that, the mother or housewife, but not a woman." These statements—with overtones closer to or further from reality—are an expression of the opposite representation of the mother as a target of oedipal hate and envy and much closer to representations of the mother as a sexually devalued woman, so common in female subjectivity and so paradoxically and confusedly represented by the religious figure of the virgin mother.

The mother as an attachment figure
and the vicissitudes of the separation–differentiation process

Discrimination of the relationship with the mother from the mother as a gender model allows preservation of the internal maternal representations as a secure attachment tie, even though the model of femininity offered by the mother is not reproduced.

Clinical vignette 2

> A woman age 40 who has decided not to have children still begins a second analysis with a female analyst (the first had been a man), because she now has doubts about her decision. Analysis reveals the threats to life implicit in maternity, since her mother suffered from an auto-immune disease (she believed that it had emerged with her first pregnancy), which had led her to be a person who was "always ill". She has a very significant dream about *a painting of a Madonna and Child in a very sweet and beatific scene, which turns into another in which the virgin appears dressed in rags, with an expression of intense suffering, while the painter observes the scene and the child is behind him.* Her associations lead the patient to think that her father never protected her mother and to connect with intense hate towards him and also towards her mother, since she adds that she can't stand "suffering women".

The choice of a female analyst by a woman with serious conflicts with maternity is frequently understood as displaying "maternal transference with heavy preoedipal colouring". The dream, which I consider an abbreviated synthesis of her process, shows what is hidden in the sacralized formula of maternity, which is helplessness, loneliness, and the emotional burden of the situation of upbringing which may make women ill.

However, in a classical perspective, the dream is understood as what the girl experienced in the attachment relation: her feelings of abandonment and frustration, the accumulated hate that makes its appearance now, since the analyst is unable to prevent her from suffering and abandons her on weekends or when she takes vacations. This means that although the analyst recognizes that in her subjectivity some traces may correspond to an experienced, historical real, the interpretations of her current anger and hate, attempting as a little girl to "not be made to suffer" centres the analysis on the patient's possible early traumatic experience as a powerful reason for her to avoid maternity. However, if we take into account her comment about "suffering women" and the presence in the dream of a painter, as seen in so many paintings of the Madonna and Child, we could broaden our understanding to other meanings, apparently detached from the suffering. We could explore whether in addition to the mother's illness she has any other ideas or fantasies about the suffering of her mother or of other women, which may not be as directly connected with maternity as a biological fact but, instead, to the relationship with men or with her father. If this were so and we valued it as an addition to her mother's real illness, then we could understand the gender aspects that lead many women to fear not only maternity, but the relationship with men as very persecutory, because of the threat of emptiness and lack of caregiving to the woman. This would mean de-centring the focus from the preoedipal relation as women's basic conflict with maternity onto gender scenarios of women who observe, judge, value, feel happy, feel sad, or are afraid of the life of other women and do not want the same for themselves—that is, who consciously or unconsciously diverge from a model of femininity often just as sacralized as the maternity represented by the Madonna and Child. Reducing our understanding to preoedipal terms may leave aside aspects of the multiform structure of the female self—wanting a child but not maternity, with its risks and privations—a self that has been configured not only on the basis of early identifications but on a dynamic, ongoing process of organization throughout life.

Distinguishing between the relationship with the mother and the mother as a gender model allows preservation of the internal maternal representations as a secure attachment tie, even though the model of femininity offered by the mother is not reproduced, as was the case with this patient, who had actually had a close relationship with her mother, who had been able to provide her daughter with adequate care and a loving relationship. The "*mother in rags*" in the dream referred much more to the mother's shadows of pain because of her frustrating marriage than to sentiments of helplessness in the patient. The other bias in the lack of discrimination between conflicts in the relational world and intra-systemic conflicts in the female self structure would be to understand the problem in terms of an unfinished process of separation–individuation and therefore to propose oneself in the countertransference as a third, to separate the daughter from her mother and so enable her access to desire—in this case, of a child. As Karlen Lyons-Ruth (1991) differentiated it so well in her revision of the stage proposed by Mahler, children do not need to separate in order to individuate, much less at 24–36 months of age; they need to transform early attachment while preserving the relationship. In order to preserve this relationship, it is essential for women to differentiate their mother in her model of femininity—which they tend to reject because of the enormous changes that have produced a real expansion of horizons of the female ego ideal—from their mother as an attachment and caregiving figure, whom they can go on loving without losing this relationship.

A different modality centred on the hypothesis of preoedipal regression would consider her as having some extraordinary claim or possession of the mother due a profound retreat from oedipal disappointment. What does oedipal disappointment mean? The implicit theory is that there is only one explanation: losing phallic desire and becoming a castrated woman. A different theory would lead us to consider that oedipal disappointment concerns the grip of the traditional model of femininity: a life devoted to others and its consequences, somatic problems (Dio Bleichmar, 2008).

The meaning of the internalized sick mother could represent the opposite of a woman envied for her sex life with the father and the product of her triumphant phallic strivings, with the stereotype of a depreciated person: something in connection with her self and the mother's self, with the female gender itself rather than her relationship with men—father or husband.

The dilemma today: expansion of models of femininity
or phallic triumph?

We often find interpretations of clinical material of female patients
in which phallic symbols appear as an indication of their use of the
phallus as a compensatory illusion supporting their triumph over
mother/analyst, dodging the experience of envy, loss, and mourning. We will examine the dream of an uncommonly beautiful, very
prestigious professional woman, married and with children:

> *She was instructing a woman, a beautiful assistant and a colleague of*
> *her husband's, how to cook, and she organized knives of different sizes,*
> *asking her for the longest and largest one, which she couldn't find; the*
> *woman went out to get one, but the stores were closing.*

A classical interpretation would be that she emerges as the superior cook compared to her husband's beautiful assistant: she is "in
the know" about everything, and this is understood as an indication of her use of the phallus as a compensatory illusion supporting her triumph over mother/analyst, avoiding the experience of
envy, loss, and mourning. Once again, her differentiation from the
representation of a devalued gender—it is possible to be beautiful
and not stupid, a professional woman and at the same time a very
good cook, even better than her mother—is considered an attack
on her mother and the analyst—not a legitimate desire of her self,
but a phallic desire based on penis envy, or, with a more benevolent
clinical ear, a agglomeration of the images of herself as male and as
female. We agree with this idea, but in the sense of a good aggre-
gate image of herself with multiple aspects of the self: emotional,
domestic, instrumental, and intellectual traits.

On the other hand, what would the interpretations be if we understood her anxiety about always being considered to be cutting
off all the other women's heads, not because of her aggressiveness,
but because of her capacities and good qualities? The knives mul-
tiply wherever she goes, and her desires could offer the hope of
finding a less competitive area.

The implicit theory of some analysts is to view certain differences
with respect to the stereotype of femininity as a woman's increased
hold on her devitalized femininity, considering it a sad irony that in
"having it all" she has nothing of real substance or satisfaction. In

other words, whatever may be understood in a contemporary conception of the expansion of feminine gender identity, the fact that by integrating feminine and masculine aspects women may access more substance and satisfaction continues to be understood in the terms of Joan Riviere who, in 1929, considered that a professional woman who enjoyed herself sexually with her husband and was an excellent mother and housewife concealed her phallic desires within a masquerade of femininity (Dio Bleichmar, 1997).

Womanliness as a masquerade

Joan Riviere, on the basis of a finding by Ferenczi—the tendency of some homosexual men to exaggerate their heterosexuality as a defence—draws a parallel with women whose endeavours in life are in activities that are traditionally reserved for men and who accentuate their seductive activity in order to fend off anxiety and avoid the revenge they fear from men. Although her study centres on a clinical case and two vignettes from everyday life, the importance of her paper resides in the scope the author attributes to her argument: femininity that fails to make maternity its principal motivation is false and is screening attacks on the father/man/analyst, the legitimate possessors of knowledge.

Riviere elaborates this paper in the frame of Melanie Klein's theory and Ernest Jones's ideas about the importance of the role of aggressiveness and the preoedipal stages. She anticipates the papers on female sexuality and femininity to be written by Freud years later, in 1931 and 1932; however, their conceptions of the phallic–masculine component of feminine subjectivity are curiously and symptomatically very much alike. The model proposed by Riviere is altogether similar to Freud's: the woman will suffer throughout life not being a man, because of her "castrated" condition, for the penis she does not have and lacks; but simultaneously, and this is the most curious aspect, the difficulties inherent to her feminine being, the rockiest and most complicated road she finds to access adequate female sexuality, resides in the excessive masculinity of her drive. It is certainly an unfortunate fate to wish for what one is not and does not have and yet to suffer for being it in excess while not knowing it.

The description of the case begins with a classification and continues with an enumeration of traits, which ends with a strange reflection:

> It is with a particular type of intellectual woman that I have to deal. Not long ago intellectual pursuits for women were associated almost exclusively with an overtly masculine type of woman, who in pronounced cases made no secret of her wish or claim to be a man. This has now changed. Of all the women engaged in professional work today, it would be hard to say whether the greater number are more feminine than masculine in their mode of life and character. In University life, in scientific professions and in business, one constantly meets women who seem to fulfil every criterion of complete feminine development. They are excellent wives and mothers, capable housewives; they maintain social life and assist culture; they have no lack of feminine interests, e.g. in their personal appearance, and when called upon they can still find time to play the part of devoted and disinterested mother-substitutes among a wide circle of relatives and friends. At the same time they fulfil the duties of their profession at least as well as the average man. It is really a puzzle to know how to classify this type psychologically. [Riviere, 1929, pp. 303–304]

Why this demand for classification? Why does Riviere feel obliged, in describing her patient, to fit her into a categorization? Having done so and found that she does not fit, she is then faced with the doubt: is she a real woman, or is she something of a man? Using today's schemes of delimitation and definition of levels of analysis, we would say that in order to support her doubt, she would need to refer to discourse, fantasies, dreams, or transference, which might show hesitation or inconsistency of her femininity in her psyche, though not in her social behaviour or activities or in the area of those activities.

Why were the conceptual instruments of psychoanalysis insufficient for Joan Riviere, and, when faced with the subject of the femininity of a certain woman—in her particular category as a singular subject, not as a general category—why does she still do so on the basis of standard configurations of femininity/masculinity? It is precisely because of this woman's unusual profile of femininity for her period—the end of the 1920s—that the question comes up for Joan Riviere. The implicit theory is that femininity/masculinity are present clearly as an established system that already exists in her mind: a code solidly standardized on the basis of what is prescribed or forbidden, adequate or inadequate for one or the other sex, since doubt about the purity of the feminine components of this woman in particular, evaluated by a psychoanalyst in particular, is established on the basis of social behaviour. The inevitable conclusion is that, even for a Kleinian analyst, there is no way for her to extricate herself from gender codes.

However, Riviere does not locate the elements of analysis within the frame of a code of classification transcending the singular subject: she believes and considers that her patient is difficult to classify as a woman. What is striking is that, following the social classification, Riviere goes on to describe how the patient defines or represents herself from a psychological point of view: she does not do so as if she were confused about being a man or a woman, but defines herself as frankly and indubitably feminine.

Therefore, we see that the first criterion applied by Riviere to establish a clear demarcation between femininity and masculinity is in terms of activities: when women fill university halls or the business world or professional life and, instead of complaining and asking for help, they do as well as any man, femininity is attacked and denaturalized. Therefore, if this is what occurs at the level of action, from a psychological viewpoint—which is the level at which she assumes she is doing her analysis—should we suspect the purity of these women's sexuality? Are they real women, or are they masked homosexuals? In the 1930s the question regarding the masculine/feminine component could find no other channel for understanding it except by centring on the drive and penis envy.

What problems did this very successful woman have? She experienced some anxiety, sometimes quite intense after her public speaking, in conferences and debates given or conducted by her, despite her undeniably good performance, intellectual qualities, practical gifts, and her capacity to interest audiences and to conduct debates. This anxiety took shape in two forms: (1) fear of having made some mistake or *faux pas*; (2) a compulsion to flirt with and seduce men, more or less discreetly—behaviour she displayed following her public appearances, which contrasted greatly with the objective and impersonal attitude she assumed in the course of them.

We need to examine the symptom in detail: in the 1930s, for a woman to have public functions, to speak in public, to conduct debates, and constantly experience situations of collective evaluation would in itself be so foreign, unfamiliar, and demanding that we can readily accept her fear of making mistakes or *faux pas*. It does not seem to be such an unjustified fear but, rather, speaks of healthy reality judging and great care in keeping up her good performance. All these traits indicate a high degree of organization of the ego–superego–ego ideal psychic agencies. Riviere seems to understand this but does not emphasize the point, considering this woman's need to seduce men and her desperation to appease them, since her fantasy was aimed at reprisals her intellectual prowess would elicit from men. The horrible fear that her father might take revenge was neutralized by the fantasm of sexual offering.

We see that the interpretation is based on her fear of something coming from her father—a product, in turn, in Kleinian terms, of her own oedipal rivalry with her father for her mother—which in adulthood she projects into men. She does not take into account the possible two-way street in her construction of the persecutory image of men: that they or her father himself might consider her an intellectual rival.

The analyst's interpretation of the meaning of this behaviour enables the patient to remember conscious fantasies during her adolescence in the Southern United States: an African–American man was going to attack her, and she would defend herself by forcing him to embrace her and make love to her. This memory of a strategy carefully planned when she was young, together with the patient's current behaviour, lead Riviere to conclude that this woman felt a secret rivalry with men, with strong and secret wishes of castration and exhibition of her own "penis". The patient's intellectual abilities are viewed by Riviere as expressions of her unconscious masculinity/homosexuality. From our perspective, the presence of anxiety or persecutory feelings in women's minds for their successes in masculine areas undoubtedly seems to respond to their fullest femininity. What other explanation could we find for her appeasement, coupled with a return to a masculine–feminine relationship in which both return to their traditional roles—that is, the sexual roles that calm and locate each in the man–woman relationship?

Why this compulsion to return to a behaviour on the basis of a clear delimitation of the gender differences, which had been erased by intellectual activity? The reason lies in the fact that the patient, like any woman in the 1930s, and in fact any woman even today who performs in areas of action traditionally reserved for men, "knows" that if she does her job well, she will elicit anything from an icy silence to the deepest indignation in her male audience, and that the possible variety of reprisals, which will depend on how secure the man feels in his acquired positions, will always include, as a constant, a doubt concerning her femininity. What is truly surprising is that this is just what Riviere—who is neither a man nor a prejudiced observer—concludes: it is a double transgression of masculinity and femininity. The psychoanalyst shares, in an ideologically and scientifically legitimate register, the assumption of both the patient and men regarding this "type" of woman.

If we invert the analytic perspective, the pieces fit together differently. In the 1930s, a woman who performed public functions in executive positions and by means of words necessarily did so in the face of a social risk that was certain to have psychological consequences. What was this risk? Not only her probably insufficient technical preparation, since social structures were not—nor are yet—prepared to receive female candidates for these functions (which women always learn on the side or by borrowing), but, more significantly, her model has not been another woman but a man. Therefore, she is performing in "a foreign place", *de facto* usurped.

This is placed in the foreground in Joan Riviere's interpretation:

> In that guise the man found no stolen property on her which he need attack her to recover and, further, found her attractive as an object of love. Thus the aim of the compulsion was not merely to secure reassurance by evoking friendly feelings towards her in the man; it was chiefly to make sure of safety by masquerading as guiltless and innocent. It was a compulsive reversal of her intellectual performance; and the two together formed the "double-action" of an obsessive act, just as her life as

a whole consisted alternately of masculine and feminine activities. [Riviere, 1929, pp. 305–306]

Nothing is closer to the truth than Riviere's conclusion, since what
the material shows is that the patient's masculinity was based not on
a hidden identity or a desire to be a man, but on the development
of activities considered masculine. It was precisely in the course of
these activities (conferences, debates) that anxiety appeared. In
other words, the theatre of operations where her disguise revealed
its weak point was well defined: during her performance of activities that put her in charge of actions socially attributed to men.

Examination of her rivalry with those of a masculine gender also
merits detailed treatment:

> She had quite conscious feelings of rivalry and claims to superi-
> ority over many of the "father-figures" whose favour she would
> then woo after her own performances! She bitterly resented any
> assumption that she was not equal to them, and (in private)
> would reject the idea of being subject to their judgement or
> criticism. [Riviere, 1929, p. 304]

For a woman to "experience" conscious feelings of rivalry towards
men does not indicate any sort of severe pathology but, rather, that
she has ambitions and aspirations in areas that have traditionally
been reserved for men. If it is men who speak and write and her
father was one of them, and if she devoted herself to public action
and writing, with whom was she going to compete (Abelin-Sas,
2008)? And why would she not compete, when without competition
she would have no way of being tested? Therefore, if this woman's
rivalry was simply one that she "experienced", with all its associated psychic consequences—self-persecution, guilt, the need for
appeasement and reassurance, the feeling that she had caused no
harm to third parties: that is to say that she was not on the receiving
end of paranoid treatment, nor was acting, nor created problems
in her interpersonal relationships. What other course could we imagine for the competition and rivalry inherent to human existence
when, as in any given instance of the many life provides us, there
is only one place for two?

In psychoanalysis rivalry between the sexes has been formulated
predominantly in genital terms, mistaking what is represented for
the form of the fantasm or conditions of psychic representabil-

ity—in other words, the signified for the signifier, the broad field of human action that masculinity symbolizes for the genital.

The implicit theory behind this conclusion is based on the conception of the meaning of phallic. Is it literally envy of the penis as a male genital organ, or is it symbolic materiality of the social difference between the genders? If we understand it, as proposed by Grossman and Stewart (1976), as a metaphor of the inequities between masculine and feminine in our culture, should we not include in our listening a legitimate desire for expansion of the feminine self and its desirable differentiation from traditionally deprecated forms of femininity?

If we are to incorporate the concept of gender, we need to broaden our listening and become better attuned to the ways women speak about restrictions on the self, the difficulties they face when they decide to differentiate themselves from their mother's model, and the importance of understanding and separating these anxieties from oedipal conflicts. This orientation could help analysis to free such women from somatic and bodily preoccupations. I think that the implicit theory that makes it difficult to fully assimilate contemporary views on female development is based upon the idea that gender is a sociological issue and failing to recognize that it is a broad and complex structure of the self configured from the outset in the unconscious intersubjective exchange between parents and their sons and daughters.

It is in this perspective that I consider that the concept of gender, which initially had only a sociological dimension—even though it was a physician who first thought about it—may be worked upon psychoanalytically, as Laplanche has begun to do. I would like to close this chapter with his current idea about the riddle of femininity: "In the adult, it is the riddle of something that is neither purely biological, nor purely psychological, nor purely sociological but an odd mixture of the three" (p. 209), and also with Fonagy's proposal:

> Psychoanalytic theory of mental function could then follow practice, integrating what is newly discovered through innovative methods of clinical work. Such a pragmatic, principally action-oriented use of theory would bring psychoanalysis more in line with modern, postempirical views of science. [Fonagy, 2003, p. 13]

10

Femininity and the human dimension

Mariam Alizade

> There is no doubt that we have left very many points over to
> be established and clarified by some future band of observers
> and enquirers. But we may console ourselves with the
> knowledge that we have worked honestly and in no narrow
> spirit, and that in so doing we have opened up paths along
> which later research will be able to travel.
>
> Freud, "Contributions to a Discussion on Masturbation"
> (1912f, p. 246)

Over the last few decades, some significant scientific contributions in psychoanalysis have called into question certain Freudian
premises concerning sexuality.

Gender studies, investigations into neo-sexuality, transsexual-
ity, and same-sex parenting, interdisciplinary studies, and queer
studies, among others, have opened up new areas of investigation. These constitute some of the paths mentioned by Freud in
1912 along which "later research will be able to travel" (1912f).
Heterogeneity, relativism, deconstruction, subjectivity, and link interactions have been converted into conceptual models that have

provided answers to many questions and have generated theoretical and clinical uncertainties.

In this chapter, I revisit the 1933 conference on femininity and give it a new validity by considering certain comments made by Freud that were thought to be relatively tangential.

The first point I would like to draw attention to is the simple fact of being human. It is my belief that psychoanalysis has not dealt in sufficient depth with this concept, which embraces a multiplicity of phenomena that go beyond the area of sexual differences and sexual options. The second point is the repeated mention of the uncertainty of knowledge concerning the sex life of women, and the third concerns the allusion to the effect of socio-cultural factors on health and pathology.

In the 1933 text, vacillations in Freud's thinking are evident, as is the fact that his theories are coloured by the consensus of opinion at that time. I will not focus on these theories here, given that they have already been questioned and reconceptualized by numerous authors: the woman as a little man, the weak super ego, penis envy, etc.

Freud's work can be understood at two theoretical levels: basic, "hard" theories (the theory of dreams, metapsychology, the concept of the unconscious) and "soft" theories influenced by historical and sociocultural variables (masculine–feminine, sex roles, male and female Oedipus complex).

Freud wrote: ". . . what constitutes masculinity or femininity is an unknown characteristic which anatomy cannot lay hold of" (1933, p. 114). The first complementary series was not sufficient to explain the vicissitudes of sexuality. Neither were the second or third series. I have proposed (Alizade, 2004b) the inclusion of a fourth complementary series, which focuses specifically on the study of the influence of society and culture on the systems of acquisition of knowledge and on the production of both mental health and pathology.

The complementary series, in line with the motivational schema of reciprocal action (Bleger, 1963), is concerned with causal overdetermination on the one hand and, on the other, with the succession and interweaving of factors deriving from various levels of integration. The consideration of a fourth series frees psychoanalysis from

the inflexibilities of psychosexual norms. Ideals, day-dreams, fantasies, desires, feelings that seemingly emanate from the individual
tend to be unconsciously impregnated with the pervasive culture
in which that individual is immersed, resulting in the subtle impo-
sition of beliefs and the production of alienating identifications.
The fourth complementary series considers the theoretical and
clinical weight of a social perspective. This takes into account the
distortion of the expression of desires behind the façade of apparent spontaneity arising from the influence—disciplinary influence,
Foucault would say—of cultural repression, from the ideologies of
power, from sexual prohibitions and permissions by society and its
culture. Freud was not unaware of these issues, and on two occasions in his 1933 lectures he drew attention to the effect of social
context in mental life.

Sexual differences also have political consequences (Saal,
1981). Let us take, for example, the notion of the "enigma of
women" (Freud, 1933, p. 131). This idea was considered paradigmatic. "Enigma" is a word with poetic resonance that expresses
mystery, ignorance, difficulty in understanding the object referred
to. "Enigma" did not explain femininity but, rather, left it as a
vague, ambiguous notion and confirmed a certain insufficiency
in the understanding of sexual matters concerning women and
femininity. The famous phrase: "What does a woman want?" attributed to Freud in his conversations with Marie Bonaparte, triggered a surge of conceptualizations with regard to femininity.
"Enigma" and "dark continent" shared the same idea of an inability to understand women, with the supposition that this lack of in-
telligibility was a quality that was characteristic of them (Alizade,
2004c).

This universal proposition constituted an *a priori* concept serv-
ing as a fantasmatic solution or a working hypothesis, which was received with a certain fascination by many schools of psychoanalytic
thought. However, this attribute of being enigmatic was relativized
thanks to the development of new concepts and clinical observations—as Toril Moi writes: "It is time to give up the fantasy of finding the key to the 'riddle of femininity'. Women are not sphinxes.
Or rather: they are no more and no less sphinxlike than men.
There is no riddle to solve" (Moi, 2004, p. 102).

Gender

The contribution of gender studies merits special mention. The term "gender" is not a simple one. The source of much controversy, it has been rejected by some schools of psychoanalysis. Psychoanalysis and gender do not neatly map onto one another. They are two terms whose relationship is one of intersection, with some areas in common and others that do not overlap. Certain areas relating to gender are independent of psychoanalysis and form part of other disciplines, such as sociology and philosophy (Alizade, 2004a). Likewise, psychoanalysis has areas of knowledge that are incompatible with the idea of gender. Gender studies and their multiple derivations have paved the way for a series of fruitful debates that have forced us to reconsider many ideas that previously seemed immutable. It could be said that behind this concept lies a sort of crystallized "agglomeration" (Lewkowicz, 1997, p. 410), a pivotal point for discussions and viewpoints arising from different disciplines. These arguments concerning sexual differences are not always clearly distinguishable, and on occasion there has been an excess of theorizing. Nevertheless, this focus on the prejudices and determinism of an era that permeates an individual's identity, role, and sexual preferences has proved to be extremely useful.

I will distinguish two aspects that do not overlap in gender studies. First, gender is rooted in a binary male–female system and reifies this difference. Gender is bound up with the cultural construction of sex. This concept is widely accepted in the field of feminism, in which there have been many studies into the social problems of the collectivity of woman. According to this approach, a woman is a woman and, as such, is subjected to specific sociocultural and historical contexts. The term "gender" was linked to the material reality of the sex of the person in accordance with the anatomical attributes with which that individual was born. This sexual–cultural notion of gender gave rise to stereotypical claims and simplistic generalizations. Second, in the more innovative and controversial sense, gender is a concept that goes beyond the binary male–female concept and constructs different subjectivities and a multiplicity of unusual heterogeneities. Gender shifts from the masculine to the feminine: the nuclear gender identity may not be firmly established, facets of sexual identity are selectively revealed, and new identities are created and proliferate. Dio Bleichmar (1991, p. 48) exemplifies this complexity when, in a sort of gender puzzle, she says: ". . . a person with a male gender attribution, with a female gender identity, with masculine interests, a male sexual object, who uses female clothes: is this person a man or a woman?"

The mind denies the normative sexual body. Sex is absorbed within gender and, from this vast fantasmatic territory, creates its own inventions. This is a gender that is constructed according to each individual. Gender acquires a plural character that brings an "imaginary morphology" into play (Butler, 1993b).

The suffering of intersexuals, forced by society from birth into one of the two normative groups, clearly shows how social pressure prevents and opposes anything outside the binary system that is considered to be natural or normal.

It is necessary to encourage the creative use of the terms masculine–feminine in order to act effectively in the clinical context. This is important when faced with an ambiguous anatomy and appearance and the complexities that spring from the shifting yet seemingly solid base of sexual normality, which give rise to unexpected and surprising associations.

Relatedly, Judith Butler has highlighted in an interview (Glocer Fiorini & Gimenez de Vainer, 2008) her concerns with respect to the univocality of the terms *masculinity* and *femininity*, saying that these are expressions that have tried to articulate a bodily difference without there being a consensus as regards the way in which this difference can be identified.

I will cite, in particular, the work of Heineman (2006), who, from the clinical observation of children of same-sex parents, puts forward the hypothesis of the rupture of the oedipal causal nexus in which the father, mother, and child occupy specific places and arouse specific fantasies according to the sex of the individual. This author proposes reconstructing our notion of the Oedipus complex and the psychosexual development of children. Her exploration of the interpretation that tends to be given to the Oedipus complex coincides with that of Freud when he writes: "And besides, you should consider how little of its sexual wishes a child can bring to preconscious expression or communicate at all" (1933, p. 121). Healthy sexual development in children brought up by a couple where both are of the same sex brings into question the linearity of causality, which is presumed to be universal.

If we take this one step further, queer studies challenge the culturally established canons and have appropriated the labels "strange", "marginal", "different", and "unconventional". Being queer implies sustaining a provocative identity that challenges cultural norms and categories, whether they be of a homosexual or heterosexual orientation. The queer individual is defined not solely in terms of sex but also of social class and roots (Sáez, 2004). The ideas arising from these studies impact on the theoretical corpus of psychoanalysis, generating questions that as yet remain unanswered. We are still far from 1933.

The human dimension

In the beginning, before having been classified as male or female, a human being is born. Even when another fellow human being looks at the genitals of the infant, placing them into one of the two sexual categories of the species, there still exists a prior instance that lies outside the realm of sex and gender. The binary division laid down by social rules does not eliminate the human character of the species. The non-sexual side of the human is sustained as an on-going quality and continues to be present over the course of the human being's life.

In this dimension, gender falls into the category of the *human gender* and loses its sexual connotation.

Freud (1933) dealt tangentially with the human aspect of the psyche when he wrote: "However, we find enough to study in those human individuals who, through the possession of female genitals, are characterized as manifestly or predominantly feminine" (p. 116), and, a little later: ". . . but we do not overlook the fact that an individual woman may be a human being in other respects as well" (p. 135).

In his metapsychology, he referred more specifically to this issue when dealing with the primary identification. He wrote:

. . . the effects of the first identifications made in earliest childhood will be general and lasting. This leads us back to the origin

of the ego ideal; for behind it there lies hidden an individual's first and most important identification, his identification
with the father in his own personal prehistory. [Freud, 1923b,
p. 31]

I would like to draw attention to the footnote that follows:

Perhaps it would be safer to say "with the parents"; for before
a child has arrived at definite knowledge of the difference between the sexes, the lack of a penis, it does not distinguish in
value between its father and its mother. . . . In order to simplify
my presentation I shall discuss only identification with the father. [Freud, 1923b, p. 31]

The pre-figuration that is independent of the binary man–woman,
mother–father regimen (Alizade, 2000a) is the human being: the
first, ineludible identification.

I propose that the notion of a pre-sexual psychic world, outside
the sex-gender system and anything connected to it, is considered
as a *transitional concept* (Green, 1990), which, by definition, "suggests a territory which is able to admit contradictions" and which
maintains "concepts of judgement in suspension while their heu-
ristic value seems irreplaceable" (p. 418).

The pre-sexual is interwoven in different ways with the sexual
world but preserves its autonomy of existence. A human being is
not permanently the product of their sex or the multiple facets
of their gender. The possibilities that derive from the sex-gender
system—nuclear identity, momentary feelings of being a man or
a woman, feminine or masculine representations—are variations
and vicissitudes of different moments which play a key role in the
structuring of the mind and which do not constitute the totality
of the field of representations. There are mental processes that lie
outside the dominion of psychosexuality. "*The universals of existence*"
constitute a common backdrop on which is drawn our journey
through life. These universals are laws or general conditions that
make up the basic life matrix of experiences and events. They are
the elements inherent in the human condition, and thus shape our
everyday life (Alizade, 2008). Helplessness, finitude, the need for
the other in order to survive, are universal elements that are not
dictated by sexual differences.

The human dimension is tied to both pre-sexual and non-sexual questions based on mechanisms and defences that spring from the interests of the ego and on the problems of the individual's existence. The interrelationship of theoretical concepts linked to sexual differences with those connected to the non-sexual dimension is logical, complex, and paradoxical.

Freudian psychoanalysis has rushed to pan-sexualize its theoretical framework and has left little margin for the exploration of the non-sexual aspects of the human being.

The contributions of many authors whom I cite or whose work I use for the purposes of exemplification have emphasized the importance of the structuring of the human being (Garbarino, 1990), the sustaining and support of the human being (Levin de Said, 2004), psychic containment (Winnicott, 1971b), and human attachment (Bowlby, 1969).

Studies into the nature of the human being have broadened the complexity of this subject. The human being constitutes not a monolithic concept but, rather, the reverse and has, as a consequence, generated a wealth of different theories. The common theme is that the individual does not necessarily need to sustain an existence on a psychosexual basis but, rather, passes along paths where the ego, the ego-being (Garbarino, 1990), the interests of the ego, the interactive force of social groups, the pre-sexual, and a-sexual dimension of the psyche, and other theoretical references all intersect.

The Oedipus complex

The end of the Oedipus complex signals an integrative resolution, a resolution of conflicts, the liberation of alienating identifications, and a superior level of mental maturity. The culmination of this process of subjectivity is marked by ego-fulfilment.

Basing my conceptualizations as regards women at the end of the Oedipus complex on clinical practice (Alizade, 1999a, 2000a), I clearly deviate from the indeterminate, incomplete ending suggested by Freud (1925j, 1931b) and postulate a concluding mental movement in which the complex is clearly demolished. I wish to draw attention to the final stage of the Oedipus complex. I do not want to focus on those concepts that Freud dealt with, such as woman–little man, penis envy, and the hegemony of the phallus, which, as I have already mentioned, have been questioned for decades in the light of clinical experience in different socio-cultural contexts and by different schools of psychoanalysis.

I am, rather, interested in discovering how women, like men, arrive at the point that Freud called (1924d) "losing the milk teeth", despite their different object vicissitudes. In her life experiences, which encompass loves, hate, rivalries with her father, mother, siblings, the subject–woman, in the final stage of the Oedipus complex, frees herself of the problem of envy, whose damaging effects consist fundamentally in the intensification of the alienation of the ego.

Penis envy loses its hegemony, both in clinical listening and in analytic interpretations, no longer constituting the central axis of female psychosexuality. A deepening of clinical listening brings to light many envy games played by both sexes and genders, which relegate the Freudian conceptualizations of the woman's great envy of the phallus, embodied in the man's penis, to the backwaters of the developmental history of psychoanalytic ideas. As Horney (1932) highlights all men have, from an early age, felt the desire to be a woman, and this has wounded their narcissism. The envy of a fertile womb can be detected in analysis. Furthermore, I would like to point out that penis envy and vagina envy are not the exclusive domain of women and men, respectively. As a result of an extensive review of the literature, I have described penis envy in men—envy of large penises, envy of erect penises, and so on—and also womb envy in men (Alizade, 2007).

In the final stages of the Oedipus complex, the woman ceases to have a compulsive desire for the penis, for a child, or for the company of an eternal, omnipresent mother. Beyond this desire *to have*, women take possession of the psychic richness of being. A state of psychic maturity is reached through the process of achieving independence and individuality. The collapse of the Oedipus complex does not require the threat of any castration: it is a maturative, cognitive process. The woman becomes separate from her husband, her children, her lover. Her object choices minimize the need to bind to an object, a need that had been a product of her previous fragility, before the resolution of the Oedipus complex. The need for fusion (Alizade, 2006) gives way to the egoic force of autonomy, and primary bonds lose their libidinal viscosity characteristic of the preoedipal period. As self-worth grows, so the compulsion for the other, originating from the maternal bond and original helplessness, gradually fades.

During this stage, women give priority to relationships with other women of the same generation and, stripped of infantile hostility, also with their own mother. A space opens up "between women" of sublimated homosexuality. This period of female bonding signals a time of mutual mirroring between women, a time of positive narcissism, whereby, in the mirror image of others, women search for ownership of themselves, free from their dependency on object bonds. During this time of inner reflection, women withdraw within themselves, to pass from this communion between women to a *lone psychic space* in which each woman strives to find herself. Fertile solitude becomes a requisite in the decline of the Oedipus complex in the woman.

Solitude and femininity find a point of intersection

The building of this lone space (Alizade, 1999b) characterizes a new psychic configuration. Women are centred on themselves and see themselves as objects in a sort of intrapsychic unfolding that generates a narcissistic backwash over the ego. The woman who arrives at the culmination of the Oedipus complex detaches herself from the demands of sexual differences, and the building of her own life takes on a quality that is both polymorphic and playful.

The female human being succeeds in dis-alienating herself from the desiderative masculine identity and cultural, patriarchal mandates and stereotypes. This "new, psychic act" modifies the mental structure.

The process undertaken in the woman's inner world at the final stage of the Oedipus complex leads to the incorporation within the ego of a *unifying identification,* a one-ego, which grants them complete power to name and fulfil their desires. The solitary woman becomes a positive image where the solitude of anxiety is transformed into a source of independence, a state of happiness in existing. From this position of freedom, women choose or re-choose their objects on the basis of need and love without the desperate demands of the other to calm the anxieties of separation. The psychic plasticity achieved enables them to pass from one to two, from masculine to feminine, and to enjoy their psychic bisexuality.

"Normal femininity", which for Freud (1933) depended on the insatiable desire for a child as a replacement for the penis, becomes independent of the maternal solution. The mental health of women was linked irreducibly to the symbolic equation penis–son, and a woman's sound mental health was the result of the substitution of the penis for a son. The end of the Oedipus complex grants women full liberty as regards their maternal desires.

In this phase of psychic immersion, mental processes that are sexual and those that lie outside the realm of sexuality coexist. There is a merging of different mental facets: that of the human being striving to attain their individuality and to realize their creative potential—at a non-sexual level—and that of the sexualized being immersed in the fantasies of castration, seduction, and envy, struggling against their neurotic manifestation.

I have the impression that there is not such a great difference between men and women at the end of the Oedipus complex. After negotiating different mental pathways between objects, drives, and fantasies, everyone arrives at a similar end point. The Oedipus complex of women as proposed by Freud is permeated with the prejudices of that era in that women's desire for professional development, for economic independence, and for freedom of object choice were attributed to penis envy and phallic competition. Freud's often-quoted 1895 passage still has resonance: "The question has to be considered of how it comes about that anaesthesia is so predominantly a characteristic of women. This arises from the passive part played by them. An anaesthetic man will soon cease to undertake any coitus; *a woman has no choice*" (1950 [1892–1899], p. 204; emphasis added).

The end of the Oedipus complex is a sort of psychic "enough is enough!" to the psycho-sexual conflicts of mental structuring.

Clinical observations

I will go on to describe some clinical vignettes in support of the ideas that I have put forward.

Clinical vignette: "Ines"

In this young woman, who was nearing 40, what could clearly be seen was a symbiotic, pre-Oedipus conflict with heightened affective ambivalence. Divorced for six years, she had not managed to find another partner, despite her conscious efforts to forge a lasting relationship. Her mother had taught her that men were unfaithful and irresponsible, and this was confirmed time and again in her encounters with men.

There was a re-edition of her dependence on the primary object in the transference that prevented the analysis from coming to an end. The process of working through, after several years of analysis, enabled her to approach new psychic territory that she was frightened to enter. The psychic step that remained to be taken for her to surmount the Oedipus complex required that she dare to confront the autonomy of her inner world. The relinquishing of conflicts with her father, mother, and siblings seemed impossible to her. They formed part of a vicious circle of representations that she would constantly come back to: the melancholy of the mother, the infidelity of the father, the rivalry with her brother. Her associations seemed to go round in circles without making new ground. Her meetings with men were characterized by a somewhat adolescent, hysterical quality, coupled with unrealistic expectations. The impossibility of concluding the Oedipus complex overwhelmed her at times, leaving her despondent and depressed. Men acquired an exaggerated phallic value, and, as a result of her submission to maternal and socio-cultural mandates, she was often disparaging of herself. Her superego demanded a parody of femininity, which she achieved by being docile, smiling, and of good character, forcing her to hide and repress her hostility. She had not succeeded in fulfilling the desire of her father, who had vehemently wished that she had been a boy.

The idealization and envy of men and the pre-Oedipus oral fixation constituted a constellation of elements that resulted in her unhappiness. The change gradually came about with the analysis of the transference of envy and the process of dis-idealization and of dis-identification with the melancholic mother.

Ines gradually experienced a state of harmonic solitude free from the habitual anxiety that tended to accompany it. In the building of her lone space, her self-esteem grew. She was able to see herself from a vantage point outside the domain of oedipal sexual conflicts. She was able to leave behind the prejudice that if she developed a greater autonomy of desires, she would be negatively labelled as masculine. The "human" dimension, beyond sex and gender, took on a positive aspect and gained a new relevance in her psychic life.

The end of analysis comprised a series of impasses in which Ines gradually developed her ability to be alone. These impasses took the form of small endings of the Oedipus complex, which were the precursors of the final termination. What was striking during the final throes of the Oedipus complex was her internal vacillations between clinging to old representational psychosexual pathways and the fear of change.

Clinical vignette: "Diana"

Diana was young and neurotic and had a liking for various drugs. She was insecure, had low self-esteem, and was constantly searching for love in her numerous sexual relationships.

After a sex party with two men in a beach house, she fantasized about having a child with one of them. This deep desire showed her compulsion for the other and her extreme affective dependency.

Two sequences of associations became indicators of change, which resulted in the dissolution of her Oedipus complex and the increase in her self-worth as a human being. While reflecting in a session when describing the man with whom she thought she was in love, she said: "He feels happy in himself. He is his own person." The various meanings of the phrase "his own person" were explored. Its implications were the recognition of a basic condition of psychic structuring tied to confidence and the ownership of oneself. "He is his own person" was synonymous with "He feels good within himself" . . . "He feels fine alone". This lucid statement was present in her representations and emotions for some months. In the analytic process, it was possible to detect how "being one's own person" did not depend neither on the difference between the sexes, nor on phallic rivalry. This discovery of "self-ness" became tied to the condition of being human.

What followed were dreams and associations that signalled her psychic progress. During the course of another session, Diana said that she had a secret that she was not going to tell anyone. She rejected all analytic intervention and kept silent. This sustained silence constituted a "demonstration" in the session of her self-affirmation. With this announcement, she constructed her lone space in the presence of the analyst and initiated a sort of "psychic exile", which enabled her to build a space of solitude and pleasure in her own company. Diana reached an internal psychoanalytic impasse: she interrupted the external process while she experimented with and practised the structural change in her inner world. The representations and affects that emerged after this stage of analysis, connected to new and different experiences in her life, were particularly striking.

Note

This chapter was translated by Lesley Speakman.

11

The persistence of tradition
in the unconscious of modern Korean women

Mikyum Kim

When I was invited to discuss the subject of feminism in Korea today, I accepted the invitation rather quickly, without much thought;
but I soon realized that it is an almost impossible task because of
the cultural complexity and lack of published clinical material on
the subject. As a result, this chapter should be seen as preliminary—the beginning rather than the end of a longer discussion.

As a Korean–American, my experience is particular—being
both inside and outside the culture into which I was born. Deeply
influenced by the Korean War and the rapid modernization and
industrialization that followed, I was more aware of the discontinuities with the past and less conscious of the persistence of the tradition. In the course of years of practice as a psychoanalyst, I have
come to observe that, in spite of all that is new and modern in the
conscious lives of my Korean women patients, there is much that is
specifically Korean in their unconscious conflicts and psychological
problems; material can be located from each of the major sources
of Korean tradition. Moreover, I have discovered that these issues
vary within each of the three generations of women's experience
that I have described.

"Today" does not exist without "yesterday", and the accumulation of yesterdays become a history of mankind. "Today" is a creation of yesterday's internal and external conflicts, where both internal world and external record of the historical action is largely unconscious.

An internal world moves slowly, often with sceptical eyes, while an external world always rushes to move to tomorrow, often without judgement and seemingly with trustful eyes. An internal world crawls, and the external world seems to fly. In this way, the transformation of the internal world seems always to be behind, always catching up with the external world.

In order to understand Korean women today, it is essential to know the history of the country, particularly its major cultural and religious traditions.

The first part of this chapter will briefly review women's lives in the traditional Korean society, and the transformation of Korean women in the modern period. The second part is a psychological understanding of the traditional, the modern, and the post-modern Korean woman, with material from the case histories of women I have treated. It will be obvious to the reader that my personal history is deeply implicated in the discussion that follows.

Background

There are three main religious traditions in Korean culture: Shamanism, Buddhism, and Confucianism; I will begin with a brief discussion of each of them.

Shamanism is the most ancient indigenous tradition of Korea, possibly derived from Siberian Ural prototypes and Palaeolithic hunter/gatherer antecedents. Gradually, Korean Shamanism became ostracized by the ruling classes and survived mainly among the poorer and rural classes.

Buddhism was first introduced to the Korean peninsula in 372 AD and gradually spread throughout the country. In the Buddhist-dominated Koryo period (918 AD–1392 AD), women held high status, both at home and in society. During the period of the "Three Kingdoms" (57 BC–668 AD),[1] married couples started their marriage in the bride's house. After the couple had children, they moved to the groom's house and lived with his family. The Koryo family was matrilocal in every social class. In that society, women were economically independent, and they controlled the upbringing and education of their children (Deuchler, 1992b).

In 1392 AD, when the Choson Dynasty was founded, the political elite adopted Confucianism. They expelled the previously powerful Buddhist elite and monopolized political power on the basis of Confucian teaching.

Confucianism as such is not an organized religion. Nevertheless, Confucian ethical values have, for well over a thousand years, served as the source of inspiration as well as the court of appeal for human interaction at all levels of Korean society.

Beginning in 1392 AD, the Neo-Confucians reorganized Korean society around the concept of agnation, or relationship through the male line. Agnation was seen as an essential moral force, sanctioned by a cosmos in which heaven (yang, man) dominates earth (yin, woman). The ultimate social value was filial piety, which required all people to honour and obey the patriarch. This value system gradually led to the widespread adoption of Namjon Yobi (the principle that men are fundamentally superior to women).

Sons inherit the family line, but daughters are "raised for others" and are considered outsiders. Namjon Yobi defines the woman's position in traditional Korea as inferior to that of the men politically, socially, economically, and culturally. The status of women as property was sanctioned by both law and tradition (Peterson, 1983). As a consequence, it was unthinkable that women would participate in societal or legal affairs. Women were not allowed to be seen alone in public. When in the public realm, they were required to cover their faces.

In the Confucian ideology, women's roles were defined by specific terms to designate normative roles: "virtuous wife", "obedient daughter-in-law", and "chaste widow". A woman was supposed to serve only one man for her entire life, regardless of circumstances. If she were to remarry after becoming a widow, it would embarrass the entire family. Society honoured a woman who sacrificed her own needs and desires and who served her in-laws and children wholeheartedly after she became a widow. A widow who expressed sexual desires was often humiliated in public or punished by the government; she was denied any possibility of getting married officially, a sanction that applied to her entire family and their offspring.

In my own family, a great aunt was married by arrangement at the age of 13. Her husband was several years younger. By custom, she went to her husband's house to live with his family to learn the family's traditions until the young groom was able to consummate the marriage. Unfortunately, her young husband died before the relationship had been consummated. I witnessed my great aunt proudly living the life of a virgin widow until her death in her late 70s.

In Choson dynasty[1] there was no public education for women. Girls were prohibited from studying Confucian philosophy because it was believed that literate women would only interfere with the men's public work.

For men, there were many educational institutes. Women stayed at home, where they were taught virtuous conduct. Such rigorous socialization was essential in preparing girls for their future roles as moral guardians of the domestic sphere and also as labourers for the physical needs of their families (Deuchler, 1992a).

What has been recorded regarding traditional Korean women is mostly limited to the upper classes; very little is known about the lives of ordinary women. In traditional society, women of the working class laboured to help their husbands. They, in effect, had two jobs: the maintenance of the household, as well as the more public role of labourers for their husbands.

Among working women, formal or informal education was permitted in three specific roles: the shaman, the kisang, and the medicine women.

Shamanism was relegated mainly to the lower class. Shamans were, in general, female, becoming a shaman through an informal tutorial process from a senior shaman.

The only official educational institution for young girls was designed to educate them in how to serve and entertain men, especially government officers, foreign ambassadors, and even kings. This role was called "kisang". Young girls who were "kisang" were in general underprivileged. They were taught art, music, calligraphy, poetry, and politics. But they were not allowed to have independent lives. Paradoxically, even though they were the most intelligent and well educated among women, they were the lowest class of people.

The medicine woman was a unique feature of traditional Korean society. After the age of 7, girls could no longer associate with boys or men. Therefore, it was a shameful thing for a woman to be examined by a male doctor. In an extreme situation, some women had chosen to die rather than be treated by a male doctor. Medicine women were taught how to diagnose illness, how to take care of patients, and how to deliver babies, but only male doctors had the privilege of prescribing medication. Medicine women were also educated by the government, but belonged to the lowest class in society.

In the late nineteenth century, Western culture began to enter traditional Korea through Christian missionaries. Schools for women were founded, but very few women attended.

As the Choson Dynasty (1392 AD–1910 AD) declined, Korea came under Japanese rule and was officially annexed in 1910. Under Japanese hegemony, women started to attend school, and some educated women began to participate in the larger political and social culture. During the Japanese colonial era, Korean women began to organize a women's liberation movement and to protest against the Japanese occupation. This was the real beginning of modernization for Korean women.

During the Japanese colonial era (1910–45) and, later, the Korean war (1950–53), many families were torn apart when men emigrated as voluntary or involuntary labourers, joined independent resistance movements, or joined the army, leaving women as *de facto* heads of the family, with heavy responsibilities (H. J. Cho, 2002).

Modern Korean women

In contemporary Korea, we can identify at least three generations. Cho Haejeong, a sociologist, delineated them as "the grandmothers' generation", "the mothers' generation", and "the daughters' and grand-daughters' generation" (H. J. Cho, 2002).

The grandmothers' generation might be represented by women who are in their mid-80s today, having been born during the 1920s under the Japanese colonial occupation. These women came of age after the liberation of 1945. They reared families, and some had young children during the Korean War (1950–53).

For women who lived through this troubled time, the patrilineal principle was maintained as a cultural ideal, even though women were in fact the centre of the family, taking care of everything from supporting the family financially to educating the children. Women in this generation were not expected to marry again even if they were widowed, lest they dishonour their family.

> In my practice, an elderly woman came for consultation. During the Korean war, as a young woman with three children, she had been widowed. She came from a very traditional Confucian family. She fell in love with a man and became pregnant with his child. Not daring to dishonour her family, she shut herself away, cutting off all relations with her original family and totally estranged herself from her own children.

The mothers' generation included women who were born in the 1940s and 1950s, who are now in their late fifties to early sixties. They experienced the Korean war as children. They reared their children in the 1960s through the 1980s, while Korea was in transition from a traditional patriarchy to a modernized and Westernized culture. During these years, in a period of rapid economic growth, the most visible transition in Korea was from the extended family to the urban nuclear family. Women worked as hard as their husbands, they were aggressive modern wives, the backstage managers of rapid industrialization, and they were largely responsible for the "Korean economic miracle".

Large numbers of young men pursued secure and well-paying jobs in the modern sector, while their young wives managed their husband's income and their children's education.

As the nuclear family system became firmly established in a rapidly urbanizing society, the wife's role gained in importance relative to that of mother and the mother-in-law. Young husbands suffered from the rift between mother and wife and came to refer to themselves as the "sandwich" generation. For the women in this generation, marriage was simply a mundane fact of life. They formed families with their children and often lacked intimate connection with their husbands.

In modern Korean society, the Confucian philosophy of patriarchy is still deeply ingrained. In 1974, one study concluded that Korea is one of three countries in the world with the highest preference for boys (Cha, Chung, & Lee, 1977). In modern Korea, the son's role is still important as successor to the family lineage, performer of family ancestor rites, provider of support for his parents in old age, as well as a source of pride in the eyes of others.

Clinical vignette: "Ann"

My patient, Ann, born in 1948, is a professional woman, married, and the mother of a girl. She came to me suffering from "anxiety". She had become very concerned about her future as a computer specialist. While her colleagues had been promoted, Ann repeatedly failed the examination. She was almost paralysed in anticipation of the examination. No matter how much she prepared for it, her mind went blank when faced with the exam.

Ann is the youngest in a middle-class Korean family of five daughters. Her parents were devastated by the birth of yet another daughter. Her mother was ashamed and felt guilty for not being able to produce a son; she initially reacted in a rejecting way by refusing to nurse her infant daughter.

The devastated mother chose to dress her daughter in masculine clothing. In Korean folk belief, if a female child is raised as if she were male in terms of her appearance, clothing, and name, she will bring a baby brother to the family. In her frustration, it seems the mother would have done almost anything to have a son. From birth, Ann was a victim of her culture in so far as she was not allowed to inhabit the gender identity to which she was born.

When Ann was 3, her mother finally gave birth to a son. The immediate family and extended family were exhilarated. As soon as the baby brother was born, Ann was forgotten. She was unhappy with the newcomer and was jealous of him. Just before his second birthday, the boy died of pneumonia. Ann's mother went temporarily insane. Ann vividly recalls the visit of shaman who performed a ritual to calm the spirit of the newly departed boy. Ann remembered feeling terrified looking into the room through a small opening as the shaman attempted to contact her dead brother. In her young mind, Ann must have been tormented by the wish that her competitor would disappear, and with feelings of guilt that her wish had come true. In her unconscious she had killed her brother. Her mother was unable to produce more children.

Suddenly, Ann became the favourite child in the family: she was seen as the prettiest and the smartest. Her distant and authoritarian father began to pay attention to her academic achievements. Her mother became totally involved in Ann's schooling, calling her, "my son". She had been a brilliant student throughout her high-school years and wound up in the most prestigious engineering school in Korea. She was the only female student in her class. Although she made many male friends, she never fell in love. In spite of her good looks, her psychic structure was quite masculine. She hated being identified as a "feminine girl": it meant being stupid, inferior, and dependent. After earning a master's degree, she came to the United States for advanced education. Although Ann had many suitors, she chose a man who was passive and unassertive. In marriage, Ann easily assumed the dominant role.

In many ways, Ann's experience was typical of that of her generation. While her particular story is unique, she has much in common with other women who did not emigrate but remain part of modernizing Korea.

The "daughters' generation" born in the late 1960s to early 1970s, came of age under the military regime. This is the first generation to fully enjoy Korea's economic miracle without the hardships of their parent's generation.

Women of this generation were exposed to student activism in their college years and the feminist movements of the 1980s. They were caught between their mothers' materialistic ambitions and their own self-realization. In this period, a new image of women emerged: women were seen as the brave partners of patriotic men engaged in student activism. In this contest, the Korean women's liberation movement was born (H. J. Cho, 2002).

Clinical vignette: "Young-Sook"

Another student, Young-Sook, was born in 1960 into an upper-middle-class family. While attending graduate school in Seoul, she was introduced to a Korean man who was studying in a graduate programme in the United States. She decided to marry him, although she knew little about him other than that they shared a common interest in books, music, and art. After the wedding, Young-Sook gave up her graduate studies in Seoul to join her husband in the United States. She soon realized that the marriage was not what she had imagined.

One of the difficult aspects of her marriage was facing the reality of her husband's life. Her husband was not particularly dedicated to his studies, and consequently completing his degree took much longer than she had been told. She realized that he was not academically inclined, but because of the family's expectations for his achievement, he was not able to give up his studies. Her role as wife and as daughter-in-law was to help him in every possible way to study, while at the same time she herself believed that her husband's academic success was his own responsibility. The husband's inability to complete his degree affected his mother's emotional and physical health. The pressure on her from his family was enormous. A year after the marriage, she decided to go back to school for her own graduate degree.

While both husband and wife were involved in pursuing advanced degrees, her husband expected her to do all of the domestic chores, even though he had done them before he was married. He became the traditional Korean husband. My patient was deeply dissatisfied, and the couple began having heated arguments. Eventually, the husband agreed to share the domestic duties with her. However, this change of heart surprised her husband's Korean friends, who seemed to pity him, labelling him as a submissive husband. People, including her husband, called Young-Sook a "feminist". Finally, after eight years, both husband and wife earned their degrees, returned to Korea, and moved into the husband's family home.

From that point onward, the conflict between mother and daughter-in-law became increasingly intense. Sharing the domestic work was seen as the wife abusing her husband. She was urged by her mother-in-law to become "de-Americanized". Her husband passively abided by his mother's wishes.

Young-Sook became frustrated, angry, helpless, and lonely. She realized that she could not lean on anyone, particularly her husband. She was alone, but ready to fight for her rights. She often thought about divorcing her husband. Today, however, she is not sure whether keeping her marriage is the solution for her loneliness, and yet she is afraid of being alone.

Looking back on her life with her mother-in-law, she is surprised that her mother-in-law's expectations for her are very different from those she has for her own daughter. Her mother-in-law was very over-protective of her daughter, especially in relation to Young-Sook and even her husband.

The daughters' generation was born in the 1980s and 1990s—a time of modernization when economic production was strongly emphasized and consumerism became the central ideology.

Korean women in this period are typically described as desiring to be "charming and sexy". Young women in this generation began to use cosmetic surgery to improve their appearance. In the mid-1990s college students became very fashion-conscious, unlike the young women of the 1980s who strived to be patriotic and intellectual (H. J. Cho, 2002).

In the 1990s, young people were freed from their sexual inhibitions relative to the previous generation. A 1994 survey of 1,500 college students revealed that 64.1% approved of premarital sex and 25.5% agreed with the idea of "free sex". There is, however, a discrepancy between the survey and reality. Ideally, young people seem to believe in premarital sex and even in "free sex", but in reality they do not appear to practice what they believe. In the 1990s, as sexual norms became more relaxed, men tended to expect sex from women more readily. Traditionally, when a woman refused sex if she was asked, a man respected that refusal, understanding it as chastity, but if a woman in the 1990s refused sex, he interpreted that refusal as a lack of love or as a sign of manipulation. In spite of being misunderstood by a man, women tended to practice chastity in order to maintain their status (Y. J. Cho, 1996).

Traditionally, the mother is seen as responsible for her daughter's behaviour. A mother's constant vigilance over her daughter's chastity was the main foundation for her daughter's sexual behaviour. On the other hand, mothers encouraged their daughters to flirt with men in order that they might enjoy their sexual relationship with their future husbands. Furthermore, mothers believed that "flirtation" would help their daughters find men more easily.

Mothers participated in preparing their daughters to become their own ideal selves: sexy externally, chaste internally (Y. J., Cho, 1996). Inadvertently, they were fostering an internal conflict in their daughters—a conflict that neither mother nor daughter fully acknowledged.

Contemporary Korean society is one in which all three generations of Korean women coexist in a time of dramatic cultural changes. It is less clear how deeply these changes have penetrated the psyche of Korean women.

Korean women and psychoanalytic theory

Penis envy begins with the discovery of the anatomical distinction between the sexes: the little girl feels inferior in relation to the boy, and she wishes to possess what he has. Subsequently, in the course of the oedipal phase, penis envy takes on two secondary forms: first, the wish to acquire a penis within oneself (principally in the form of the desire to have a child) and second, the wish to enjoy the man's penis in coitus (Laplanche & Pontalis, 1973).

The first mention of penis envy is in Freud's work "On the Sexual Theories of Children" (1908c), where he draws attention to the little girl's interest in the boy's penis, an interest that "falls under the sway of envy. . . . When a girl declares that "she would rather be a boy", we know what deficiency her wish is intended to put right" (1908c).

By the time Freud used this concept (1914c) to denote the expression of the castration complex in the girl, the term "penis envy" had already gained acceptance in psychoanalytic parlance.

In the paper "On the Transformation of Instinct, As Exemplified in Anal Erotism" (1917c), however, the term was no longer restricted to the female's desire to have a penis like the boy's, but also referred to the main derivative versions of penis envy: namely, the wish for a child, in accordance with the symbolic equivalence of penis and child, and the desire for the male as an "appendage to the penis" (1917c).

Freud's view of female sexuality (1925j, 1931b, 1933) gives penis envy an essential place in the psychosexual development towards becoming a woman, a development which involves a change in erotogenic zone (from the clitoris to the vagina) and a change of object (a preoedipal attachment to the mother giving way to the oedipal love for the father). The castration complex and penis envy at different levels serve as the crux of this double reorientation.

On one level, there is resentment towards the mother who has failed to provide the daughter with a penis; on another, there is depreciation of the mother, who now appears castrated. There is also, according to Freud, a renunciation of phallic activity—clitoral masturbation—as passivity takes over symbolic equivalence between having a penis and having a child.

> The wish with which the girl turns to her father is no doubt originally the wish for the penis which her mother has refused her and which she expects from her father . The feminine situation is only established, however, if the wish for a penis is replaced by a wish for a baby, in accordance with an ancient symbolic equivalence. [Freud, 1933, p. 128]

Although the concept of penis envy is strongly debated in the literature, my focus is not on further exploration of this controversy but focusing on penis envy as it appears among Korean women.

The sociologist Cha Jae-Ho and colleagues (Cha, Chung, & Lee, 1973) have studied the issue of the widespread preference for boys in Korean society. His study suggests that in spite of rapid economic growth and modernization, the traditional preference for boys remains central to the "spiritual life of the Korean people" and that the tragedies and comedies of human existence are continually played out around this motive in the private lives of Korean couples. The most vexing aspect of this bias is that "not only men but also women themselves tend to recognize the inferiority of women, at least unconsciously" (Kim, 1988, p. 4).

In traditional society, the life cycle of the Korean woman appears to be comprised of two stages. In the first, the young woman is helpless, innocent, and at the mercy of her family of origin. The second begins with her entry into her husband's family. Her fate is not the outcome of intra-psychic development but, rather, the culturally imposed norm assigned to women.

How does lacking a penis in this patrilineal culture affect a young woman's psyche? Freudian theory has been interpreted as defining women as essentially castrated males, envious of the penis, and in this sense destined for neurosis. In the context of Korean Namjon Yobi, however, a woman's feelings of inferiority and her desire to gain power and identity through males are considered not only normal but also virtuous.

In traditional Korean society, the second stage of woman's life begins at marriage. Marriage was the precondition for adulthood, and to remain unmarried was to be socially stigmatized. For a woman the wedding was a rite of passage from childhood to adulthood and allowed her to become a full member of society. Once she was married, the mother-in-law became the most important individual in the life of the young bride. For a woman, a mother-in-law stood at the apex of female social prestige and authority, while the young bride was at the lowest level. The daughter-in-law was to strive to follow the mother-in-law's orders precisely, and she was taught to avoid situations that might give rise to scolding. The young daughter-in-law, sometimes facing harsh and inhumane treatment from her husband's family (particularly from her mother-in-law), had no place to turn for relief from her bonds of obedience. She had only one choice: to endure and survive within her husband's family (Deuchler, 1977).

A daughter-in-law gained an identity as a respectable person by producing a son who would grow up and take a wife of his own. A woman then assumed the position of mother-in-law, essentially becoming the very person who tormented her in the years before she added a male heir to the patriarchal line. Thus a sado-masochistic relationship, a relationship of dominance and submission, comes full circle, with the new daughter-in-law playing the role of the tormented victim. For the new mother-in-law, the son becomes her identity and her repository of worth, as well as her source of social and economic power: he becomes her phallus.

As the mother and son become closely intertwined for life, the son also comes to represent a narcissistic object choice for the mother.

Thus, there are two kinds of women in this society: women before marriage, who do not possess a "penis" and are, as a result, helpless, powerless, and without identity, and women after marriage, who become mothers to a son (or sons) and gain power, respect, and identity through this son. A married woman who does not have a son/sons remains powerless and without respect.

> In the Choson dynasty, the maternal role was extremely important in determining the overall status of women. Women, through their maternal identity and role, could receive considerable respect not only in the family but also in the larger society. Filial piety was upheld as the ultimate value in Korean Confucianism. Filial piety extended to both sexes indiscriminatingly. As mothers were highly regarded and rewarded, a woman's life goal, naturally, was to produce successful sons. [H. J. Cho, 1998]

A woman who never had a son was without filial piety. Hence, a son is a mother's symbolic penis. She was born without a penis, but by becoming a mother of a son, she acquired a penis.

In my clinical practice in the 1980s and early 1990s I saw many cases where a woman's modern view of marriage had collided with the traditional view of her mother-in-law and husband. The traditional mother feels entitled to dominate the life of her son, who is bound by filial piety to accede to her wishes. Even moving to a new country and setting up a separate home may not prevent the mother–son relationship from overwhelming the new marriage. And a young wife who has not yet produced a son has won no influence of her own in the traditional family system.

Clinical vignette: "Hae-Young"

> Hae-Young was a 28-year-old married woman, a graduate student in computer science with a bachelor of art degree from a university in Seoul. She was born into a wealthy family where she was the youngest of three children (two older brothers and herself). After coming to the United States for graduate school, she fell in love with a graduate student and married him.

Since the young bride refused to live with her husband's parents, the couple moved into a second-floor apartment in a private house owned by a Korean woman. In her daily visits, the mother-in-law snooped around the apartment, cooked her son's favourite meals, and told the daughter-in-law how to take proper care of him. She also gossiped with the landlady, complaining that an unworthy young woman had stolen her beloved son.

She openly complained that the daughter-in-law's wedding gifts to the groom's family were not good enough. Hae-Young believed that her mother-in-law was stuck in a terrible marriage of her own and had therefore directed her affections and interests towards her son. Worse still, Hae-Young's husband took a passive position towards his mother's intrusiveness and said that he felt sorry for his mother.

Hae-Young was deeply upset and ready to give up on the marriage. One morning, while thinking about her mother-in-law's criticism of her, she felt her face burning and her heart pounding. She feared she was losing her mind and nearly fainted.

At the end of eight months of a weekly psychotherapy, Hae-Young packed her belongings and left her husband.

Unlike traditional Korean women, who simply absorbed their mothers-in-law's outrageous behaviour without complaint, Hae-Young argued with her husband about the intrusiveness of his mother. She expressed her unhappy feelings and questioned whether or not she should stay in her marriage.

Ultimately, she came to see that she had a choice for her future.

How are these transformations reflected in the Korean woman's unconscious? In spite of these drastic changes in external appearance, the Korean woman's cultural ideal (ego-ideal) does not appear to have changed as quickly as external appearances would indicate. In last 60 years, Korean women seem to have been freed from many aspects of Confucian morals and values. But for women in the grandmother's generation, a heavy price was paid for freedom from the traditional norms and ideals. I have already presented the story of a young married woman with children who had become a widow during the Korean war. She fell in love with a man, with whom she had a child. In order to protect her very traditional Confucian family's honour, she had to remove herself from the family and became estranged from her children. It was very high price for her pay. In her traditional family, attaining the cultural ideal was far more important than gratifying individual needs.

An example of woman's liberation in modern Korean society can be found in the life of a patient I will refer to as Hyun-Joo.

Clinical vignette: "Hyun-Joo"

In her late 30s, Hyun-Joo was married to a man who was the only son in a very traditional Confucian family. Right after the arranged marriage, the couple came to the United States for her husband's education. Even though she had a graduate degree in chemistry from a university in Korea, Hyun-Joo became a housewife. Within a few years, she became pregnant and had a daughter. It took 10 years in the United States for her husband to finish a doctorate degree in engineering and his post-doctorate training. By then, she had become a mother of two children, a daughter and a son.

Upon returning to Korea, the family moved into the husband's parents' house. Since he was the only child in a traditional family, it was unthinkable for him to live separately from his parents. His strong obligation was to take care of his elderly parents and to worship his ancestors.

Hyun-Joo had grown up in a family that did not have the rigid tradition and religion of her husband's family. She considered herself a liberal and a feminist. She began her new life with a certain idealism, but soon realized that life with her in-laws was not what she had imagined. She was expected to be a daughter-in-law in the very traditional Korean style of previous centuries. Her mother-in-law's unspoken expectations for Hyun-Joo, as the one and only daughter-in-law in a traditional Confucian family, were unbearable. She became confused and felt that her life was nothing but doggedly carrying out the traditional obligations

Mikyum Kim

and duties expected of her. Her husband was not helpful. Three years of virtual imprisonment that she experienced with her in-laws lead her to lose her sense of reality. Her self-esteem and self-worth were shattered, and her identity was gradually being lost. She no longer knew who she was. She began to believe that her mother-in-law was persecuting her, and she responded with aggression, both verbal and physical. The proud mother-in-law could not reveal the horrendous family secret of her daughter-in-law's unthinkable behaviour.

The mother-in-law sought professional help and had to give up living with her son's family.

Only by giving up her own sanity was Hyun-Joo able to liberate herself from the traditional value system.

In modern Korea, married women divorce their husbands if they are not happy in their marriage, and they are allowed to remarry if the opportunity arises. The boy-preferring Korean culture has been changing for the past two decades. Married women have eagerly embraced the idea of having only one or two children regardless of gender. Some Koreans have decided not to have children at all. Married couples often, and increasingly, have extramarital affairs.

From the late 1970s to the late 1980s, the Christian population in Korea grew explosively. As Christianity has become more pervasive, Confucian rituals such as ancestor worship have begun to disappear.

The modern Korean mother-in-law does not seem to have the same extent of power over her daughter-in-law as in traditional society. However, the strong tie between Korean mothers and their sons persists.

The power of the phallus is very strongly present throughout Korean history. In traditional Korean society, a woman's ultimate goal was to marry and have a son or sons, and the son became her phallus. A modern Korean woman's goal is either to marry a successful man and through her husband gain power and wealth, or through higher education, become a professional person herself and gain her own power and independence.

For modern Korean mothers, educating their children, either male or female, has been very important. They sacrifice their lives, often their marriages, in order to give their children better and higher education. A mother's devotion to her children's higher education is one way of gaining phallic power.

My grandmother, who was very bright and intelligent, became a widow in her mid 30s; as a result, she had a very hard life. Upon her biological daughter's premature death during the Korean war, she raised me as though I were her own daughter. As a woman, she was not allowed the opportunity to have the official education she desperately wanted.

As a teenager, I remember having heated discussions with my grandmother, who strongly believed that the male gender is superior to the female. I disagreed with my grandmother with my strong convictions that both sexes are equal. My grandmother persisted in her belief that the male gender is superior. But although she was an uneducated and helpless woman, my grandmother also believed in women's education and their right to become professionals. In my view, my grandmother was envious of men and wished to have a man's power through education and a respectable profession. Without any doubt, her wishes were transmitted to me, and as a result my life-long mission has been in achieving a high level of education and becoming a respectable professional.

To summarize

In the fifteenth century, the Choson dynasty embraced Neo-Confucianism. From the seventeenth century onward, Confucian practice in Korea became pervasive and widely accepted as a way of life. In that society, Korean women were confined to the home.

Since liberation from Japan in 1945 and in the Korean war of 1950, Korea has gone through drastic transformations politically, culturally, economically, and religiously. In the meantime, Korea has rapidly industrialized and experienced an economic miracle. Korean culture was transformed from the extended family to the urban nuclear family. Women's lives have also been transformed drastically. Korean women seem to have been freed from many aspects of Confucian morals and values.

In this rapidly transforming Korean society, we have seen three generations coexisting: a mother sacrificing her life for her family, especially for her children, who would grow up to be successful citizens both professionally and financially. Women who married these successful men became competitive consumers, aggressive investors, and ambitious for their children's education and marriage. Women who grew up in prosperous Korea became consumer-oriented people and created a new femininity based on being attractive, sexy, and compliant.

In spite of these drastic changes in external appearance, the Korean woman's cultural ideal (ego-ideal) does not appear to be changing as quickly as external appearances would indicate.

In each of the clinical examples we can find specific instances of the survival of cultural values from each of the major periods in Korean history. We see that these values persist in the unconscious minds of three generations of Korean women, both in Korea itself and in the United States. Unconscious allegiance to ancient tradition plays itself out in the marital conflicts of these women as well as in their ideal images of the lives they would most like to lead.

Note

1. Korean written history began in the "Three Kingdoms": Goguryeo, Baeje, and Silla Kingdom, which coexisted during that time. In 668 the Three Kingdoms were united under the Silla hegemony, which lasted until 935. This hegemony was replaced by the Koryo, which came to power in 918 and lasted until 1392, when it gave way to the Choson dynasty. The Choson dynasty declined in 1910, when Korea was annexed by Japan.

REFERENCES

Abelin, E. (1971). The role of the father in the separation–individuation process. In: J. McDevitt & C. Settlage (Eds.), *Separation–Individuation* (pp. 229–252). New York: International Universities Press.

Abelin, E. (1980). Triangulation, the role of the father and the origins of core gender identity during the rapprochement subphase. In: R. F. Lax, S. Bach, & J. A. Burland (Eds.), *Rapprochement* (pp. 151–170). New York: Jason Aronson.

Abelin-Sas, G. (1994). The headless woman: Scheherezade's syndrome. In: A. K. Richards & A. D. Richards (Eds.), *The Spectrum of Psychoanalysis: Essays in Honor of Martin S. Bergmann*. New York: International Universities Press.

Abelin-Sas, G. (2004). Malignant passionate attachments. *Aperturas Psicoanalíticas, 1*.

Abraham, K. (1966). *On Character and Libido Development: Six Essays*, ed. with intro. by B. D. Lewin, tr. D. Byran & A. Strachey. New York: W. W. Norton.

Aisenstein, M. (2006). The indissociable unity of psyche and soma: A view from the Paris Psychosomatic School. *International Journal of Psychoanalysis, 87*: 667–680.

Akhtar, S. (1999). The distinction between needs and wishes: Implications for psychoanalytic theory and technique. *Journal of the American Psychoanalytic Association, 47*: 113–151.

Alizade, A. M. (1999a). *Feminine Sensuality*. London: Karnac.

Alizade, A. M. (1999b). *La mujer sola. Ensayo sobre la dama andante en Occidente* [The lone woman: Essay on the woman walking in the West]. Buenos Aires: Lumen.

Alizade, A. M. (2000a). Algunas consideraciones para enmarcar el estudio de los sexos y los generos [Some considerations on sex and gender]. In: *Cénarios Femininos*. Brazil: Ed Imago.

Alizade, A. M. (2000b). "El final del complejo de Edipo en la mujer. De la duplicación a la individuación" [The end of the Oedipus complex in the woman: From duplication to individuation]. Paper presented at the Argentine Psychoanalytical Association.

231

Alizade, A. M. (2004a). Relaciones lógicas y controversias entre género y psicoanálisis [Logical relations and controversies between gender and psychoanalysis]]. In: A. M. Alizade & T. Lartigue (Eds.), *Psicoanálisis y Relaciones de Género* (pp. 17–36). Buenos Aires, Lumen.

Alizade, A. M. (2004b). *La cuarta serie complementaria en psicoanálisis* [The fourth complementary series in psychoanalysis]. Unpublished.

Alizade, A. M. (2004c). Enigma de mujer. Enigma de la creación [The enigma of woman: Creation's enigma]. *Revista Agenda-Imago, 81:* 25–30.

Alizade, A. M. (2006). El deseo fusional en las mujeres [The wish for fusion in women]. *Revista Actualidad Psicológica, 31* (345): 30–32.

Alizade, A. M. (2007). Escenarios masculinos vulnerables [Vulnerable masculine scenarios]. *Revista de Psicoanálisis, Sociedad Peruana de Psicoanálisis, 5:* 25–39.

Alizade, A. M. (2008). *La pareja rota. Estudio sobre el divorcio* [The broken couple: An essay on divorce]. Buenos Aires: Editorial Lumen.

André, J. (1995). *Aux origines féminines de la sexualité* [The female origins of sexuality]. Paris: Presses Universitaires de France.

Aristophanes (411 BC). *Lysistrata.* Harmondsworth: Penguin Classics, 1973.

Bacal, H. A., & Newman, K. M. (1990). *Theories of Object Relations: Bridges to Self Psychology.* New York: Columbia University Press.

Baker Miller, J. (1976). *Toward a New Psychology of Women.* Boston, MA: Beacon Press.

Balsam, R. H. (1996). The pregnant mother and the body image of the daughter. *Journal of the American Psychoanalytic Association, 44:* 401–427.

Balsam, R. H. (2000). The mother within the mother. *Psychoanalytic Quarterly, 69:* 465–492.

Balsam, R. H. (2001). Integrating male and female elements in a woman's gender identity. *Journal of the American Psychoanalytic Association, 49:* 1335–1360.

Baranger, M., & Baranger, W. (2009). *The Work of Confluence: Listening and Interpreting in the Psychoanalytic Field,* ed. L. Glocer Fiorini. London: Karnac.

Barnett, M. C. (1966). Vaginal awareness in the infancy and childhood of girls. *Journal of the American Psychoanalytic Association, 14:* 129–141.

Beauvoir, S. de (1949). *The Second Sex,* tr. H. M. Parshley. Harmondsworth: Penguin, 1972; New York: Random House, 1974. New York: Alfred A. Knopf, 1993. [Originally published as *Le deuxième sexe.* Paris: Gallimard.]

Beebe, B., Lachman, F., & Jaffe, J. (1997). Mother–infant interaction structures and presymbolic self and object representations, *Psychoanalytic Dialogues, 7:* 133–192.

Beebe, B., Rustin, J., Sorter, D., & Knoublauch, S. (2005). *Forms of Intersubjectivity in Infant Research and Adult Treatment.* New York: Other Press.

Bégoin-Guignard, F. (1988). Le rôle des identifications maternelles et féminines dans le devenir de la masculinité du garçon [The role of maternal and feminine identifications in the evolution of masculinity in boys]. *Adolescence, 6* (1): 49–74.

Bem, S. L. (1993). *The Lenses of Gender.* New Haven, CT: Yale University Press.

Benjamin, J. (1988). *The Bonds of Love: Psychoanalysis, Feminism and the Problem of Domination.* New York: Pantheon.

Benjamin, J. (1991). Father and daughter: Identification with difference. A contribution to gender heterodoxy. *Psychoanalytic Dialogues, 1*: 3.

Benjamin, J. (1995). *Like Subjects, Love Objects.* New Haven, CT: Yale University Press.

Benjamin, J. (1998). *Shadow of the Other: Intersubjectivity and Gender in Psychoanalysis.* New York: Routledge.

Benjamin, J. (2004). Deconstructing femininity: Understanding "passivity" and the daughter position. *Annual of Psychoanalysis, 32*: 45–57.

Bergmann, M. (2000). *What I Heard in the Silence: Role Reversal, Trauma and Creativity in the Lives of Women.* Madison, CT: International Universities Press.

Bernardez-Bonesatti, T. (1978). Women and anger: Conflicts with aggression in contemporary women. *Journal of American Women Analysts, 33*: 215–219.

Bernstein, D. (1990). Female genital anxieties, conflicts and typical mastery modes. *International Journal of Psychoanalysis, 71*: 151–165.

Bernstein, D. (1993). *Female Identity Conflict in Clinical Practice.* Northvale, NJ: Jason Aronson.

Bleger, J. (1963). *Psicología de la Conducta* [The psychology of behaviour]. Buenos Aires: Eudeba, 1966.

Bokanowski, T. (1998). *De la pratique psychanalytique.* Paris: Presses Universitaires de France. [*The Practice of Psychoanalysis*, tr. D. Alcorn. London: Karnac, 2006.]

Bourdieu, P. (1998). *Masculine Domination,* Cambridge: Polity Press, 2001.

Bowlby, J. (1969). *Attachment and Loss, Vol. 1: Attachment.* New York: Basic Books.

Braunschweig, D., & Fain, M. (1975). *La nuit, le jour. Essai psychanalytique sur le fonctionnement mental* [Night, day: A psychoanalytic essay on mental functioning]. Paris: Presses Universitaires de France.

Britton, R. (1989). The missing link: Parental sexuality in the Oedipus complex. In: *The Oedipus Complex Today,* ed. J. Steiner (pp. 83–101). London: Karnac.

Brown, L. J. (2002). The early oedipal situation: Developmental, theoretical, and clinical implications. *Psychoanalytic Quarterly, 71*: 273–300.

Burch, B. (1993). Gender identities, lesbianism, and potential space. *Psychoanalytic Psychology, 10*: 359–375.

Burch, B. (1997). *Other Women*. New York: Columbia University Press.

Butler, J. (1990). *Gender Trouble*. New York: Routledge.

Butler, J. (1993a). *Bodies that Matter: On the Discursive Limits of Sex*. London: Routledge.

Butler, J. (1993b). Introduction. In: *Bodies that Matter: On the Discursive Limits of Sex*. New York: Routledge.

Butler, J. (1995). Melancholy gender-refused identification. *Psychoanalytic Dialogues*, 5: 165–180.

Cartwright, D. (2004). The psychoanalytic research interview: Preliminary suggestions. *Journal of the American Psychoanalytic Association*, 52: 209–242.

Castoriadis, C. (1998). *Figures of the Thinkable*. Stanford, CA: Stanford University Press, 2007.

Castoriadis, C. (2002). *Sujeto y verdad en el mundo histórico-social* [Subject and truth in the socio-historical world]. Buenos Aires: Fondo de Cultura Económica, 2004.

Cha, J. H., Chung, B. M., & Lee, S. J. (1977). Boy preference reflected in Korean folklore. In: S. Mattielli (Ed.), *Virtues in Conflict: Tradition and the Korean Woman Today*. Seoul: Royal Asiatic Society.

Chasseguet-Smirgel, J. (1970). Feminine guilt and the Oedipus complex. In: J. Chasseguet-Smirgel (Ed.), *Female Sexuality: New Psychoanalytic Views* (pp. 94–134). Ann Arbor, MI: University of Michigan Press.

Chasseguet-Smirgel, J. (2005). *The Body as Mirror of the World*, tr. S. Leighton. London: Free Association Books.

Cho, H. J. (1998). Male dominance and mother power: The two sides of Confucian patriarchy in Korea. In: W. H. Slote & G. A. DeVos (Eds.), *Confucianism and Family* (pp. 190–201). Albany, NY: State University of New York Press.

Cho, H. J. (2002). Living with conflicting subjectivity: Mother, motherly wife, and sexy woman in the transition from colonial-modern to postmodern Korea. In: L. Kendall (Ed.), *Under Construction: The Gendering of Modernity, Class, and Consumption in the Republic of Korea*. Honolulu: University of Hawaii Press.

Cho, Y. J. (1996). *New Writings about Marriage*. Seoul: Another Culture.

Chodorow, N. J. (1978). *The Reproduction of Mothering: Psychoanalysis and the Sociology of Gender*. Berkeley, CA: University of California Press.

Chodorow, N. J. (1989). *Feminism & Psychoanalytic Theory*. New Haven, CT: Yale University Press.

Chodorow, N. J. (1994a). Family structure and feminine personality. In: *The Homeric Hymn to Demeter* (pp. 243–265). Princeton, NJ: Princeton University Press.

Chodorow, N. J. (1994b). *Femininities, Masculinities, Sexualities: Freud and Beyond*. London: Free Association Books.

Chodorow, N. J. (1996). Theoretical gender and clinical gender: Epistemological reflections on the psychology of women. *Journal of the American Psychoanalytic Association, 44S*: 215–238.

Chodorow, N. J. (2000). Reflections on the reproduction of mothering: Twenty years later. *Studies in Gender and Sexuality, 1*: 337–348.

Cixous, H., & Clément, C. (1986). *The Newly Born Woman*, tr. B. Wing. Manchester: Manchester University Press.

Clower, V. (1990). The acquisition of mature femininity. In: M. Notman & C. Nadelson (Eds.), *Women and Men: New Perspectives on Gender Differences* (pp. 75–88). Washington, DC: American Psychoanalytic Press.

Coates, S. (2006). Developmental research on childhood gender identity disorder. In: P. Fonagy, R. Krause, & M. Leuzinger-Bohleber (Eds.), *Identity, Gender, and Sexuality, 150 Years after Freud*. London: IPA.

Coates, S., & Wolfe, S. M. (1995). Gender identity disorder in boys: The interface of constitution and early experience. *Psychoanalytic Inquiry, 15*: 6–38.

Corbett, K. (2001). Nontraditional family romance, *Psychoanalytic Quarterly, 70:* 599–624.

Cornell, D. (1991). *Beyond Accommodation: Ethical Feminism, Deconstruction and the Law*. New York: Routledge.

Cournut, J. (2001). *Pourquoi les hommes ont peur des femmes* [Why men are afraid of women]. Collection "Quadrige". Paris: Presses Universitaires de France, 2006.

Cournut-Janin, M., & Cournut, J. (1993). La castration et le féminin dans les deux sexes [Castration and the feminine dimension in both sexes]. (Report delivered at the 53rd Congress of French-speaking Psychoanalysts from the Romance Language countries.) *Revue Française de Psychanalyse, 57:* 1335–1558. [Special Congress Issue]

Creith, E. (1996). *Undressing Lesbian Sex: Popular Images, Private Acts and Public Consequences*. London: Cassell.

David-Ménard, M. (1997). *Les constructions de l'universel.* Paris: Presses Universitaires de France. [*Constructions of the Universal,* tr. D. Davis. Albany, NY: SUNY Press.]

Deleuze, G. (1995). *Conversaciones* [Conversations]. Valencia: Pre-Textos.

Deleuze, G., & Guattari, F. (1980). *Mil Mesetas* [A thousand plateaux]. Valencia: Pre-Textos, 1994.

Deleuze, G., & Parnet, C. (1977). *Diálogos.* Valencia: Pre-Textos, 1980. [*Dialogues*. London: Athlone, 2002].

de Marneffe, D. (1997). Bodies and words: A study of young children's genital and gender knowledge. *Gender & Psychoanalysis, 2*: 3–33.

Derrida, J. (1987). *Deconstruction and Philosophy: The Texts of Jacques Derrida.* Chicago: University of Chicago Press, 1989.

Deuchler, M. (1977a). The tradition: Women during the Yi Dynasty. In: S. Mattielli (Ed.), *Virtues in Conflict: Tradition and the Korean Woman of Today*. Seoul: Royal Asiatic Society.

Deuchler, M. (Ed.) (1977b). *Virtues in Conflict: Tradition and the Korean Woman Today*. Seoul: Royal Asiatic Society.

Deuchler, M. (1992a). Confucian legislation: The consequences for women. In: *The Confucian Transformation of Korea: A Study of Society and Ideology*. (Harvard-Yenching Institute Monograph Series published by the Council on East Asian Studies.) Cambridge, MA: Harvard University Press.

Deuchler, M. (1992b). The pre-Confucian past: A reconstruction of Koryo society. In: *The Confucian Transformation of Korea: A Study of Society and Ideology*. (Harvard-Yenching Institute Monograph Series published by the Council on East Asian Studies.) Cambridge, MA: Harvard University Press.

Deutsch, H. (1932). Homosexuality in women. *International Journal of Psychoanalysis, 14* (1933): 34.

Diamond, M. (2004). The shaping of masculinity: Revisioning boys turning away from their mothers to construct male gender identity. *International Journal of Psychoanalysis, 85*: 359–380.

Diamond, M., & Sigmundson, H. K. (1997). Sex reassignment at birth: Long-term review and clinical implications. *Archives of Pediatric and Adolescent Medicine, 151* (3): 298–304.

Dimen, M. (1991). Deconstructing difference: Gender, splitting and transitional space. *Psychoanalytic Dialogues, 1*: 335–353.

Dinnerstein, D. (1976). *The Rocking of the Cradle and the Ruling of the World*. London: Women's Press, 1987.

Dio Bleichmar, E. (1991). *El Feminismo Espontáneo de la Histeria* [The spontaneous feminism of hysteria]. Madrid: Siglo XXI.

Dio Bleichmar, E. (1992). What is the role of gender in hysteria? *International Forum of Psychoanalysis, 1*: 155–162.

Dio Bleichmar, E. (1995). The secret in the constitution of female sexuality: The effects of the adult sexual look upon the subjectivity of the girl. *Journal of Clinical Psychoanalysis, 4*: 331–342.

Dio Bleichmar, E. (1997). *La sexualidad femenina. De la niña a la mujer* [Feminine sexuality: From the girl to the woman]. Barcelona: Paidós.

Dio Bleichmar, E. (2002). Sexualidad y género. Nuevas perspectivas en el psicoanálisis contemporáneo [Sexuality and gender: New perspectives in contemporary psychoanalysis]. *Aperturas Psicoanalíticas, 11* (www.aperturas.org).

Dio Bleichmar, E. (2006). The place of motherhood in primary femininity. In: A. M. Alizade (Ed.), *Motherhood in the Twenty-First Century*. London: Karnac.

Dio Bleichmar, E. (2008). Relational gender compensation of the imbalanced self. *Studies in Gender and Sexuality, 9* (3): 258–273.

Domenici, T., & Lesser, R. C. (1995). *Disorienting Sexuality: Psychoanalytic Reappraisals of Sexual Identities*. London: Routledge.

Dorsey, D. (1996). Castration anxiety or genital anxiety? *Journal of the American Psychoanalytic Association, 44*: 283–302. [Supplement: The Psychology of Women]

Easser, R. (1975). "Womanhood." Paper presented to the American Psychoanalytic Association Annual Meeting, as part of a panel on "The psychology of women: Late adolescence and early adulthood." *Journal of the American Psychoanalytic Association, 24*: 631–645, 1976.

Edgecumbe, R., Lunberg, S., Markowitz, R., & Salo, F. (1976). Some comments on the concept of the negative oedipal phase in girls. *Psychoanalytic Study of the Child, 31*: 35–61.

Elise, D. (1997). Primary femininity, bisexuality and the female Ego Ideal: A re-examination of the female developmental theory. *Psychoanalytic Quarterly, 66*: 489–517.

Elise, D. (1998a). Gender configurations: Relational patterns in heterosexual, lesbian and gay couples. *Psychoanalytic Review, 85*: 253–267.

Elise, D. (1998b). Gender repertoire: Body, mind, and bisexuality. *Psychoanalytic Dialogues, 8*: 353–371.

Elise, D. (2007). The black man and the mermaid. *Psychoanalytic Dialogues, 17*: 791–809.

Erasmus of Rotterdam (1511). *The Praise of Folly*. Harmondsworth: Penguin Classics, 1993.

Fast, I. (1979). Developments in gender identity: Gender differentiation in girls. *International Journal of Psychoanalysis, 60*: 443–453.

Fast, I. (1984). *Gender and Identity: A Differentiation Model*. Hillsdale, NJ: Analytic Press.

Fast, I. (1990). Aspects of early gender development: Toward a reformulation. *Psychoanalytic Psychology, 78*: 105–107.

Faure-Oppenheimer, A. (1980). *Le choix du sexe* [Gender selection]. Paris: Presses Universitaires de France.

Ferenczi, S. (1938). Thallassa: A theory of genitality. *Psychoanalytic Quarterly, 2*: 361–364.

Fischer, R. S. (2002). Lesbianism: Some developmental and psychodynamic considerations. *Psychoanalytic Inquiry, 22*: 278–295.

Fliegel, Z. O. (1982). Half a century later: Current status of Freud's controversial views on women. *Psychoanalytic Review, 69* (1): 7–28.

Foley, H. P. (1994). *The Homeric Hymn to Demeter*. Princeton, NJ: Princeton University Press.

Fonagy, P. (2003). Some complexities in the relationship of psychoanalytic theory to technique. *Psychoanalytic Quarterly, 72*: 13–47.

Fonagy, P. (2008). A genuinely developmental theory of sexual enjoyment and its implications for psychoanalytic technique. *Journal of the American Psychoanalytic Association, 56*: 11–36.

Foucault, M. (1966). *The Order of Things*. London: Routledge, 2001.

Frenkel, R. S. (1996). A reconsideration of object choice in women: Phallus or fallacy. *Journal of the American Psychoanalytic Association, 44*: 133–156.

Freud, S. (1895d). *Studies on Hysteria. S.E., 2.*

Freud, S. (1896b). Further remarks on the neuro-psychoses of defence. *S.E., 3:* 159.

Freud, S. (1896c). The aetiology of hysteria. *S.E., 3:* 189.

Freud, S. (1900a). *The Interpretation of Dreams. S.E., 4.*

Freud, S. (1905d). *Three Essays on the Theory of Sexuality. S.E., 7:* 135–243.

Freud, S. (1906a). My views on the part played by sexuality in the aetiology of the neuroses. *S.E., 7:* 271.

Freud, S. (1908c). On the sexual theories of children. *S.E., 9.*

Freud, S. (1909b). Analysis of a phobia in a five-year-old boy. *S.E., 10.*

Freud, S. (1910a [1909]). Five lectures on psychoanalysis. *S.E., 11:* 9–59.

Freud, S. (1910h). A special type of choice of object made by men (Contributions to the psychology of love, I). *S.E., 11:* 167.

Freud, S. (1912d). On the universal tendency to debasement in the sphere of love (Contributions to the psychology of love, II). *S.E., 11:* 179.

Freud, S. (1912f). Contributions to a discussion on masturbation. *S.E., 12:* p. 243.

Freud, S. (1912–13). *Totem and Taboo. S.E., 13.*

Freud, S. (1913f). The theme of the three caskets. *S.E., 12:* 289–301.

Freud, S. (1913i). The disposition to obsessional neurosis. *S.E., 12:* 313.

Freud, S. (1914c). On narcissism: An introduction. *S.E., 14.*

Freud, S. (1914d). On the history of the psycho-analytic movement. *S.E., 14:* 3.

Freud, S. (1915a [1914]). Observations on transference-love (Further recommendations on the technique of psycho-analysis, III). *S.E. 12:* 149.

Freud, S. (1915c). *Instincts and Their Vicissitudes. S.E., 14.*

Freud, S. (1916–1917). *Introductory Lectures on Psycho-Analysis. S.E., 15 & 16.*

Freud, S. (1917c). On transformations of instinct as exemplified in anal erotism. *S.E., 17.*

Freud, S. (1918a [1917]). The taboo of virginity (Contributions to the psychology of love, III). *S.E., 11:* 198–199.

Freud, S. (1919e). A child is being beaten. *S.E., 18:* 67–144.

Freud. S. (1919h). The uncanny. *S.E., 17.*

Freud, S. (1920g). *Beyond the Pleasure Principle. S.E., 18:* 1.

Freud, S. (1921c). *Group Psychology and the Analysis of the Ego. S.E., 18:* 67.

Freud, S. (1923b). *The Ego and the Id. S.E., 19.*

Freud, S. (1923e). The infantile genital organization: An interpolation into the theory of sexuality. *S.E., 19.*

Freud, S. (1924c). The economic problem of masochism. *S.E., 19:* 157.

Freud, S. (1924d). The dissolution of the Oedipus Complex. *S.E., 19.*

Freud, S. (1925d [1924]). *An Autobiographical Study. S.E., 20:* 3.

Freud, S. (1925j). Some psychical consequences of the anatomical distinction between the sexes. *S.E. 19*: 248–258.

Freud, S. (1930a [1929]). *Civilization and Its Discontents. S.E., 21:* 59–145.

Freud, S. (1931b). Female sexuality. *S.E. 21*: 221–243.

Freud, S. (1933). Femininity [Lecture XXXIII]. In: *New Introductory Lectures on Psycho-Analysis. S.E., 22:* 112–134.

Freud, S. (1933a). *New Introductory Lectures on Psycho-Analysis. S.E., 22:* 1–182.

Freud, S. (1937c). Analysis terminable and interminable. *S.E., 23*: 209–253.

Freud, S. (1940a [1938]). *An Outline of Psycho-Analysis. S.E.,* 23: 141.

Freud, S. (1950a [1887–1902). *The Origins of Psycho-Analysis.. S.E., 1.*

Freud, S. (1950 [1892–1899]). Extracts from the Fliess Papers [Draft G, Melancholia]. *S.E., 1.*

Freud, S. (1950 [1895]). Project for a scientific psychology. *S.E. 1.*

Freud, S. (1963). *Letters of Sigmund Freud.* New York: Basic Books, 1960.

Fritsch, E., Ellman, P., Basseches, H., Elmendorf, S., Goodman, N., Helm, F., et al. (2001). The riddle of femininity: The interplay of primary femininity and the castration complex in analytic listening. *International Journal of Psychoanalysis, 82*: 1171–1183.

Galenson, E. (1971). A consideration of the nature of thought in childhood play. In: J. B. McDevitt & C. F. Settlage (Eds.), *Separation–Individuation: Essays in Honor of Margaret S. Mahler* (pp. 41–49). New York: International Universities Press.

Galenson, E., & Roiphe, H. (1971). The impact of early sexual discovery on mood defensive organization and symbolization. *Psychoanalytic Study of the Child, 26:* 195–216.

Galenson, E., & Roiphe, H. (1974). The emergence of genital awareness during the second year of life. In: R. C. Friedman, R. M. Richart, & R. L. Van de Wiele (Eds.), *Sex Differences in Behavior* (pp. 223–231). New York: Wiley .

Galenson, E., & Roiphe, H. (1976). Some suggested revisions concerning early female development, *Journal of the American Psychoanalytic Association, 24* (Suppl.): 29–57.

Garbarino, H. (1990). *El ser en psicoanálisis* [The self in psychoanalysis]. Montevideo: Eppal Ltda.

Gedo, J. (1988). *The Mind in Disorder: Psychoanalytic Models of Pathology.* Hillsdale, NJ: Analytic Press.

Gedo, J. (1989). *Portraits of the Artist.* New York: Guilford Press.

Gedo, J. (1996). The artist and the emotional world: Creativity and personality. In: A. Cooper & S. Marcus (Eds.), *Psychoanalysis and Culture.* New York: Columbia University Press.

Gilligan, C. (1982). *In a Different Voice: Psychological Theory and Women's Development.* Cambridge, MA: Harvard University Press.

Glocer Fiorini, L. (1994). La posición femenina: Una construcción heterogénea [The feminine position: A heterogeneous construction]. *Revista de Psicoanálisis, 51* (3): 587–603.

Glocer Fiorini, L. (1996). En los límites de lo femenino. Lo otro [At the edge of the feminine: The other]. *Revista de Psicoanálisis, 53* (2): 429–443.

Glocer Fiorini, L. (1998). The feminine in psychoanalysis: A complex construction. *Journal of Clinical Psychoanalysis, 7*: 421–439.

Glocer Fiorini, L. (2001a). El deseo de hijo. De la carencia a la producción deseante [The desire for a child: From lack to wishful reproduction]. *Revista de Psicoanálisis, 58* (4): 965–976.

Glocer Fiorini, L. (2001b). *Lo femenino y el pensamiento complejo* [The feminine and the complex thought]. Buenos Aires: Lugar Editorial.

Glocer Fiorini, L. (2006). Las mujeres en el contexto y el texto freudianos [Women in the Freudian context and text]. *Revista de Psicoanálisis, 63* (2): 311–323.

Glocer Fiorini, L. (2007). *Deconstructing the Feminine: Psychoanalysis, Gender and Theories of Complexity.* London: Karnac.

Glocer Fiorini, L. (2008). Verso una decostruzione del femminile inteso come altro [Towards a deconstruction of the feminine as an other]. *Psicoterapia Psicoanalitica* (Bologna), *15*: 2.

Glocer Fiorini, L., & Gimenez de Vainer, A. (2008). Entrevista a Judith Butler [Interview with Judith Butler]. In: L. Glocer Fiorini (Ed.), *El cuerpo. Lenguajes y silencios* [The body: Languages and silences] (pp. 83–91). Buenos Aires: APA & Lugar Editorial.

Goldner, V. (1991). Toward a critical relational theory of gender. *Psychoanalytic Dialogues, 1*: 249–272.

Goldner, V. (2005). Ironic gender, authentic sex. In: L. K. Toronto, G. Ainslie, M. Walsh Donovan, M. Kelly, C. Kieffer, & N. McWiliams (Eds.), *Psychoanalytic Reflections on a Gender-free Case: Into the Void* (chap. 17). London: Routledge.

Green, A. (1986). Féminité et masculinité [Femininity and masculinity]. *Bulletin de la Société Psychanalytique de Paris, 9*: 21–30.

Green, A. (1990). Lo originario en el psicoanálisis [The originary in psychoanalysis]. *Revista de Psicoanálisis, 47* (3): 413–418.

Green, A. (1995). *La métapsychologie revisitée* [Metapsychology revisited]. Paris: Champ Vallon.

Green, A. (1997). *The Chains of Eros: The Sexual in Psychoanalysis,* tr. L. Thurston. London: Karnac, 2000.

Greenacre, P. (1950). Special problems of early female sexual development. In: *Trauma, Growth and Personality* (pp. 237–258). New York: International Universities Press, 1969.

Greenacre, P. (1952). *Trauma, Growth, and Personality.* New York: International Universities Press, 1969.

Greenacre, P. (1958). Early physical determinants in the development of the sense of identity. In: *Emotional Growth* (pp. 113–127). New York: International Universities Press, 1971.

Greenson, R. (1968). Dis-identifying from mother: Its special importance for the boy. *International Journal of Psychoanalysis, 49*: 370–374.

Grossman, W. I., & Kaplan, D. M. (1988). Three commentaries on gender in Freud's thought. In: H. Blum, Y. Kramer, A. K. Richards, & A. D. Richards (Eds.), *Fantasy, Myth and Reality* (pp. 339–370). Madison, CT: International Universities Press.

Grossman, W. I., & Stewart, W. A. (1976). Penis envy: From childhood wish to developmental metaphor. *Journal of the American Psychoanalytic Association, 24*: 193–213. Also in: H. Blum (Ed.), *Female Psychology* (pp. 193–212). New York: International Universities Press. .

Guignard, F. (1997). *Épître à l'objet* [Epistle to the object]. ("Épîtres" series.) Paris: Presses Universitaires de France.

Harris, A. (1991). Gender as contradiction. *Psychoanalytic Dialogues, 1*: 197–233.

Heineman, T. (2006). Reconstructing Oedipus? Considerations of the psychosexual development of boys of lesbian parents. In: *Motherhood in the Twenty-First Century* (pp. 85–96). London: Karnac.

Héritier, F. (2007). *Masculino–Femenino, II* [Masculine and Feminine, II]. Buenos Aires: Fondo de Cultura Económica.

Herzog, J. (2001). Dr. C: Trauma and character. In: *Father Hunger: Explorations with Adults and Children*. Hillsdale, NJ: Analytic Press.

Herzog, J. (2005). Triadic reality and the capacity to love. *Psychoanalytic Quarterly, 74*: 1029–1052.

Hoffman, L. (1999). Passions in girls and women. *Journal of the American Psychoanalytic Association, 47*: 1145–1168.

Holtzman, D., & Kulish, N. (1996). Nevermore: The hymen and the loss of virginity. *Journal of the American Psychoanalytic Association, 44*: 303–332.

Holtzman, D., & Kulish, N. (1997). *Nevermore: The Hymen and the Loss of Virginity*. Northvale, NJ: Jason Aronson.

Holtzman, D., & Kulish, N. (2000). The feminization of the female oedipal complex, Part 1: A reconsideration of the significance of separation issues. *Journal of the American Psychoanalytic Association, 48*: 1413–1437.

Holtzman, D., & Kulish, N. (2003). The feminization of the female oedipal complex, Part II: A reconsideration of the significance of aggression. *Journal of the American Psychoanalytic Association, 51*: 1127—1151.

Horney, K. (1924). On the genesis of the castration complex in women. *International Journal of Psychoanalysis, 5*: 50–65. Also in: H. Kelman (Ed.), *Feminine Psychology* (pp. 37–53). New York: W. W. Norton, 1993.

Horney, K. (1926). The flight from womanhood: The masculinity complex in women as viewed by men and women. *International Journal of Psychoanalysis, 7*: 324–329. Also in: H. Kelman (Ed.), *Feminine Psychology* (pp. 54–70). New York: W. W. Norton, 1967.

Horney, K. (1932). The dread of woman. In: H. Kelman (Ed.), *Feminine Psychology* (pp. 133–146). New York: W. W. Norton, 1967.

Horney, K. (1933). The phallic phase. *International Journal of Psychoanalysis, 14*: 1–33.

Irigaray, L. (1985a). *Female Hom(m)osexuality: Speculum of the Other Woman*, tr. G. Gill (pp. 98–104). Ithaca, NY: Cornell University Press.

Irigaray, L. (1985b). *This Sex Which Is Not One*, tr. C. Porter. Ithaca: Cornell University Press.

Israël, L. (1979). *La histeria, el sexo y el médico* [Hysteria, sex, and the physician]. Barcelona: Toray-Masson.

Jacobson, E. (1968). On the development of the girl's wish for a child. *Psychoanalytic Quarterly, 37*: 523–558 (1950).

Jones, E. (1927). The early development of female sexuality. *International Journal of Psychoanalysis, 8*: 459–472.

Jones, E. (1933). The phallic phase. *International Journal of Psychoanalysis, 14*: 1–13.

Jones, E. (1935). Early female sexuality. *International Journal of Psychoanalysis, 16*: 263–273.

Kantrowitz, J. J. (1997). A different perspective on the therapeutic process: The impact of the patient on the analyst. *Journal of the American Psychoanalytic Association, 45*: 127–153.

Kaplan, D. M. (1990). Some theoretical and technical aspects of gender and social reality in clinical psychoanalysis. *Psychoanalytic Study of the Child, 45*.

Kaplan, L. J. (1991). *Female Perversions: The Temptations of Emma Bovary*. New York: Doubleday.

Kavaler-Adler, S. (2000). *The Compulsion to Create Women Writers and Their Demon Lovers*. New York: Other Press.

Kestenberg, J. (1956). Vicissitudes of female sexuality. *Journal of the American Psychoanalytic Association, 4*: 453–476.

Kestenberg, J. (1968). Outside and inside, male and female. *Journal of the American Psychoanalytic Association, 16*: 456–520.

Kestenberg, J. (1982). The inner-genital phase: Prephallic and preoedipal. In: D. Mendell (Ed.), *Early Female Development: Current Psychoanalytic Views*. New York: Spectrum.

Kim, C. U. (1988). On male chauvinistic cultural attitudes. In: *Korean Women Today, Vol. 19*. Seoul: Korean Women's Development Institute.

Kleeman, J. A. (1976). Freud's views on early female sexuality in the light of direct child observation. *Journal of the American Psychoanalytic Association, 24S*: 3–26.

Klein, M. (1928). Early stages of the oedipal conflict. In: *The Psychoanalysis of Children* (pp. 179–209). New York: Grove, 1960.

Klein, M. (1945). The Oedipus complex in the light of early anxieties. *International Journal of Psychoanalysis, 26*: 11–33.

Kramer-Richards, A. (1996). What is new with women? *Journal of the American Psychoanalytic Association, 44*: 1227–1241.

Kristeva, J. (1984). *Revolution in Poetic Language,* tr. M. Waller. New York: Columbia University Press. Also in: *The Kristeva Reader,* ed. T. Moi. Oxford: Blackwell, 1986.

Kristeva, J. (1989). *Black Sun: Depression and Melancholia.* New York: Columbia University Press.

Kubie, L. S. (1974). The drive to become both sexes. *Psychoanalytic Quarterly, 43*: 349–426.

Kubie, L. S. (1975). The language tools of psychoanalysis: A search for better tools drawn from better models. *International Review of Psycho-Analysis, 2*: 11–24.

Kulish, N. (2000). Primary femininity: Clinical advances and theoretical ambiguities. *Journal of the American Psychoanalytic Association, 48*: 1355–1379.

Kulish, N. (2006). Frida Kahlo and object choice: A daughter the rest of her life. *Psychoanalytic Inquiry, 26*: 7–31.

Kulish, N., & Holtzman, D. (1998). Persephone, the loss of virginity and the female oedipal complex. *International Journal of Psychoanalysis, 79*: 57–71.

Kulish, N., & Holtzman, D. (2008). A *Story of Her Own: The Female Oedipus Complex Reexamined and Renamed.* New York: Jason Aronson.

Lacan, J. (1955–56). The hysteric's question (II): What is a woman? In: *The Seminar, Book III: The Psychoses.* New York: W. W. Norton, 1993.

Lacan, J. (1964). *The Four Fundamental Concepts of Psychoanalysis,* tr. A. Sheridan. New York: Norton; London: Hogarth Press, 1978.

Lacan, J. (1966). The function and field of speech and language in psychoanalysis. In: *Ecrits.* New York: W. W. Norton, 2007.

Lacan, J. (1972–73). *The Seminar, Book XX: Encore.* New York: W. W. Norton, 2000.

Lacan, J. (1977). The significance of the phallus. In: *Ecrits: A Selection,* tr. A. Sheridan (pp. 281–91). New York: W. W. Norton, 2007.

Lampl-de Groot, J. (1927). The evolution of the Oedipus complex in women. *International Journal of Psychoanalysis, 9* (1928): 332.

Laplanche, J. (1980). *Problématiques II: Castration-Symbolisations* [Problematics II: Castration–symbolization]. Paris: Presses Universitaires de France.

Laplanche, J. (1992). *La révolution Copernicienne inachevée* [The unfinished Copernican revolution]. Paris: Aubier.

Laplanche, J. (1997). The theory of seduction and the problem of the other. *International Journal of Psychoanalysis, 78*: 653–666.

Laplanche, J. (2007). Gender, sex and sexuality. *Studies in Gender and Sexuality, 8*: 201–219.

Laplanche, J., & Pontalis, J.-B. (1973). *The Language of Psychoanalysis*. London: Hogarth Press; reprinted London: Karnac, 1988.

Laqueur, T. (1990). *Making Sex: Body and Gender from the Greeks to Freud*. Cambridge, MA: Harvard University Press.

Lasky, R. (2000). Body ego and the pre-oedipal roots of feminine gender identity. *Journal of the American Psychoanalytic Association, 48*: 1381–1412.

Lax, R. F. (1990). An imaginary brother, his role in the formation of a girl's self-image and ego ideal. *Psychoanalytic Study of the Child, 45*: 257–272.

Lax, R. F. (1995). Freud's views and changing perspectives on femaleness and femininity: What female analysands taught me. *Psychoanalytic Psychology, 12*: 393–406.

Lax, R. F. (1998). *On Becoming and Being a Woman*. New York: Jason Aronson.

Lerner, H. E. (1976). Parental mislabeling of female genitals as a determinant of penis envy and learning inhibitions in women. *Journal of the American Psychoanalytic Association, 24S*: 269–283.

Lerner, H. E. (1980). Internal prohibitions against female anger. *American Journal of Psychoanalysis, 40*: 137–148.

Lévinas, E. (1947). *Time and the Other*. Pittsburgh, PA: Duquesne University Press, 1990.

Levin de Said, A. (2004). *El sostén del ser* [The support of the self]. Buenos Aires: Paidós, Psicología Profunda.

Lewis, R. W. B. (1985). *Edith Wharton*. New York: Fromm International.

Lewkowicz, I. (1997). El género en perspectiva histórica en sexualidad y género [Gender in historical perspective in sexuality and gender]. *Revista Asociación Psicoanalítica de Buenos Aires, 19* (3): 427.

Lichtenberg, J. (2004). Commentary on "the superego": A vital or supplanted concept? *Psychoanalytic Inquiry, 24*: 328–339.

Lichtenstein, H. (1961). Identity and sexuality: A study of their interrelationship in man. *Journal of the American Psychoanalytic Association, 9*: 197–260.

Lombardi, K. (1998). Mother as object, mother as subject: Implications for psychoanalytic developmental theory. *Gender and Psychoanalysis, 1*: 33–46.

Lorde, A. (1982). *Zami: A New Spelling of My Name. A Biomythography*. New York: Persephone Press.

Lyons-Ruth, K. (1991). Rapprochement or approachment: Mahler's theory reconsidered from the vantage point of recent research on early attachment relationship. *Psychoanalytic Psychology, 8*: 1–23.

Lyons-Ruth, K. (1999). The two-person unconscious: Intersubjective dialogues, enactive relational representation and the emergence of new forms of relational organization. *Psychoanalytic Inquiry, 19*: 576–617.

Lyons-Ruth, K. (2006). The interface between attachment and intersubjectivity: Perspective from the longitudinal study of disorganized attachment. *Psychoanalytic Inquiry, 26*: 595–616.

Mahler, M. (1963). Thoughts about development and individuation. *Psychoanalytic Study of the Child, 18*: 307–324.

Mahler, M., Pine, F., & Bergman, A. (1975). *The Psychological Birth of the Human Infant.* London: Hutchinson.

Mahon, E. J. (1991). The "dissolution" of the Oedipus complex: A neglected cognitive factor. *Psychoanalytic Quarterly, 60*: 628–634.

Masson, J. M. (1985). *The Complete Letters of Sigmund Freud to Wilhelm Fliess, 1887–1904.* Cambridge, MA: Harvard University Press.

Mayer, E. L. (1985). Everybody must be just like me: Observations on female castration anxiety. *International Journal of Psychoanalysis, 66*: 331–347.

Mayer, E. L. (1995). The phallic castration complex and primary femininity: Paired developmental lines toward female gender identity. *Journal of the American Psychoanalytic Association, 43*: 17–38.

McDougall, J. (1979). The homosexual dilemma. In: I. Rosen (Ed.), *Sexual Deviation* (pp. 206–245). New York: Oxford University Press.

McDougall, J. (1993). Sexual identity, trauma, and creativity. *International Forum of Psychoanalysis, 2*: 69–79.

McDougall, J. (1995a). The artist and the outer world. *Contemporary Psychoanalysis, 31*: 247–262.

McDougall, J. (1995b). *The Many Faces of Eros: A Psychoanalytic Exploration of Human Sexuality.* London: Free Association Books.

Meissner, W. (2005). Gender identity and the self. II. Femininity, homosexuality, and the theory of the self. *Psychoanalytic Review, 92*: 29–66.

Milner, M. (1950). *On Not Being Able to Paint.* Madison, CT: International Universities Press.

Mitchell, J. (1974). *Psychoanalysis and Feminism.* New York: Pantheon.

Mitchell, J. (1982). Introduction. In: J. Mitchell & J. Rose (Eds.), *Feminine Sexuality: Jaques Lacan & the Ecole Freudienne.* London: Macmillan.

Moi, T. (2004). From femininity to finitude: Freud, Lacan, and feminism, again. *Signs: Journal of Women in Culture and Society, 29* (3): 841–878. Also in: I. Matthis (Ed.), *Dialogues on Sexuality, Gender and Psychoanalysis* (pp. 93–135). London: Karnac.

Money, J. (1955). Hermaphroditism, gender and precocity in hyperadrenocorticism: Psychology findings. *Bulletin of the Johns Hopkins Hospital, 96*: 253–264.

Money, J. (1965). *Sex Research: New Developments.* New York: Holt, Rinehart & Winston.

Money, J. (1988). *Gay, Straight, and In-between.* New York: Oxford University Press.

Money, J., Hampson, J. G., & Hampson, J. I. (1955). An examination of basic sexual concepts: The evidence of human hermaphroditism. *Bulletin of the Johns Hopkins Hospital, 97*: 301–319.

Money, J., & Ehrhardt, A. (1972). *Man and Woman, Boy and Girl: The Differentiation and Dimorphism of Gender Identity from Conception to Maturity.* Baltimore, MD: Johns Hopkins University Press.

Money-Kyrle, R. (1971). The aim of psychoanalysis. *International Journal of Psychoanalysis, 52*: 103–106.

Morin, E. (1990). *Introducción al pensamiento complejo.* [Introduction to complex thought]. Barcelona: Gedisa, 1995.

Moulton, R. (1970). A survey and reevaluation of penis envy. *Contemporary Psychoanalysis, 7*: 84–104.

Mugo, M. G. (1976). From a Zulu woman's diary. In: *Daughter of My People Sing.* Nairobi: East African Literature Bureau.

O'Connor, N., & Ryan, J. (1993). *Wild Desires & Mistaken Identities: Lesbianism and Psychoanalysis,* London: Virago.

Ogden, T. (1994). The analytic third: Working with intersubjective clinical facts. *International Journal of Psychoanalysis, 75*: 3–19.

Orbach, S., & Eichenbaum, L. (1982). *Outside In, Inside Out: A Feminist Psychoanalytic Approach to Women's Psychology.* Harmondsworth: Penguin.

Parens, H. (1990). On the girl's psychosexual development: Reconsiderations suggested from direst observation. *Journal of the American Psychoanalytic Association, 38*: 743–772.

Parens, H., Pollock, L., Stern, J., & Kramer, S. (1976). On the girl's entry into the Oedipus complex. *Journal of the American Psychoanalytic Association, 24*: 79–107.

Payne, S. A. (1935). A conception of femininity. *British Journal of Medical Psychology, 15*: 18–33.

Person, E. S. (2000). "Issues of Power and Aggression in Women." Paper presented at the Winter Meetings of the American Psychoanalytic Association, New York, December.

Person, E. S., & Ovesey, L. (1983). Psychoanalytic theories of gender identity. *Journal of the American Psychoanalytic Association, 11*: 203–226.

Peterson, M. (1983). Women without sons: A measure of social change in Yi Dynasty Korea. In: L. Kendall & M. Peterson (Eds.), *Korean Women: View from the Inner Room.* New Haven, CT: East Rock Press.

Plato (2003). *The Symposium.* Harmondsworth: Penguin Classics.

Plaut, E. A., & Hutchinson, F. L. (1986). The role of puberty in female psychosexual development. *International Review of Psychoanalysis, 13*: 417–432.

Pruett, K. D. (1998). Role of the father. *Pediatrics [Research perspectives], 102*: 1253–1261.

Puget, J. (2003). Intersubjektivität. Krise der Repräsentation [Intersubjectivity: Crisis of representation]. *Psyche: Zeitschrift für Psychoanalyse und Ihre Anwendungen, 9/10*: 914–934.

Raphael-Leff, J. (1986). Facilitators and regulators: Conscious and unconscious processes in pregnancy and early motherhood. *British Journal of Medical Psychology, 59*: 43–55.

Raphael-Leff, J. (1991). *Psychological Processes of Childbearing* (4th edition). London: Anna Freud Centre, 2005.

Raphael-Leff, J. (1993). *Pregnancy—The Inside Story.* London: Karnac, 2001.

Raphael-Leff, J. (1997). The casket and the key: Thoughts on gender and generativity. In: J. Raphael-Leff & R. J. Perelberg (Eds.), *Female Experience: Four generations of British Women Psychoanalysts on Their Work with Female Patients.* New York: Routledge, 2008.

Raphael-Leff, J. (2000a). "Behind the shut door": A psychoanalytical approach to premature menopause. In: D. Singer & M. Hunter (Eds.), *Premature Menopause: A Multidisciplinary Approach.* London: Whurr.

Raphael-Leff, J. (2000b). "Climbing the walls": Puerperal disturbance and perinatal therapy. In: J. Raphael-Leff (Ed.), *Spilt Milk: Perinatal Loss and Breakdown.* London: Routledge.

Raphael-Leff, J. (2002). Eros & ART. In: J. Haynes & J. Miller (Eds.), *Inconceivable Conceptions: Psychotherapy, Fertility and the New Reproductive Technologies.* London: Routledge.

Raphael-Leff, J. (2007). Freud's prehistoric matrix: Owing "nature a death". *International Journal of Psychoanalysis, 88*: 1–28.

Raphael-Leff, J. (2010a). "The Dreamer by Daylight"—Imaginative play, creativity and generative identity. *Psychoanalytic Study of the Child, 64*.

Raphael-Leff, J. (2010b). Parental orientations: Mothers' and fathers' patterns of pregnancy, parenting and the bonding process. In: S. Tyano, M. Keren, H. Herman, & J. Cox (Eds.), *Parenthood and Mental Health: A Bridge between Infant and Adult Psychiatry.* London: Wiley.

Reenkola, E. M. (2002). *The Veiled Female Core.* New York: Other Press.

Reich, A. (1940). A contribution to the psychoanalysis of extreme submissiveness in women. *Psychoanalytic Quarterly, 9*: 470–480.

Reich, A. (1953). Narcissistic object choice in women. *Journal of the American Psychoanalytic Association, 1*: 22–44.

Renik, O. (1993). Analytic interaction: Conceptualizing technique in light of the analyst's irreducible subjectivity. *Psychoanalytic Quarterly, 62*: 553–571.

Richards, A. (1996). Primary femininity and female genital anxiety. *Journal of the American Psychoanalytic Association, 44S*: 261–282.

Ritvo, S. (1989). Mothers, daughters, and eating disorders. In: H. Blum, Y. Kramer, A. K. Richards, & A. D. Richards (Eds.), *Fantasy, Myth, and*

Reality: Essays in Honor of Jacob A. Arlow (pp. 371–380). Madison, CT: International Universities Press.

Riviere, J. (1929). Womanliness as a masquerade. *International Journal of Psychoanalysis, 10*: 303–313. Also in: J. Raphael-Leff & R. J. Perelberg (Eds.), *Female Experience: Four Generations of British Women Psychoanalysts on Their Work with Female Patients.* New York: Routledge. And in: V. Burgin, J. Donald, & C. Kaplan (Eds.), *Foundations of Fantasy.* London: Methuen.

Robbins, M. (1996). Nature, nurture and core gender identity. *Journal of the American Psychoanalytic Association, 44S*: 93–117.

Rocah, B. (2009). *The Professor Is Not Always Right (H. D. 1956): Rethinking Freud's 1933 Paper on Femininity.* Unpublished manuscript.

Roiphe, H., & Galenson, E. (1981). *Infantile Origins of Sexual Identity.* Madison, CT: International Universities Press.

Roussillon, R. (2008). Postface. In: J. Schaeffer, *Le refus du féminin (La sphinge et son âme en peine)* (5th edition). Paris: Presses Universitaires de France. [*The Universal Refusal: A Psychoanalytic Exploration of the Feminine Sphere and Its Repudiation,* tr. D. Alcorn. London: Karnac, forthcoming.]

Rubin, G. (1975). The traffic in women: Notes on the "political economy" of sex. In: R. R. Reiter (Ed.), *Toward an Anthropology of Women.* New York: Monthly Review Press.

Saal, F. (1981). Algunas consecuencias políticas de la diferencia psíquica de los sexos. In: M. Lamas & F. Saal (Eds.), *La bella (in)diferencia* (pp. 10–34). Mexico: Siglo XXI.

Sáez, H. (2004). *Teoria queer y psicoanalisis* [Queer theory and psychoanalysis]. Madrid: Editorial Sintesis.

Sandler, J. (1967). Trauma, strain and development. In: S. Furst (Ed.), *Psychic Trauma* (pp. 154–174). New York: Basic Books.

Schaeffer, J. (1997). *Le refus du féminin (La sphinge et son âme en peine)* (5th edition). Paris: Presses Universitaires de France, 2008. [*The Universal Refusal: A Psychoanalytic Exploration of the Feminine Sphere and Its Repudiation,* tr. D. Alcorn. London: Karnac, forthcoming.]

Schaeffer, J. (1998). Que veut la femme? *ou* Le scandale du féminin [What does a woman want? Or, The scandalous nature of the feminine dimension]. In: *Clés pour le féminin (femme, mère, amante et fille). Débats de psychanalyse* [A key to the feminine dimension (Woman, mother, lover and daughter): Psychoanalytic debates.] Paris: Presses Universitaires de France.

Schaeffer, J. (2008). Une symbolisation du sexe féminin est-elle possible? [Can the female sex be symbolized?]. In: B. Chouvier & R. Roussillon (Eds.), *Corps, acte et symbolisation* [Body, acts and symbolization]. Brussels: De Boeck University Editions.

Scharff, J. (1994). *The Autonomous Self: The Work of John D. Sutherland.* Northvale, NJ: Jason Aronson.

Schore, A. (2001). The effects of early relational trauma on right-brain development, affect regulation, and infant mental health, *Infant Mental Health Journal, 22:*, 201–269.

Sherfey, M. J. (1966). The evolution and nature of female sexuality in relation to psychoanalytic theory. *Journal of the American Psychoanalytic Association, 14:* 28–128.

Sherman, E. (2002). Homoerotic countertransference: The love that dare not speak its name? *Psychoanalytic Dialogues, 12:* 649–666.

Siegel, D. (2001). Toward an interpersonal neurobiology of the developing mind: Attachment relationships, "mindsight", and neural integration. *Infant Mental Health Journal, 22* (1–2); 67–94.

Socarides, C. (1978). *Homosexuality,* New York: Jason Aronson.

Spinoza, B. (1677). *Ethica Ordine Geometrico Demonstrata* [The ethics]. Project Gutenberg (www.gutenberg.org).

Spitz, R. A. (1962). Autoerotism re-examined. *Psychoanalytic Study of the Child, 17:* 283–315.

Stein, R. (2007). Moments in Laplanche's theory of sexuality. *Studies in Gender and Sexuality, 8:* 177–200.

Stern, D. (1985). *Interpersonal World of the Infant.* New York: Basic Books.

Stoller, R. (1968a). A further contribution to the study of gender identity. *International Journal of Psychoanalysis, 49:* 364–368.

Stoller, R. (1968b). *Sex and Gender.* London: Karnac, 1984.

Stoller, R. (1976). Primary femininity. *Journal of the American Psychoanalytic Association, 24:* 59–78.

Stoller, R. (1985). *Presentations of Gender.* New Haven, CT: Yale University Press.

Stuart, J. (2007). Work and motherhood: Preliminary report of a psychoanalytic study. *Psychoanalytic Quarterly, 76:* 439–485.

Sweetnam, A. (1996). The changing contexts of gender between fixed and fluid experience. *Psychoanalytic Dialogues, 6:* 437–459.

Talbot, M. (2002). Girls just want to be mean. *New York Times,* 24 February, p. 24.

Tessman, L. (1989). Fathers and daughters: Early tones, late echoes. In: S. H. Cath, A. Gurwitt, & L. Gunsberg (Eds.), *Fathers and Their Families* (pp. 197–225). Boston: Little Brown.

Ticho, G. (1976). Female autonomy and young adult women. *Journal of the American Psychoanalytic Association, 24S:* 139–155.

Todorov, T. (1995). *La vida en común* [Life together]. Madrid: Taurus.

Torok, M. (1979). The significance of penis envy in women. In: J. Chasseguet-Smirgel (Ed.), *Female Sexuality: New Psychoanalytic Views.* Ann Arbor, MI: University of Michigan Press.

Trad, P. V. (1990). On becoming a mother: In the throes of developmental transformations. *Psychoanalytic Psychology, 7*: 341–361.

Trevarthen, C., & Aitken, K. J. (2001). Infant intersubjectivity: Research, theory and clinical applications. *Journal of Child Psychology and Psychiatry, 42*: 3–48.

Tronick, E. (1989). Emotions and emotional communication in infants. *American Psychology, 44*: 112–119. Also in: J. Raphael-Leff (Ed.), *Parent–Infant Psychodynamics—Wild Things, Mirrors and Ghosts* (chap. 4). London: Whurr.

Tyson, P. (1982). A developmental line of gender identity, gender role and choice of love object. *Journal of the American Psychoanalytic Association, 30*: 59–84.

Tyson, P. (1994). Bedrock and beyond: An examination of the clinical utility of contemporary theories of female psychology. *Journal of the American Psychoanalytic Association, 42*: 447–467.

Tyson, P. (1996). Female psychology: An introduction. *Journal of the American Psychoanalytic Association, 44*: 11–20.

Tyson, P. (2003). Some psychoanalytic perspectives on women. *Journal of the American Psychoanalytic Association, 51*: 1119–1126.

Tyson, P., & Tyson, R. L. (1990). *Psychoanalytic Theories of Development: An Integration.* New Haven, CT: Yale University Press.

Vaillant, G. E. (2005). *Ego Mechanisms of Defense: A Guide for Clinicians and Researchers.* Washington, DC: American Psychiatric Press.

Winnicott, D. W. (1959). The fate of the transitional object. In: *Psycho-Analytic Explorations,* London: Karnac, 1989.

Winnicott, D. W. (1960). Ego distortion in terms of true and false self. In: *The Maturational Processes and the Facilitating Environment* (pp. 140–152). London: Hogarth Press, 1965; reprinted London: Karnac, 1990.

Winnicott, D. W. (1966). The split-off male and female elements to be found in men and women. In: *Playing and Reality* (pp. 72–85, in chap. 5, "Creativity and Its Origins"). London: Routledge, 1971. Also in: *Psycho-Analytic Explorations.* London: Karnac, 1989.

Winnicott, D. W. (1971a). Creativity and its origins. In: *Playing and Reality* (pp. 65–85). London: Tavistock Publications.

Winnicott, D. W. (1971b). *Playing and Reality.* London. Routledge.

Woolf, V. (1929). *A Room of One's Own.* San Diego: Harcourt Brace, 1989.

Young-Bruehl, E. (2003). Are human beings by nature bisexual? In: *Where Do We Fall When We Fall In Love?* (pp. 179–212). New York: Other Press.

Zolla, E. (1981). *Androginia.* Madrid: Debate, 1990.

INDEX

Abelin, E., 44, 145
Abelin-Sas Rose, G., 1–6, 144–159
abortion, 76, 72, 105, 107, 156
Abraham, K., 158
adolescence, 51–53, 63, 70, 119, 166, 194
aggression and competition, 46–47
aggressiveness, 20, 27, 47, 138, 190, 191
   in females, 11–17, 40
   in males, 11–12
agnation, 214
Aisenstein, M., 67
Aitken, K. J., 61
Akhtar, S., 174
Alizade, M., 6, 198–211
Allen, W., 58
ambition, 64, 122, 155
   in women, 29
ambivalence, 16, 20, 29, 39, 105, 153, 156, 171, 172, 180, 209
ambivalent father transference, 126
anal sadistic stage, 130
analyst's meta-theories, 79–96
analytic field, 84
anatomical heterogeneity, 95
anatomy as destiny, 2, 162
André, J., 129
Andreas-Salomé, L., 74, 131
androgyny, 83, 119, 127
Anna O, 66
anthropogeny, 70
après coup, 63, 70
archaic mother, seductive, 75
Aristophanes, 82
asexual conception, 78
asexuality, 69
assertion, concept of, 152–155
assignment vs. symbolization, 180
assisted conception, 1, 59
attachment (*passim*):
   infantile, 185
   to mother, 159, 161, 174, 187–189
      pre-Oedipus, 15, 25, 30, 36, 164, 223
      symbiotic, 114
   primary female homosexual, 67
   theory, 176

transfer of, from mother to father, 15, 17, 20, 29, 145
attunement, 61, 166
auto-eroticism, 101
autonomous self, 6, 163, 164, 172, 173, 175
autonomy:
   development of, 164, 175
   egoic force of, 207
   feminine, 6, 160–176
   true and false, 163, 173, 174, 175

baby, wish for, girls', 24–27, 29–30, 36, 223
Bacal, H. A., 164
Baker Miller, J., 158
Balsam, R. H., 49, 50, 172
Baranger, M., 84
Baranger, W., 84
Barnett, M. C., 75
Beauvoir, S. de, 57, 93, 132
bedrock, repudiation of femininity as, 5, 43, 98, 100, 110, 129, 130, 132, 134
Beebe, B., 61, 178
Bégoin-Guignard, F., 100
Bem, S. L., 65
Benjamin, J., 44, 49, 65, 75, 159, 175, 177, 180
Bergman, A., 78
Bergmann, M., 158
Bernardez-Bonesatti, T., 46
Bernays, M., 86
Bernstein, D., 48, 75
biogenetic determinism, 77
biological factors, 15, 27, 42, 43, 58
biotechnology, 63, 73, 82
bisexual fluidity, 75
bisexuality, 5, 10, 11, 12, 27, 43, 44, 57, 67, 69, 70, 71, 75, 76, 160, 162
   in analytic situation, 97–111
   and creativity, 112, 113, 119, 124–128
   psychic, 64, 73–74, 87, 98, 100, 131, 208
      primary, 2
   work of, in psychoanalytic treatment, 109–110
Bleger, J., 199
bodily schemata, 60–62